Healing the Broken Family of Abraham:

New Life for Muslims

By
Don McCurry

This work is dedicated
to all of those
who down through the years
have given their lives
to help Muslims come to Jesus.

Healing the Broken Family of Abraham _____

ACKNOWLEDGMENTS

First of all, my praise and thanks go to God, my Savior, who called me to Himself and thrust me, as His worker, into the Muslim world. He has faithfully sustained and led me throughout these amazing years, including the project of writing this book.

Without the steady encouragement of my wife, Mary Jo, this work would not have been completed. The same could be said for Greg Roth, and the other members of the Board of Trustees of Ministries to Muslims: Robert Pickett, Bryce Herndon, Rollo Entz, Gerald Swank, and Ron Kernaghan.

Also, without the faithful prayer warriors and support partners who sustained us while we simultaneously ministered and worked on this project, this work would not have been possible.

It was Ralph Winter, friend and professor at Fuller Seminary's School of World Mission, who first suggested I make time to research new methods in Muslim evangelism. His suggestion was heartily endorsed by Arthur Glasser and Charles Kraft. Also at Fuller was Peter Wagner, who first encouraged me to dream of what could be done in the Muslim world. This led to the Glen Eyrie Consultation on Muslim Evangelization, out of which the Zwemer Institute was formed. I am deeply indebted to all the board members of Zwemer, who were so supportive in the seven years I served there. A special thanks goes to Robert Douglas, who with his wife June, helped draft the original proposal for the Lausanne Committee that led to the Glen Eyrie Consultation. Without the invaluable help of Edward Dayton of World Vision, the planning and holding of the Glen Eyrie Consultation would never have happened. We all learned so much from the 40 study papers that fed that consultation. Many thanks to each of you who took time out of your busy lives to write those papers.

I owe so much to my former students both at Fuller Seminary and the Zwemer Institute, who, coming from their overseas field experiences, brought so many valuable insights with them into the classroom.

A profound word of thanks goes to Charles Kraft, my ever-patient, chief mentor. He, too, was a constant source of encouragement throughout this arduous process. And I am also grateful to Dudley Woodberry and Dean Gilliland, for their invaluable suggestions as they served with Charles Kraft on my dissertation committee.

Finally, a word of deep gratitude to the countless Muslim friends from whom I have learned so much over the years, several of whom are now fellow citizens with us in the Body of Christ.

TABLE OF CONTENTS

PART FOUR: MINISTERING TO MUSLIMS: THE QUESTION OF ATTITUDE

PART FIVE: APPROACHES TO SPECIFIC KINDS OF MUSLIMS

INTRODUCTION

This is a book about winning Muslims to Christ. It is about healing for the broken family of Abraham. It is a book to help Christian workers learn to work with the sons and daughters of Ishmael, who were given this name because Muhammad and his followers chose to identify with Abraham's family through the lineage of Hagar and Ishmael. The book is not for the scholar; it is for the worker. It is designed to be an introduction to ministries with Muslims. For those rare workers who have the privilege of having undertaken graduate study in Islam, or for those workers who have taught themselves as they went along by keeping abreast of current reading, this book will hold nothing new. But for those workers who have had neither the privilege of graduate study in missiology and Islamics, nor access to the latest books in the field, this volume is designed to fill the gaps in their preparation.

The history of humanity's redemption begins and ends with Jesus Christ, the Alpha and Omega, the beginning and the end of God's activity in relation to the human race. But that history is sketched out against the background of the family of Abraham. Abraham is held up to us as the one who believed God and it was counted to him as righteousness (Gen. 15:6). At the end of human history, all the redeemed are gathered at a marvelous feast where we will sit down with Abraham (Matt. 8:11).

Today, Christianity, Judaism and Islam all boast of their links to Abraham. But Jesus, in His controversy with the Jews of His day, said, "If you were Abraham's children, then you would do the things Abraham did" (John 8:39). So apparently, being racially linked does not qualify one for being a child of Abraham in God's eyes. The unbelieving Jews were disqualified from being members of Abraham's true family because of their rejection of Christ. Muslims, likewise, will not be automatically included in the kingdom because of any supposed racial linkage with Abraham. The key to being included in the true family of Abraham has to do with how one relates to Abraham's greatest son, Jesus Christ. This book will take up in careful detail what Muhammad and Muslims ever since Christ have done with Him. And, of course, it will suggest ways for bringing

1

Muslims into the family of Abraham.

The roots of this story carry us back four thousand years to a domestic tragedy in the tents of Abraham, the "Friend of God." This is the story of the rivalry between two mothers and their respective sons. The flames of this ancient rivalry, resulting in the eviction of Hagar and her son from the immediate family, have never died. They burn on in the breasts of Abraham's embittered progeny to this present day. Hovering over the growing conflagration of the Middle East is the enormous shadow of a mighty man, Ishmael, desert prince, the slave-son of Abraham by Hagar. First child of the circumcision, beloved by his father, Ishmael was the would-be heir of Abraham.

But it was not meant to be. Isaac was born to Sarah. And what Ishmael took for granted was soon taken away. Rival mothers, rival sons, child of the flesh and child of faith could not coexist in the same cluster of tents. Hagar and Ishmael would have to go. Fierce, wild, free, untamable, implacable Ishmael, disinherited by Abraham and Sarah, was adopted by God Himself. He grew up in the wilderness of the desert. This was no ordinary man. Desert kings came from his loins.

A thousand years later, his name and his sons' names lived on, carefully chronicled in the genealogies of the Holy Text (1 Chron. 1:29-31). Prophets remembered mighty Nebaioth and greater Kedar, Ishmael's first and second sons. They would be gathered with their flocks to the Messiah's fold in the day of harvest (Isa. 42:11; 60:7). Isaiah even links Kedar with the Arab people (Isa. 21:13-17). Two and a half millennia later, an orphaned Arab would arise to champion the cause of his illustrious ancestor. Muhammad, staunchly independent of Jew and Christian, traced his monotheism back to Ishmael and his father Abraham.

Strong and fierce, this Semitic gentile warrior seemed destined to avenge Ishmael's shame. Both Jew and Christian would feel the Muslim sword. Defiant, bold, imaginative, the golden tongue of unshakable will, a religious genius who wed prayers to swords, Muhammad, founder of Islam, was first of the Muslims. He was the prophet-king who would attempt to reclaim the lost place of Ishmael in Abraham's family. Death took him by surprise. But his words lived on, spearheaded by Arab pride. Within a hundred years of his death, Muslim armies swept on to Samarkand and Sind, to Jerusalem and Spain. The world trembled before these mighty idol smashers. Mirthless and without music, their mosques, for a time, appeared to have won out over synagogue and church.

But what Muhammad built on Arab pride could not withstand the dangers of worldly success. Riches were too tempting to his fighting heirs. Religion gave way to the whims of flesh for both caliphs and sultans. The door was opened for many divisions to come into what Islam called the "Household of the Believers." Islam split, and split and split again. Legalism, pietism, mysticism, materialism—all threaded their way through the changing fortunes of Arab, Persian, Turkish and Moghul kings. Ethnicity, language, race and pride would take their toll on Islam's growing empires.

Islam suffered the blight of fatal syncretisms. It began to wear many faces with matching costumes as it intermingled with the religions of its subject races and the spirits that empowered them. Today, we count at least four hundred and eight distinct ethnolinguistic peoples among these more than one billion Muslims of our world (Weekes 1984:913-927). They live in forty-nine countries, either as the majority population, or as a plurality—a minority that controls the government. But that only accounts for seventy-seven percent of them; the other twenty-three percent live as minorities in scores of other countries. How do we reach such a vast melange of races, tongues and tribes? That is what this book is all about.

We begin by taking up the study of the family of Abraham. One of the early themes will be the focus on the "cry of Ishmael." In Genesis 21:17, Scripture says, "God heard the boy crying ..." The boy's name was "God Hears" (Ishmael). Here we will use "Ishmael" in a generic way in speaking about all Muslims who claim him as either their physical or spiritual ancestor, or both.

Since God heard the original Ishmael cry, we believe He also hears the present-day cry of Ishmael's prolific children scattered across the face of the earth: the Muslims. And as God's agents of reconciliation on earth, we, too, hear their cry and will find ways to respond so that Muslims can be truly brought into the family of Abraham. In this work we will detail suggestions and ideas gleaned from Scripture, as well as various related insights and experiences for the Christian worker to use in reaching Muslims.

We have both biblical and practical grounds for believing God for a great harvest among Muslims; and that leads to the second major theme of this study: The broken family of Abraham will be healed by the atoning sacrifice of Jesus on the cross. There He has made available the reconciliation of all things, including the reconciliation of Muslims to the Lord Jesus Christ, Son of God (Col. 1:20).

In this work, I accept the idea that Muhammad sought to establish his kinship with Abraham through Ishmael. As an aside, I should point out that some scholars, such as Chapman, question whether Muhammad could trace his genealogy to Ishmael (1989:50-57). Others, such as Hamada in his book, *Understanding the Arab World*, sketch out in some detail the Semitic background of the Arabs, and hence the possibility of Muhammad being descended from Abraham through Ishmael. However, he also points out that Ishmaelite intermarriage with other ethnic peoples makes it virtually impossible to trace a pure line (1990:58). The point in this study is that Muslims themselves, especially Arab Muslims, claim identity with Ishmael. It is in this sense, then, that we use Ishmael in a generic way for Muslims. Since we are working with Muslims who believe it, we will start with them where they are. Accordingly, we accept the link from Muhammad to Abraham through Ishmael.

In the second and third sections of this book, I detail the life and accomplishments of this amazing Arab man and the religion he has bequeathed to the world. Then I describe the major divisions and sects that have arisen in Islam.

The fourth section serves as a transition to the practical aspect of ministry, tackling the problem of attitudes. As we set out to win Muslims to Christ, how should we relate to them? What is our message? What do we do with the challenge of culture, ours and theirs? How do we deal with the great spiritual powers behind this rival system?

Then, in the fifth section of the book, we will see how to apply these principles to the various kinds of Muslims. As there may be as many kinds of Muslims as there are Christians, we will not be able to cover them all. Therefore, we have chosen to single out eight major theological types of Muslims for our considerations.

The sixth section of the book deals with the great theological problems that exist between Islam and Christianity. These center on the Trinity, the deity of Christ, the incarnation, the idea of atonement, the crucifixion and Muslim charges that the Bible has been corrupted.

The final section presupposes a harvest. We have already begun to see Muslims come to Christ from all the major branches of Islam. In fact, we are seeing Muslims come to Jesus in numbers never before dreamed of in the decades and centuries preceding ours. But in many places, these Muslim friends pay a frightening price for declaring their allegiance to Christ. And the cost to the discipler may also be very high. These topics, along with discussions on the goals of discipling and models of incorporating these believers into the body of Christ, are the subject matter of this seventh section.

The book closes with a final challenge. Will we have the strength, the heart, the energy, the persistence required to complete the winning of Muslims from every tongue, tribe, people and nation found in the household of Islam? My assumption is that we have no choice. Christ has commanded us to go and has given hope of a harvest. Therefore, I believe we shall see teams of Christian workers reach every ethnolinguistic group of Muslims in the coming years, and that the rate of Muslims coming to Christ across the world is going to accelerate.

I also believe that militant, fundamentalist Islam is going to grow stronger. Now that Communism has collapsed, the new confrontation is going to occur between Islam and the West. As Islam seeks to define itself against the massive impact of Western culture, it will return to the fundamental teachings from which it sprang. The holy warriors will have their day. There will be much suffering and bloodshed in the coming wars between Muslims and fellow Muslims, and between Muslims and their neighbors. This is the downside of Islam's identification with Ishmael. Even though Muslims may not know this prophecy about Ishmael, by choosing to identify with him, they somehow have taken on his characteristics: "His hand will be against everyone ..." (Gen. 16:12).

As we all know, war and bloodshed are characterized by cruelty and pain. Many of Ishmael's children will tire of this endless cycle of destructive behavior and will want to truly reconcile with the other members of Abraham's family. Disillusioned by Muhammad's seventh-century attempt to improve the world through both preaching and sword, Muslims will turn to Jesus, the Savior of the world and the world's rightful Lord. It is my hope and prayer that this volume, in the hands of Christian witnesses, will be a helpful tool in the harvest fields of the Muslim world. Both Abraham's prayer for Ishmael and God's answer serve as a perennial model of how we, too, like our father Abraham, should pray for those who claim to be Ishmael's children today. "If only Ishmael might live under your blessing" (Gen. 17:18)! And may we hear God's answer as did Abraham of old: "Yes ... I have heard you: I will surely bless him ..." (Gen. 17:19, 20).

PART ONE

THE FAMILY OF ABRAHAM

CHAPTER 1

ABRAHAM, THE FRIEND OF GOD

> For I have chosen him, so that he will direct his children and his household after him to keep the way of the Lord by doing what is right and just, so that the Lord will bring about for Abraham what he has promised him (Gen. 18:19).

No one can underestimate the importance of Abraham to the three great monotheistic faiths of the world—and even to the world itself. Jesus Christ was called the "Son of David," the "Son of Abraham" (Matt. 1:1). Jesus Himself said, "Abraham rejoiced at the thought of seeing my day; he saw it and was glad" (John 8:56). Muhammad is quoted in the Quran as saying, "Without doubt, among men, the nearest of kin to Abraham, are those who follow him, as are also this Apostle [Muhammad] and those who believe [Muslims]: and God is the Protector of those who have faith [Muslims]" (Q. 3:68). (Words found inside brackets were added by the author for clarity.) Who is Abraham? What is his significance to God? To man? Why does everyone want to belong to the family of Abraham? In this chapter, we shall attempt to answer these questions.

Abraham's Call
God singled this man out to be the means of blessing to all people. Let us look closely at His call to this first missionary.

> Leave your country, your people and your father's household and go to the land I will show you. I will make you into a great nation and I will bless you; I will make your name great, and you will be a blessing. I will bless those who bless you, and whoever curses you I will curse; and all peoples on earth will be blessed through you (Gen. 12:1-3).

This call has profound implications for the whole human race. Everyone will either be blessed or cursed depending on how they relate to Abraham. What is so significant about him? Abraham said "Yes" to God; "Yes" to leave all and follow God; "Yes" to God's plan to bless all peoples on earth through him; and "Yes" to the idea of suffering "shame for that name."

In Abraham, God found a man with whom He could begin His plan to recover (bless) lost humankind, a man who would believe in Him, a man who would faithfully teach His children about the one true God, a man who would walk by faith and not according to the flesh, and, ultimately, a man through whom the Messiah of all people would come: Jesus of Nazareth.

Abraham, the Friend of God

God promised the land of Canaan to Abraham and his descendants, but Abraham remained childless. He talked to God about it, and God said, "a son coming from your own body will be your heir ..." Then God took him outside and spoke again: "Look up at the heavens and count the stars—if indeed you can count them ... So shall your offspring be" (Gen. 15:4, 5).

Then God instructed Abraham to prepare animals and birds for a special sacrifice. God manifested Himself between the split pieces of the animals and birds, thus sealing His covenant of friendship with Abraham (Gen. 15:1-19). From this unusual ceremony, Abraham was given the name, "Friend of God." He is mentioned in Scripture as such, and he is also known in Islam as *Khalil Ullah*, ("The Friend of God"). But unlike Jews and Christians, Muslims claim their identity with Abraham through Hagar and Ishmael, rather than through Sarah and Isaac. And this is the root of the alienation which exists between Christians and Muslims, both of whom claim to be the heirs of Abraham.

Who is a True Heir of Abraham?

In due time, Jesus was born, as the long promised "seed" of Abraham (Gal. 3:16). How we relate to Jesus becomes the determining factor in whether or not we truly belong to God. The Jews of Jesus' day had trouble with this claim. They said to Jesus, "We are Abraham's descendants ... "

(John 8:33). Jesus replied to them, "I know you are Abraham's descendants. Yet you are ready to kill me, because you have no room for my word. I am telling you what I have seen in the Father's presence, and you do what you have heard from your father" (John 8:37, 38).

In response, they said to Jesus, "Abraham is our father" (John 8:39). Jesus took the discussion further and said,

> If you were Abraham's children, then you would do the things Abraham did. As it is, you are determined to kill me, a man who has told you the truth that I heard from God. Abraham did not do such things. You are doing the things your own father does (John 8:39-41).

In response, the Jews insisted, "We are not illegitimate children … The only Father we have is God Himself" (John 8:41). Jesus minced no words in His reply: "You belong to your father, the devil, and you want to carry out your father's desire … " (John 8:44). As the controversy developed, the Jews reached the point where they asked, "Are you greater than our father Abraham? He died, and so did the prophets. Who do you think you are?" (John 8:53). Jesus, of course, answered these questions with a stunning claim: "Your father Abraham rejoiced at the thought of seeing my day; he saw it and was glad" (John 8:56). And, "I tell you the truth," Jesus answered, "before Abraham was born, I am!" (John 8:58).

The True Child of Abraham Believes In Jesus

The apostle Paul further clarified this issue in his letter to the Galatians: "The promises were spoken to Abraham and to his seed. The Scripture does not say 'and to seeds,' meaning many people, but 'and to your seed,' meaning one person, who is Christ" (Gal. 3:16). All the promises to Abraham are fulfilled in Jesus. It is through Abraham's Greater Son, Jesus, that the blessing spoken of in Genesis is going to reach the peoples of the world. Paul summarizes this so decisively: "You are all sons of God through faith in Christ Jesus, for all of you who were baptized into Christ have clothed yourselves with Christ … If you belong to Christ, then you are Abraham's seed, and heirs according to the promise" (Gal. 3:26, 27, 29).

Heirs of the World

The mention of the word "heirs" leads us on, then, to a much wider discussion of eternity. Above, we dealt with the question of who is to be an heir of Abraham. Now we take up the question of how one receives salvation. The Jews, and we might add, the Muslims, mistakenly think they will be saved by keeping the law, whereas the Bible unequivocally points out that salvation is only by faith in Christ. In Abraham's case, the Scripture says, "Abram believed the Lord and he credited it to him as righteousness" (Gen. 15:6). Paul shows clearly that faith in Christ is the key to obtaining this righteousness:

> The words "it was credited to him" were written not for him alone, but also for us, to whom God will credit righteousness—for us who believe in him who raised Jesus our Lord from the dead. He was delivered over to death for our sins and was raised to life for our justification (Rom. 4:23-25).

The implications of this "righteousness by faith" are far-reaching. "It was not through law that Abraham and his offspring received the promise that he would be heir of the world, but through the righteousness that comes by faith" (Rom. 4:13). And the object of our "saving faith" is Jesus Christ. Only believers in Christ are the true children of Abraham, and will receive forgiveness of their sins, and inherit the world.

Abraham and the Endtimes

The teaching above implies that how you relate to Jesus Christ determines whether or not you are a true child of Abraham and thus, an heir of the promise. Jesus, in speaking of endtimes, spells out this sharp distinction between those who will sit with Abraham and those who will not.

> I say to you that many will come from the east and the west, and will take their places at the feast with Abraham, Isaac and Jacob in the kingdom of heaven. But the subjects of the kingdom will be thrown outside, into the

darkness, where there will be weeping and gnashing of teeth (Matt. 8:11, 12).

The Jews of Jesus' day perceived themselves to be citizens of the kingdom of God, just as Muslims do today. But, the truth is that all those who reject Jesus as the King will be thrown out of the kingdom.

Paul, in his letter to the believers in Rome, summed it all up in these words:

> Therefore, the promise comes by faith, so that it may be by grace and may be guaranteed to all Abraham's offspring—not only to those who are of the law but also to those who are of the faith of Abraham. He is the father of us all. As it is written: "I have made you a father of many nations" (Rom. 4:16, 17).

In the light of such Scriptures, Abraham emerges as the first man of faith, the model for us all. This, of course, is not to take anything away from Abraham's "seed," Jesus Christ, without whom our salvation and inheritance would never have come.

As much as we would like to see Judaism, Christianity and Islam as branches of one big happy "family of Abraham," it cannot be. The stumbling block is Jesus Christ, the "seed of Abraham." When the Jews rejected Him, they put themselves outside the family of Abraham. The Muslims, on the other hand, have been more generous in the things they have said about Jesus, but the good effect of those words was nullified by the adamant stance Islam has taken against the very heart of the Gospel message. This book will address later the specifics of that stance: Islam's denial of the deity of Christ, incarnation, atonement, the crucifixion and the question of God as Father, Son and Spirit.

The schism between Islam and Christianity exists because Muslims have departed from the Scriptures and denigrated Christ. Far beyond doctrinal differences, they have set up a rival religion which seeks to supplant Christianity. Muhammad sought to give legitimacy to Islam by identifying with Abraham and his other son, Ishmael. He attempted to replace the Law of Moses with his own laws, and finally, consciously or unconsciously, to replace Jesus Christ as God's provision for our salvation with a false law that leads only to bondage and eternal death.

Let us look into the circumstances that laid the groundwork for this development. Abraham, like the rest of us, was a flawed human being, subject to error and bad judgment. If in his faith he typified the model believer, in his flesh, he forgot God's ways.

CHAPTER 2

THE FRIEND OF GOD FALTERS

So after Abram had been living in Canaan ten years, Sarai
his wife took her Egyptian maidservant Hagar and gave
her to her husband to be his wife. He slept with Hagar,
and she conceived (Gen. 16:3, 4).

On a certain occasion I preached in a large, wealthy church in
California. Five minutes before I was to stand up and speak, the
minister next to me asked, "Don, did you know that two-thirds of the
people in this congregation are single and the majority of these are
divorced?"

This information struck like a thunderbolt. I thought to myself, "Good
grief, what are all these terrible, mixed up people doing here in this attractive
'house of God?'" That was not the right reaction, of course. I turned to
the Lord and asked, "How do you see this?" He said, "You should have
praised me; I finally got them here where they belong." Then I prayed,
"Lord, please give me an opening sentence for this unusual congregation."

This is what He gave: "How many of you think God cares for every
person in a domestic tragedy when the man of the house sleeps with the
maid?" Instantly, everyone's attention was riveted on this unusual question.
Then I said, "This is the story of your father, (long pause) Abraham."

Seven Steps to Tragedy
The audience followed with rapt attention as we walked through the
chain reaction of faltering faith in the lives of Sarai, Abram and Hagar.
Let us look at these seven steps to tragedy in Genesis 16:1-6:

One. Sarai loses all hope of God's promise being fulfilled
in her life. God has spoken to her husband, saying,

"A son will come from your own body."

Sarai must have thought, "God only spoke to my husband; He didn't speak to me. My time is gone; I am beyond the age of childbearing. What should I do?" She counsels her husband to sleep with her Egyptian maidservant Hagar. "I can build a family through her."

Two. No questions asked. No consultation with the Lord. Just do what the neighbors do. "He slept with Hagar, and she conceived."

Three. "When she [Hagar] knew she was pregnant, she began to despise her mistress [Sarai]." The rivalry begins.

Four. Sarai blames Abram for this development: "You are responsible for the wrong I am suffering ... May the Lord judge between you and me."

Five. Abram shamelessly absolves himself from all responsibility, washing his hands of the whole affair. He says to Sarai, "Your servant [Hagar] is in your hands ... Do with her whatever you think best."

Six. "Then Sarai mistreated Hagar." Anger, frustration, violence, either verbal, physical, or both, rule the day.

Seven. "She [Hagar] fled from her [Sarai]." Abram was chosen to be the instrument of blessing to all mankind. Hagar fled from her only source of blessing.

What a list of missteps:

1. Take matters into your own hands. (Sarai)
2. Do not bother to consult the Lord. (Abram)
3. Be proud. Become a rival. (Hagar)
4. Blame someone else for your mistake. (Sarai)
5. Refuse to accept responsibility for your child. (Abram)
6. Give way to anger. Be abusive. (Sarai)
7. Do not repent. Run away. (Hagar)

Some people think the episode should have ended there. Abram made a mistake. The pregnant slave girl ran away. That should have been the end of the story.

An Angel Sent to Hagar

Wrong. God does not work that way. He was watching the whole scene. He loved Abram. He loved Sarai. He loved Hagar, too. Many statements in Scripture tell us what God is like: "God is love ..." (1 John 4:16), and "God our Savior ... wants all men to be saved and to come to a knowledge of the truth" (1 Tim. 2:3, 4), and "He is patient with you, not wanting anyone to perish, but everyone to come to repentance" (2 Peter 3:9).

Would God handle this matter in an honorable way? Yes! He sent an angel to minister to Hagar. How kind. Scripture says, "Are not all angels ministering spirits sent to serve those who will inherit salvation?" (Heb. 1:14). In fact, God made great promises to Hagar. Her descendants would be too numerous to count (Gen. 16:10). Today, one-fifth of the human race identifies with Hagar.

God Heard Hagar's Misery

In Semitic cultures, names have great significance. God Himself named Hagar's unborn son, and it was to be "God Hears." From the Hebrew language, that is transliterated as "Ishmael." The Lord chose this name because He had heard Hagar's misery. What a comment on the compassion of God.

God asked her to go back and to submit to Sarai. She obeyed the Lord, but before she went back, she gave a name to the place where her

17

great encounter with the Lord had occurred. She called it "The Well of the Living One Who Sees Me." Because this book has to do with Muslims, a word which means "one who has submitted," it is interesting to note that the passage could be recast as "Go back and become a 'submitter' or a 'Muslim' to Sarai."

God acted so humanely, so compassionately, so lovingly. He gave them all a second chance to live together in harmony. The years rolled by. Abram trained Ishmael in the ways of God. He loved him. Ishmael was his firstborn son and, as far as he knew, the one through whom God's promises would be fulfilled.

Surprise

When Abram was ninety-nine years old and Sarai was eighty-nine, God appeared to them. He reconfirmed His covenant with Abram, giving circumcision as the sign of this covenant. Abram and Ishmael were circumcised that same day. Then God changed Abram's name to Abraham; from "Exalted Father" to "Father of Many."

Then came the surprise. Sarai was given a new name too. She was to be called "Princess" (Sarah). But what was far more important was that she, also, was going to bear a son. Because it seemed so physically improbable, Abraham and Sarah both laughed at this impossible development. God gave the name "Laughter" (Isaac) to this coming miracle baby. A year later, "Laughter" was born.

Now Ishmael had a rival. He stood to lose everything because the real wife, the first wife, had a son. Things simmered along until the day of Isaac's weaning ceremony. It was Ishmael's turn to make a mistake. He made fun of his little half-brother. That was too much for Sarah. She made an irrevocable decision: "Get rid of that slave woman and her son, for that slave woman's son will never share in the inheritance with my son Isaac" (Gen. 21:10).

What did this mean? Did it mean that Ishmael was to be denied the blessing of salvation? Or was Sarah thinking only about wealth, the family fortune? We think it was the family wealth. For there are too many "sons of Ishmael" who have become Christians for it to mean they would be denied salvation.

Naturally, Abraham was upset. He loved his son Ishmael. In his time of distress, God spoke to him.

> Do not be so distressed about the boy and your maidservant. Listen to whatever Sarah tells you, because it is through Isaac that your offspring will be reckoned. I will make the son of the maidservant into a nation also, because he is your offspring (Gen. 21:12, 13).

In the beginning of the relationship, Abraham listened to his wife, and it turned out to be bad counsel. Now God was asking him to listen to his wife and expel Hagar and Ishmael from the home. If this had not been God speaking, Abraham might well have turned a deaf ear. But it was the Lord, so Abraham, "The Friend of God," believed and obeyed.

Hagar's Expulsion

The next morning Abraham released Hagar and her son Ishmael from his service. He gave them provisions and sent them on their way. What a shattering blow to everyone involved. Hagar's pregnancy was all Sarah's idea. Abraham complied. Ishmael was named by God Himself. Ishmael was the first child circumcised in Abraham's family. Hagar was even called Abraham's wife (Gen. 16:3). And now a heart-wrenching expulsion.

Worse was to come. Hagar became disoriented and lost in the desert of Beersheba. The provisions were all used up. Death stared Hagar and Ishmael in the face. Hagar made arrangements for both of them to die separately. Ishmael began to cry. Hagar began to sob. Again, the problem of Abraham and Sarah's mistake looked like it would be solved with the two tragic deaths. But again, God had other ideas. God heard a teenaged boy, whom He himself had named "God Hears," crying. He was not going to let this tragic mother and son die. He had made promises to Hagar and her son. He intended to keep His word. God opened Hagar's eyes and she saw a well of water; again, by God's personal intervention, their lives were spared. This God-blessed and resourceful single-parent family survived by God's grace. Scripture even says that "God was with the boy as he grew up …" (Gen. 21:20).

Our concern in this study is the question of healing broken relationships. Hagar and Ishmael, even though they both had committed

19

grave errors, had been victimized by Sarah's poor counsel and Abraham's irresponsible behavior. How does the question of salvation bear on this tragic separation? Does it mean that blessing is only to reside in Isaac's side of the family tree, and that nothing but curses and an eternity in hell await all the descendants of Ishmael? Hardly! Abraham was singled out not only to receive blessings from God, but to be the instrument of blessing to all others, even Hagar.

God's Great Love for Hagar

Many indications in this story show God's great love for Hagar and Ishmael. Twice He sent angels to minister to them and save their lives. He gave Ishmael a beautiful name and was with him as he grew up. There is no question that God desired to bless them. But another consideration figures into the question of healing this broken family, one which concerns the very nature of God's call upon Abraham to be a missionary. Let us look at that for a moment.

> I will make you into a great nation and I will bless you; I will make your name great, and you will be a blessing. I will bless those who bless you, and whoever curses you I will curse; and all peoples on earth will be blessed through you (Gen. 12:2, 3).

Abraham was not chosen to establish an exclusive family line, but rather to be the instrument of blessing to all other families on the earth. Isaac and Ishmael, one a miracle child and the other the result of a very human decision, neither having anything to do with the circumstances attending their births, were not intended to be rivals. Isaac, who received the same call as his father, was chosen to bless others, including Ishmael and his descendants. "God ... wants all men to be saved and to come to a knowledge of the truth" (1 Tim. 2:3, 4).

Reconciliation: The Question

Reconciliation is not out of the question—it *is* the question. Christ, Abraham's seed, is the Savior of all. He came to reconcile all things to Himself, including the people who call themselves Muslims (Col. 1:20).

Unfortunately, from Ishmael's line sprung a man, Muhammad, who had other ideas. He initially founded Islam as a religion for the Arab people. Later, he tried to universalize it and impose it on all mankind. In Islam, Jesus is reduced to a mere prophet: By making himself equal to Jesus and ultimately superior to Him, Muhammad perpetuated the spirit of rivalry, not reconciliation. The roots of this present-day alienation go back to the tragic events surrounding the breakup of Abraham's family. Islam became the venue for the aggrieved and alienated members of this family to redress the shame of that early expulsion from the tents of Abraham. Even more than that, Islam is committed to an attempt to dominate the world.

In spite of the spread of Islam among such a large segment of the earth's population (approximately one-fifth in the 1990s), it is still characterized by many spiritual inadequacies. Because of their religion's inability to satisfy the deepest needs of the human heart, increasing numbers of Muslims are open to Jesus and the wonderful ways He ministers to human needs. In the end, Jesus will win. We know, for example, the accolades that will be given to Christ at the end of this age:

> You are worthy to take the scroll and to open its seals, because you were slain, and with your blood you purchased men for God from every tribe and language and people and nation. You have made them to be a kingdom and priests to serve our God, and they will reign on the earth (Rev. 5:9, 10).

There will be Muslims, descendants of Ishmael, in that great heavenly gathering of people from every tribe, language, people and nation. The broken family of Abraham will be reconciled through the atoning blood of Jesus Christ. Nevertheless, for fourteen centuries, Islam has defied Christendom's best efforts to affect that reconciliation. It is, undoubtedly, the thorniest challenge facing Christian missions and the Church today.

As we respond to this challenge, let us take a closer look at the primary figures in this early domestic tragedy under Abraham's tents. What do we need to know about God's relationship to both Hagar and Ishmael? What clues can we find in the scriptural account that could influence our approach to Muslims? God our Father truly does care for every party in

CHAPTER 3

THE TRAGEDY OF HAGAR

Hagar, servant of Sarai, where have you come from, and where are you going? "I'm running away from my mistress Sarai," she answered (Gen. 16:8).

What is the matter, Hagar? Do not be afraid; God has heard the boy crying as he lies there. Lift the boy up and take him by the hand, for I will make him into a great nation (Gen. 21:17, 18).

One of the most remarkable relationships in all the Scriptures is that between God and Hagar. Why would God be interested in an Egyptian slave girl? What does this say about Him? What does it say to us as we look at the people today who claim either physical descent from her or a spiritual affinity with her?

God's Concern for Hagar

What is of immense interest to us is the concern God showed for this unfortunate woman. Twice He intervened to save her: the first time, He sent her back to submit to Sarai, her mistress. The second time, He spared her and Ishmael's lives when they were perishing in the desert.

Our premise is that if God was so concerned to save the life of this Egyptian slave girl and her son, we should be just as concerned today to reach those who claim to be her children. I believe the explanation for this concern can be found in the opening chapter of Genesis. There we read that not only man, but also woman was made in the image of God (Gen. 1:27). Hagar, in spite of her lowly estate as an Egyptian slave, and marred by the propensity to sin (as we all are), still bore that noble image of her Creator God. He valued her. She was important to Him. If Abraham was chosen to be the agent of blessing to the rest of humankind, Hagar was representative of those who were to receive that blessing.

23

God Not Willing That Any Should Perish

It is apparent from Scripture that Abraham and Sarah were willing for Hagar to perish. It was Peter who taught us that God was "not wanting anyone to perish, but everyone to come to repentance" (2 Peter 3:9). Abraham and Sarah had a lot to learn about God's love from this episode in their own lives. God wanted this first missionary couple to learn the value He places on human life. He would not allow them to treat life so cheaply. Later, Jesus came to express God's concern in these unforgettable words, "Are not five sparrows sold for two pennies? Yet not one of them is forgotten by God. Indeed, the very hairs of your head are all numbered. Don't be afraid; you are worth more than many sparrows" (Luke 12:6, 7). Then in real life He exhibited this concern for the "woman at the well" in Samaria (John 4:1-42). Jesus found a "Hagar" in his own day with whom He could demonstrate the Father's same loving concern.

Hagar and the Woman at the Well

The similarities between the story of Hagar and the "woman at the well" in Samaria are striking and deserve comment. Both women were outcasts of society; the one an expelled slave girl, the other a woman who moved from man to man, finally living with one to whom she was not married. Both encounters took place at wells. To Hagar, the Lord provided life-sustaining water; to the other, Jesus offered "living water." Hagar said, "I have now seen the One who sees me" (Gen. 16:13). The Samaritan woman said: "He told me everything I ever did" (John 4:39). God opened Hagar's eyes, and she saw a well of water that gave life to her and her dying son Ishmael. Jesus opened the eyes of the woman at the well to reveal Himself to her as the Messiah.

From this beginning of redemptive history, anticipating Jesus' teaching on the Father's love, God demonstrated to Abraham and Sarah His great love for the unfortunate.

God's Love for Hagar's Daughters

Today, this lesson needs to be learned by all Muslim women, who constitute about one out of every five women of the world. We know that God surely kept His promise to Hagar when He said, "I will so increase your descendants that they will be too numerous to count" (Gen. 16:10).

24

As was pointed out earlier, not all Muslim women can claim physical descent from Hagar, but they claim a spiritual affinity with her.

Hagar's Story Preserved in Pilgrimage

Hagar is never mentioned by name in the Quran. But the *Hadith* (the Traditions) correctly name her as the mother of Ishmael. In the pilgrim rites at Mecca, all Muslims re-enact Hagar's desperate search for water as they run between the hills of Safa and Marwa. The search is climaxed as they reach the well of Zamzam where they drink in memory of God's mercy to Hagar.

For us who know Jesus as the Fountain of Living Water, the Muslim pilgrim scene is painfully poignant on one hand, yet pregnant with hope on the other. The pain comes in watching the pilgrims re-enact this search for physical water, knowing all the while that God longs to give them spiritual water. Jesus is the true end of that search, and Islam denies Muslims that knowledge. Our hope is that God will, in His mercy, satisfy the deepest thirst of their souls, as we bring them to Jesus to drink the "living water."

In bringing this chapter to a close, I would like to share from a rare and moving selection of Dutch poetry found in Isaac da Costa's (died 1860) brilliant poem, "Hagar." This selection captures the pathos that I think we would do well to emulate as we think about Hagar's daughters today.

> Before the poet's eyes, a scene recalled,
> A precarious hour—Of barren wilderness
> With everything in perfect stillness,
> Untouched by wind or storm.
>
> A woman utterly alone, wracked with grief
> And sorrow, and the pain of shattered pride,
> Reflects the shaming humiliation from inner depths,
> As she stumbles on with unsteady steps.
>
> A flattened waterskin, long since empty,
> Flaps loosely on her swelling breasts.
> Pangs of hunger doubled by the new life within
> Aches for the bread too soon spent.

A pathetic contrast to the scene before,
When in thoughtless pride, You Sarah scorned.
O haughty one! Where will you go?
You who reaped this curse of woe?

Cast out in fitting chastisement
From the blessing of Abraham's tent.
Do not go back to the land of Ham,
Refuge find in Mamre's stand.

Humble yourself before God at Sarah's feet,
There your supply will be replete
In godly faithfulness of water and bread,
And for your soul, support and comfort spread.

In willingness serve and your seed will prosper,
For in Abraham's tent there's more than one promise.
What springs forth from Abraham's loin
Portends a mighty chieftain yet to be born.

O Mother of Ishmael, I see you once more,
Wandering the frightening desert, forlorn,
Unconsoled, despairing, in agony's grip,
Tossed in the tempest of mental torment.

You, too, gave glory to the God of heaven.
The veil was rent. He came; He spoke to you:
"At Sarah's feet you will repent
And confess your foolish pride ill-spent."

It is only in the folds of Abraham's tent
You obtain the blessing of God's covenant.
Yes. The moment you cry, your spirit is free:
"O God of my life! Have compassion on me."

CHAPTER 4

ISHMAEL: GOD HEARS

> The angel of the Lord also said to her: "You are now
> with child and you will have a son. You shall name him
> Ishmael, for the Lord has heard of your misery" (Gen.
> 16:11).

Ishmael. Translated from the Hebrew, it reads "God hears." This is the
name given by God Himself to the unborn son of Hagar, the abused,
pregnant runaway maidservant of Sarah, the wife of Abraham. The child
she was carrying was Abraham's. In this unfolding domestic tragedy, how
God relates to each person is of supreme importance. For here, in His
dealings with Abraham and his family, we find early intimations of God's
rich love, mercy and compassion. In the preceding chapter, we learned of
God's love for Hagar. In this one, we are going to look at the amazing way
in which God showed His love to Ishmael.

Ishmael, Part of the Covenant Family

Ishmael was born to Hagar, just as God had promised. He grew up at
his father's side as part of the covenant missionary family worshiping the
one true God. When Ishmael was thirteen years old, God appeared to his
father and gave to them the covenant of male circumcision. As members
of one family, Ishmael and his father Abraham were circumcised on the
same day. What is so striking today is that even though circumcision is
not mentioned in the Quran, Muslims, following this early family pattern,
circumcise all their male children.

"I Will Surely Bless Him"

During this same visit, Ishmael was a subject of conversation. God
had told Abraham that Sarah, even in her old age, was going to have a
son. Abraham's immediate response was, "If only Ishmael might live under

your blessing!" (Gen. 17:18) Having earlier been willing for Hagar and her unborn son to be banished, it is wonderful to see that Abraham has developed a truly fatherly heart and asks God to bless Ishmael. God's answer is a resounding "Yes." After discussing the future role of Isaac in His covenant plan for blessing the human race, God takes up the matter of Ishmael again: "And as for Ishmael, I have heard you: I will surely bless him; I will make him fruitful and greatly increase his numbers. He will be the father of twelve rulers, and I will make him into a great nation" (Gen. 17:20).

Sadly, in stark contrast to these words of scripture, the majority of Christians seem to believe that God has cursed Ishmael, or at least bypassed him, and that he is of no consequence. God is not like that, especially with Abraham's own son. Ishmael is to be blessed. Furthermore, he is going to become the father of twelve rulers whose descendents will form a great nation. The mysterious promise that God will establish His covenant with Isaac still prevails, but without excluding Ishmael from God's blessing. Isaac, like his father, is to be the agent of blessing, as will his ultimate descendant, Jesus, in whom and through whom we finally see the nature and magnitude of that blessing.

Ishmael in Islam

Ishmael is mentioned several times in the Quran and is powerfully memorialized in the rites connected with the annual pilgrimage to Mecca. He is frequently listed along with the other patriarchs. The one Quranic passage that treats Ishmael at length is worth quoting:

> Also mention in the Book (the story of) Ismail: He was (strictly) true to what he promised, and he was an apostle (and) a prophet. He used to enjoin on his people Prayer and Charity, and he was most acceptable in the sight of his Lord (Q. 19:54, 55).

In another section of the Quran, Muhammad cites Abraham and Ishmael in designating the Kaaba as the pilgrim center for Muslims:

> Remember We made the House a place of assembly for men and a place of safety; and take ye the Station of

Abraham as a place of prayer; and We covenanted with
Abraham and Ismail, that they should sanctify my House
for those who compass it round, or use it as a retreat, or
bow, or prostrate themselves (therein in prayer) (Q.
2:125).

The Pilgrimage Commemorates Ishmael

The greatest feast of Islam, *Id al-Adha*, occurs at the conclusion of the
pilgrimage. Each Muslim is supposed to participate in a sacrifice, whether
it be a sheep, goat or camel. The sacrifice commemorates Abraham's
willingness to offer up his son to God. This sacrifice is observed
simultaneously throughout the whole Muslim world, by pilgrims in Mecca
as well as by Muslims in their own homes. Thus all Muslims are linked
with the family of Abraham through this commemorative feast. Anyone
familiar with the biblical account of these events knows full well that
these events did not occur in Mecca, but elsewhere, and that it was Isaac,
not Ishmael, who was the designated sacrifice (Gen. 22:2). Ishmael had
been expelled from the home years before (Gen. 21:14). As misplaced as
these rituals and beliefs may appear in light of biblical material, they are,
nevertheless, profoundly insightful. Deep within the psyche of Muhammad
and the Arab people, and subsequently all Muslims, whether Arab or not,
is an intense longing to be counted in the family of Abraham, "the Friend
of God."

The Cries of Ishmael's Children Today

In the latter chapters of this book, we shall be discussing various ways
that Muslims can become true members of Abraham's family. Meanwhile,
let us listen with our Heavenly Father who first heard "God Hears" crying.
In the quiet hush of myriads of mosques, the droning voices of Muslims
intone: "There is no God but God and Muhammad is the Messenger of
God." In slavish imitation of their Arab "prophet," they mime the words,
while their hearts cry silently that God would count their endless
prostrations for good on Judgment Day.

Not far away, in the shadow of the mosque, at the tomb of a dead
"saint," a daughter of Ishmael weeps. She strokes her hands on the "holy"
tomb in the hope that blessing will rub off on her. Then she strokes her

face and breasts, crying out, "O God, answer my prayer for …"

Deep in the forest, Sufis gather in a circle. Matching the rhythm of their incessant rocking to and fro, they chant "*Allah hua,*" "God is!"—two hundred thousand times!—until they enter a psychic state of ecstasy, which they believe means they have achieved union with God.

Far from Mecca, in the jungles of Java, the cry is unearthly, piercing. All the ritual prayers of the Muslim *mullahs* (priests), all the blood of many sacrifices with their magical incantations, have not delivered this daughter of Ishmael from the torment of demons. Hers is the helpless scream of the demon-possessed from which Islam has no power to deliver.

In Ramalah, Palestine, it is not Rachel, but Riffat weeping for her children because they are no more. Israeli bullets have obliterated their lives on the dusty roads of the West Bank. It is the cry not only for children forever gone, but also for bulldozed fruit trees and leveled homes. Senseless slaughter, senseless destruction! The cry is for justice and fairness. The cry is that age-old question, "Will not the God of the whole earth do right?"

And in the dismal camps of the dispossessed, the refugee cries for his ancestral home. Ishmael has been driven from his land—not just in Palestine, but in Lebanon, Afghanistan, Kosovo, Iraq, Ethiopia, Eritrea, Sudan, Chad. And through economic disaster, hundreds of thousands more from Pakistan, Bangladesh, India, Egypt, Algeria, Tunisia, Morocco. The cries of Ishmael's children go up endlessly.

From the garbage dumps of glutted cities—Cairo—Calcutta— Dacca— Karachi—the cry is more of a moan as the utterly destitute, scavenging among the refuse and rats, are too tired to even whimper their question, "Where are you, O God?" Does God hear? Yes! Ishmael. He named this unwanted child "God Hears!" He hears! Hallelujah! He hears! God grant that we, too, may hear!

CHAPTER 5

HOSTILITY TOWARD THE BRETHREN

He will be a wild donkey of a man; his hand will be against everyone and everyone's hand against him, and he will live in hostility toward all his brothers (Gen. 16:12).

This ancient prophecy about the unborn Ishmael is cause for much thought. Did God arbitrarily predetermine Ishmael's behavior? Or is it possible that God foresaw the inevitable consequences of the broken relationships in this family? The answers to these two questions are not far apart, for God is the one who created us to function the way we do, and He knows the dynamics of human relationships. In this sense, He saw the inevitability of what was going to happen to Ishmael and foretold it.

Twists in Ishmael's Personality

A spirit of rivalry was born as soon as Hagar knew she was pregnant. In the culture of that day, a woman's fulfillment was in bearing children, especially sons. A woman who could not bear children was considered a failure in life. Hagar prematurely drew the conclusion that God had favored her and had withheld this blessing from Sarah. She gave way to pride and began to hold her mistress in contempt. Sarah, deeply hurt by Hagar's behavior, responded abusively with anger, causing Hagar to flee from her presence. So, even before he was born, Ishmael witnessed the emotional trauma—tongue-lashings from Sarah, the refusal of Abraham to defend her, and then, the sense of utter abandonment as she fled from the family. Fear, anger, and hostility caused tremendous emotional upheaval inside of Hagar while Ishmael grew in her womb.

After Ishmael's birth, things seemed to settle down. Ishmael grew up at his father Abraham's side, fully believing that, as the firstborn, he was to be the heir. He was circumcised on the same day as his father at the age of thirteen, and undoubtedly considered himself an important part of this special family.

Later, the stability of the family was shattered by the news that Sarah was going to have a baby boy named "Laughter" (Isaac). Ishmael now had to live with the possibility that he, as a son of a slave woman, might be preempted from his role as the firstborn by the son of the legitimate "first wife." Undoubtedly, Hagar's old feelings of rivalry were reawakened by this new threat. She may have helped engender feelings of jealousy and contempt in Ishmael towards Sarah's son. By the time of Isaac's weaning feast, Ishmael could no longer contain his feelings and he mocked Sarah and her son (Gen. 21:9). As a result, Hagar and Ishmael were provisioned, dismissed from service, and set free. Who can gauge the depth of bitterness and resentment that must have filled Hagar's and Ishmael's hearts? The prophetic utterance concerning the behavior of Ishmael is rooted in these events.

Ishmael's Legacy Today

In mid-2000, Muslims numbered more than one billion people and, no doubt, constitute the largest threat facing the Christian Church today. Is there any link between the characteristics of Ishmael and that of Islam, which has embraced him as one of its patriarchs? As strange as it may seem, I think there is. History seems to bear this out. Lest we be too harsh on Ishmael's descendants, let us remember our own sorrowful history. The two World Wars of this century began in the West. Until the collapse of the Soviet Union, the two most feared and dangerous powers in the world today were both considered to be Western powers, the Soviet Union and the United States. We must be careful not to judge Islam for what we ourselves have been guilty of.

What is this dynamic of violence, both ours and theirs, and of hostility that feeds it? For the following explanation, I am indebted to Edward Hunter and his unique book, *Brainwashing in Red China* (1953). Hunter's analysis was prompted by the dismay felt in America when we learned that some of our troops, captured during the Korean War, were successfully brainwashed and turned against our country. Hunter demonstrates how the Chinese learned to use psychiatric discoveries about the cycle which leads from a sense of sin (real or induced) to violence. Parenthetically, even though many scholars say that Muslims are characterized more by a "shame and honor" set of values than a "sin and obedience" one, this writer believes that all have sinned against the real God, and such sin entails real guilt. Woodberry supports this idea in his investigative work in the Quran and extra-Quranic resources (1989:150-159). Therefore, I believe the following material explains the cycle of sin and violence in the lives of Muslims.

It works something like this. Sin, real or imagined, engenders a sense of guilt. Guilt, if not dealt with, breeds fear. This fear, if not removed, leads to a vague sense of hostility. In due time, this hostility will begin to focus either inwardly, causing psychosomatically induced illnesses or suicidal tendencies, or it will project itself outward on some designated hate object. Eventually, if the person is not delivered from this fateful dynamic, the hostility can be triggered to commit acts of violence, either against a person (homicide) or against a people (genocide or war).

Ishmael's hostility and propensity to violence were rooted in the sin of his own scoffing and jealous attitude towards his brother Isaac. This vicious cycle has today been perpetuated in the lives of contemporary Muslims. They have voluntarily chosen to identify with Ishmael and have, consciously or unconsciously, embraced the spirit of that ancient and bitter rivalry.

What makes Islam unique is that it has institutionalized and even blessed this propensity to violence in the form of *jihad* (holy war), violent acts committed in the name of God. Hunter's analysis explains the reason for violence, but it was Muhammad who incorporated it as religious duty in Islam.

Muhammad, a True Descendent of Ishmael

Let us look again at that verse about Ishmael's characteristics: "He will be a wild donkey of a man ..." (Gen. 16:12). What does that mean? God, in His withering rebuke to Job, spoke of the wild donkey:

> Who let the wild donkey go free? Who untied his ropes?
> I gave him the wasteland as his home, and the salt flats as
> his habitat. He laughs at the commotion in the town; he
> does not hear a driver's shout. He ranges the hills for his
> pasture and searches for any green thing (Job 39:5-8).

Ishmael was to be strong, wild and free. He also would be difficult, holding his brother in contempt, despising town life, loving his freedom to the point of fighting with his own kin or anyone else. One commentary states: "The Ishmaelites live in an incessant state of feud ... with one another or with their neighbours," and in the same passage, "Ishmael would maintain an independent standing before [in the presence of] all the descendants of Abraham" (Keil and Delitzsch, Reprint, 1954, 1:220).

Note that both monotheism and the use of force, were characteristics of Ishmael. By spending the early years at Abraham's side, Ishmael learned monotheism. But after his expulsion from the family, the hostile and warlike tendencies began to develop.

In the light of these characteristics, Muhammad was a true descendant of Ishmael. While trying desperately to tie into the genealogical tree of biblical prophets, he fiercely maintained his independence as an "Arab prophet" with an "Arabic Quran" (Q. 12:2; 20:113; 41:44; 46:12). Moreover, Muhammad stoutly maintained that he was neither of the Jews nor the Christians but of the "Religion of Abraham" (Q. 2:135). In taking this position, Muhammad attempted to establish his own identity as a legitimate prophet. He borrowed from the traditions of each, and separated himself from both, in order to supersede all his predecessors and become the Seal of the Prophets, that is, the end of the prophetic line, and therefore, the final voice of God to the human race. At first, Muhammad attempted to woo both Jews and Christians. When he was unsuccessful, he not only turned away from them, but in the case of the Jews, he dispossessed two of the tribes, banished them, massacred all the men of a third, and made slaves of the women and children. In the case of the Christians, he reduced them to second-class citizens (*dhimmis*) and attempted to destroy the very heart of the Christian message. These points will be more fully addressed later. Having made himself odious to both Jews and Christians, Muhammad then took the step of enshrining violence forever among his followers by sanctifying vengeance (Q. 42:39) and fighting (Q. 2:216; 4:74; 9:5; 61:4). (There are more than fifty separate references in the Quran on the duties and conditions of holy war [Whitehouse 1981:50, 51]).

"I Will Surely Bless Him"

Abraham's prayer was not in vain. He prayed, "If only Ishmael might live under your blessing!" And God said, "Yes ... I have heard you: I will surely bless him" (Gen. 17:18-20). God waits for us today to ask Him to bless the sons of Ishmael—the Muslims—through the preaching of the Good News of Jesus Christ. In faith, we believe there will be a harvest among our hostile brethren, and healing will come to the broken family of Abraham, the father of us all.

PART TWO

ISHMAEL'S MOST ILLUSTRIOUS SON

CHAPTER 6

MUHAMMAD: THE FIRST MUSLIM

> Say: "Shall I take for my protector any other than God, the Maker of the heavens and the earth? And He it is that feedeth but is not fed." Say: "Nay! but I am commanded to be the first of those who bow to God (in Islam), and be not thou of the company of those who join gods with God" (Q. 6:14).

Muhammad, in the above quote, designates himself as the first Muslim, or the first in Islam. This could be interpreted in two ways: either he is the preeminent Muslim of all time, or he is the founder of a new religion called Islam. Because Muhammad presents Abraham and many biblical figures as Muslims (those who prostrate themselves before God), including Jesus, it would appear that he is giving himself preeminence.

Yet historically, the religion of Islam did not exist before Muhammad. The Muslim calendar, for example, does not start with Abraham, but with the year in which Muhammad assumed political power and military leadership of the Muslims in Medina, which was in 622. Thus, in two ways, Muhammad became the first of the Muslims: first in terms of leadership, and first in terms of being the originator of Islam.

The word "Muslim" calls for some kind of definition here. Semantically, the basic meaning of the word as found in a dictionary, is "someone who has submitted." In its Islamic context, it means "someone who has submitted to God and Muhammad." Since, in the Quran, the names of God and Muhammad are inextricably linked, it means, in short, someone who has submitted to Muhammad and his teaching as found in the Quran and the *Hadith*. Thus, Muhammad is perceived to be the founder and primary advocate of Islam.

A Sketch of Muhammad's Life

Over and over again, Muslims will ask you, the Christian worker, "What do you think of Muhammad?" You may not want to answer that question, but at least you should be able to say that you have read about him. The following sketch is based upon material from a number of biographies. (See the References Cited section at the end of this book.)

Muhammad was born in Mecca, Arabia, about the year A.D. 570. His father died before he was born, and his mother died two years later. He was raised in the desert by various relatives of the prominent Quraysh tribe. This tribe is reputed to have learned the ways of the Bedouins—the migratory, tent-dwelling Arabs characterized by their hospitality and mercy to the poor. Later, as a young man, he led caravans on behalf of rich merchants and distinguished himself for his honesty and astuteness in his dealings with others.

In the year A.D. 595, he married his wealthy employer, the widow Khadijah, who was fifteen years his senior. He was utterly faithful to her until her death in A.D. 619. From his youth, Muhammad was known as a contemplative person. His marriage to this wealthy widow afforded him the leisure time he wanted. He often withdrew to a cave at the base of Mount Hira outside of Mecca to meditate. At the age of forty (A.D. 610), Muhammad had his first ecstatic experience. Many scholars think he was referring to this experience in what he wrote in the Surah entitled, "The Star:"

> He was taught by one mighty in power, endued with wisdom: for he appeared (in stately form) while he was in the highest part of the horizon: then he approached and came closer, and was at a distance of but two bow-lengths or (even) nearer: so did (God) convey the inspiration to his servant—(conveyed) what he (meant) to convey. The (Prophet's) (mind and) heart in no way falsified that which he saw (Q. 53:5-11).

This experience initially deeply troubled Muhammad and he wondered whether he had gone mad or become possessed by a *jinn* (an evil spirit). After consultations with his wife and her Christian relative, Waraqa bin

Naufal, he was persuaded that during this experience, he was actually receiving a "revelation" from God through the intermediary role of the angel Gabriel. These "revelations" came at irregular intervals, and during this period, his wife and a few intimate friends came to believe in him as an "Apostle of God." After three years of secrecy, Muhammad felt he was receiving the command to begin public preaching (A.D. 613) This preaching went on for about six years without being seriously challenged by the leaders of the Quraysh Tribe.

Opposition to Muhammad's strong monotheistic and moralistic preaching began among the Quraysh's powerful ruling elders in A.D. 619. At that time, Mecca was a shrine center for all of Arabia and the trade associated with pagan shrines was being threatened by Muhammad's monotheistic preaching. The power struggle between Muhammad and the Quraysh leaders intensified over the next three years, culminating in their plan to assassinate him. This was in the year A.D. 622. Muhammad, warned in advance by friends, fled Mecca in June of that year, accepting the invitation to serve as a leader-arbitrator to the warring Arab tribes in the city of Yathrib, later called Medina, about two hundred miles to the north (Barton 1974:130).

Muhammad gained ascendancy among those warring tribal chieftains in Yathrib and successfully united them to challenge the supremacy of the Meccans. By the year A.D. 630, Muhammad was powerful enough to lead ten thousand men to Mecca, where he took control without a fight. In the year A.D. 632, just ten years after his emigration from Mecca to Medina, Muhammad fell ill and died under mysterious circumstances. He was approximately sixty-two years old. He had made no provision for who should succeed him in leadership, or by what rules new leaders should be chosen. This lack of foresight has plagued Islam ever since with endless power struggles, assassinations and turmoil.

Throughout these turbulent years, Muhammad displayed an unshakable tenacity in his sense of calling as the last of all the monotheistic prophets. He displayed unusual courage in battle and was extremely astute in negotiating with friend and foe. In spite of his rapidly growing list of wives (eleven, plus two concubines) following the death of Khadijiah, he was distinguished for his piety in prayer, alms, fasting and generosity.

The system of practices and code of beliefs he built and exemplified in his own life were a brilliant synthesis of worship patterns and popularly-

41

held religious ideas he assiduously cultivated from his contacts with Jews, a wide variety of Christians, Zoroastrians and of course, his own heritage as an Arab.

He had many gifts, the greatest of which was his facility with words. He was a master of the Arabic language, apparently unexcelled in his day, in the style of semi-poetic Arabic oratory. He must have had a magnificent voice and the ability to mesmerize audiences with his style of speech. He often challenged his detractors to match the quality of his utterances.

CHAPTER 7

MUHAMMAD'S BOOK: THE QURAN

> Blessed is He Who sent down the Criterion [the Quran] to his servant [Muhammad], that it may be an admonition to all creatures; —He to Whom belongs the dominion of the heavens and the earth: no son has He begotten, nor has He a partner in his dominion (Q. 25:1, 2).

If the Christian worker wants to learn why Muslims tend to be so resistant to the Good News of Jesus Christ, he or she needs to become familiar with the Quran. The average Western Christian reader will find this book puzzling. This is because we have been taught a completely different pattern of thinking than that exhibited in the construction of the Quran. Culturally, we are rationalists. We expect things to flow in logical progression. And biblically, we have been conditioned to believe redemptive history unfolds through time. The exceptions are the grouping of the "major" and "minor" prophets in the Old Testament, and the sequence of some of the Epistles in the New Testament.

The Flow of the Bible

The Christian is accustomed to a Bible that starts with the creation of the world. It describes the origins of the races and explains the reasons for various languages. It shows how and why God chose Abraham to be the first missionary to the whole world. Moses, law-giver and deliverer, comes next. History moves on through Joshua and the conquest of Canaan. The earthly kingdom of Israel is finally established through David and his line. Worship and hymnology come into being. Wisdom literature is developed. Then prophets are raised up to deal with the problem of apostasy. Divine punishment comes through devastating conquest and exile. Restoration, rebuilding and a return to the Law of God prevail for a while, only to give way to further backslides.

Throughout, there are prophecies of a Messiah to come, then silence for four hundred years. The people are left to their own choices and suffer miserable defeats. Palestine is finally occupied by the Romans and the stage is set for the coming of the Messiah. John the Baptist paves the way for Jesus, the Lamb of God, who came to take away the sin of the world.

Jesus, fully man and fully God, manifests the mighty works of God, binds Satan, overpowers demons, heals the sick, raises the dead, controls the wind and the sea, turns water into wine and multiplies loaves and fishes. He forgives people of their sins and creates new hope in human hearts. In short, Jesus conquers every known enemy of humankind temporarily in His lifetime, and permanently through His crucifixion and resurrection from the dead. Finally, He ascends to glory, and with the Father pours out the Holy Spirit on believers, empowering them to do "greater works" than He Himself did (John 14:12).

The first generation of apostles write the inspired "Good News." Other witnesses then help interpret the meaning of Christ through their New Testament writings, and finally Christ visits John, "the Apostle of Love," with a final message to his age. It all flows. There is a finality to it. It is sufficient for the rest of human history.

The Structure of the Quran

The Quran is, simply put, the collected sayings of Muhammad. The first ecstatic utterance came at the age of forty (A.D. 610) and the last came in the year of his death in A.D. 632. At the time of Muhammad's death, the Quran had not been properly written down, much less arranged (Burton 1977:119). This work was left to his survivors, and their arrangement of the material is quite unique.

It is very difficult to reconstruct the sequence of themes on which Muhammad preached, because of the unusual ways in which his successors compiled his ecstatic utterances. With the exception of the first chapter of the Quran, called the "Opening", the remaining 113 chapters are arranged by length, with total disregard for chronology. The chapters are arranged with the longest one first and the shortest one last, with the exception of chapter one. It is generally agreed that the longer chapters are compilations of utterances given at differing times. Nevertheless, there is some consensus among scholars as to what came early and what came later. In general, the powerful emotive utterances with a strong moralistic tone and fierce emphasis on monotheistic faith came early, and the more prosaic chapters dealing with organizational, legal and administrative matters came later. The later chapters are also thought to have dealt with the controversies with the Jews and Christians, the preoccupation with war, and intimations of the universality of Islam. Throughout, one will find repeated references to Muhammad's defense of his prophethood, and the constant linking of his name with that of Allah as the one to be obeyed.

Why wouldn't Muhammad's survivors arrange the Quran chronologically? The answer is found in Muhammad's and the Muslims' concept of revelation. To them, "The language of the Koran is God's language, and its eloquence is miraculous … it is an infallible guide to conduct … it is therefore absolutely and uniquely consistent …" (Margoliouth 1928:63). Unlike Christians, who believe the Spirit of God moved on the minds of men, inspiring them to write in their own words and style the intent of God, the majority of Muslims believe the Quran is eternal, the original copy possibly written on "preserved tablets" placed beside the Throne of God (Hitti 1970:26). They believe that in due time, these "revelations" were moved from the highest heaven to the lowest heaven and dispatched to earth through the agency of an angel, presumably, Gabriel, as they were needed for guidance in the unfolding events in Muhammad's life.

As-Suyuti (A.D.1445-1505), the great Muslim Quranist, is quoted in *Islam from within:* "There is no disagreement among intellectuals that the Book of God [the Quran] most exalted is a miracle which no one can imitate when challenged to do so" (Cragg and Speight 1980:18). More recently, Rahman, has written, "The Quran is thus pure Divine Word … The Divine Word flowed through the Prophet's heart" (Rahman 1979:33).

This latter Muslim concept of the Quran as miracle has made it easy for them to compile Surahs according to their own perceptions of what constitutes a chapter. If it is miracle (magic), then chronology is not important. It will work wherever you put it. Arberry, in his preface to *The Koran Interpreted*, approaching the problem from a unique literary position, has written, "I have disregarded this accepted fact [that is, the gathering in one chapter passages from widely differing periods of time], wishing to show each Surah as an artistic whole, its often incongruous parts constituting a rich and admirable pattern" (Arberry 1955:25).

It is this mysterious artistic thread that wreaks havoc with any concept of narration on any kind of a time line. A few scholars, like Richard Bell (1958), have valiantly attempted to rearrange the Quran according to the events as they occurred in the life of Muhammad, and any interested student may do the same, with great profit. For to place the words of the Quran in the context of what was going on in Muhammad's life makes the words far more understandable. Unfortunately, Muslim scholars are seldom given to this kind of reconstruction, and because they have this unusual view about the words themselves being the actual words of God, they do not appreciate outsiders tampering with their book. So, the non-Muslim student of the Quran is left to his own devices in systematizing and analyzing the contents. To add to the confusion, according to common understanding, later "revelations" could abrogate earlier utterances of the Quran (Guillaume 1954:184). So readers should not look for total consistency in the Quran.

Here is a simple illustration of how mutually contradictory material has been brought together in the Quran without regard for chronology or contradiction. In the beginning of his career, when Muhammad was trying to woo the Christians and Jews to believe in him as an authentic prophet of God, he said such things as:

> Nearest among them in love to the Believers [Muslims] wilt thou find those who say, "We are Christians": Because amongst these are men devoted to learning and men who have renounced the world, and they are not arrogant (Q. 5:85).

But later on, after Muhammad failed to persuade the Jews and Christians that he was a true prophet of God, he turned against them, and this is reflected in such sayings as:

> O ye who believe [Muslims]! Take not the Jews and the Christians for your friends and protectors: they are but friends and protectors to each other. And he amongst you that turns to them (for friendship) is of them. Verily God guideth not a people unjust (Q. 5:54).

Both of these are found in the same Surah, but in reverse chronological order! Obviously, they were gathered together in a chapter that touched on Muhammad's dealings with Jews and Christians, as well as many other themes. And that is not to say that everything he said on this subject is confined to this chapter.

The story of how the first caliphs, beginning with Abu Bakr, gathered these sayings from people's memories, pieces of leather, stones, palm fronds and writings on the flat bones of animals and caused them to be written down is fascinating. But because the vowel points were not written into the text at that time, variant readings developed over the years. It was another one hundred and fifty years before a standard text was decided on.

Sources of Quranic Material

In spite of the fact that Muslims regard the Quran as the eternal Word of God, to the average Westerner, it merely reflects the brilliant responses of a gifted and sensitive religious and political genius to the events transpiring in his environment of early seventh century Arabia. For the interested Westerner, several valuable books trace the sources of the Quranic material. From the missionary perspective, three older missionary sources are worthy of mention here:

> *The Mizan-ul-Haqq* (Balance of Truth) by C. G. Pfander, first written in Persian in 1835, later translated and revised by W. St. Clair Tisdall in 1910, London: The Religious Tract Society.
> *The Original Sources of the Quran* by W. St. Clair Tisdall, London: Society for Promoting Christian Knowledge, 1911.
> *The Sources of Islam* by John C. Blair, Madras: The Christian Literature Society for India, 1925.

The latter two each build on the work of his predecessor. Blair's work, therefore, is the most well documented; and from it, the researcher can actually trace most of the material in the Quran to identifiable sources existing at the time of Muhammad in and around Arabia.

For the interested scholar, there are secular texts, such as C. C. Torrey's collected lecture series entitled, *The Jewish Foundation of Islam* (1933);

The Origin of Islam in its Christian Environment, by Richard Bell. London: Frank Cass and Company Limited, 1926; *Christianity Among the Arabs in Pre-Islamic Times,* by J. Spencer Trimingham, Longman's, London, 1979 and *Studies on Islam,* Editor, Merlin L. Swartz (Henninger's article, "Pre-Islamic Bedouin Religion"). New York: Oxford University Press, 1981.

Without going into a great deal of detail, the following summary is derived from Blair's work.

The "Christian" material in the Quran is largely attributed to matters arising out of the Christological controversies of the day between the Monophysites and the Nestorians, plus material either refuting or taken from heretical Gospels. The Monophysites believed Christ had only one nature and it was divine. They concluded the divine Christ could not be crucified—it only appeared so. The Nestorians believed that Christ had two natures and that the divine nature was given to Christ at His baptism and taken up to heaven from the cross before Jesus died.

The "Jewish" material is virtually all found in various places in the *Talmud* and the *Mishnah.* Even so, some confusion is evidenced in Muhammad's assumption that "Maryam" the sister of Moses (1440 B.C.) was the same "Maryam," the Mother of Jesus at the beginning of the Christian Era, an idea that cannot be blamed on either the *Talmud* or *Mishnah.*

Muhammad's sensuous concept of heaven, with unlimited numbers of beautiful dark-eyed virgins for every man, may be the most often quoted example of material borrowed from Zoroastrianism. And in spite of Muhammad's claim that the Quran was "pure" Arabic, scholars have now identified several words from Ethiopic, Sanskrit, Chaldee and Syriac (Jeffrey:1938).

This information is valuable to the Christian confronted with the claims Muslims make for the Quran. It also helps defend Muhammad against the charge of being unusual, because we now know where he gleaned his material. We have come to realize that he was not making things up, but was accurately reflecting what he had learned by word of mouth from his contemporaries. His genius was not in his sources, but in his ability to weave all this material together in such a way that it had an almost mesmeric effect on his Arabian hearers. The secret of its effect was in the evocative imagery that could touch a native Arabic speaker's heart.

The Power of the Quran

When Muslims claim that the Quran is not translatable, they mean that the literary subtleties fail to come through with the same rich, emotive power they hold in the original. This is true of brilliant poetry in almost any language. Too much is lost in translation. In this respect only, their point is valid. In all other respects, the Quran *is* translatable and has been translated into about a hundred different languages.

In trying to further explain the grip of the Quran on its Arabian listeners, A. J. Arberry's comments are most apropos:

> First let us look again at the rhythm; for it is to the rhythm that I constantly return as I grope for a clue to the arresting, the hypnotic power of the Muslim scriptures ... a wide range of rhythmic patterns, all used with seemingly effortless ease, and each eliciting a distinctive response from the listener ... Rhythm runs insistently through the entire Koran; but it is a changeful, fluctuating rhythm, ranging from the gentle, lulling music of the narrative and legislative passages, through the lively counterpoint of the hymns of praise, to the shattering drum-rolls of the apocalyptic movements (1980:Volume II, 8, 9).

The average Western reader, unacquainted with the subtleties and rich complexities of Arabic prosody, loses all of this in English translation. Arberry's translation of the Quran (1955), along with selected passages from Dawood (1956), and rare but exquisite translations from Cragg (1988), come close at times to capturing some of this "hypnotic" power of words in English, but the Christian worker will really have to become proficient in classical Arabic to appreciate what a Muslim experiences while listening to the recitation of the Quran.

The Content of the Quran

With regard to the content of the Quran, there is no substitute for reading the whole of it for one's self. Anyone who seeks to work with Muslims should be able to say to his friend, "Yes, I have read the Quran." To hundreds of millions of Muslims, Muhammad comes across as the last and greatest prophet. The Quran reflects a fierce monotheism, a higher ethical standard than that of his contemporaries, a seductive promise of a sensuous paradise against frightening pictures of a gruesome hell, a great collection of religious dicta, and an exclusivism that divides the world into two groups: the "House of Islam" and the "House of War." It is through this book, about two-thirds the size of the New Testament, as well as through his personal example, that Muhammad imparted to his followers a passion for world conquest in the name of Islam.

The Authority of the Quran

The apparent unwillingness of Muslims to look at biblical texts can be attributed to the Muslim attitude concerning the finality of the Quran. As far as we know, Muhammad never saw a Bible in the Arabic language. Hence, he could blithely claim of the Quran: "To thee we sent the scripture in truth, confirming the scripture that came before it, and guarding it in safety ..." (Q. 5:51). Also, note the following:

This Quran is not such as can be produced by other than God; on the contrary it is a confirmation of (revelations) that went before it, and a fuller explanation of the Book [The Bible]— wherein there is no doubt— from the Lord of the Worlds (Q. 10:37).

In other words, Muhammad saw the Quran as a continuation of all that went before, and as the climax of it all. But in addition to this, he saw the Quran as all-sufficient, in and of itself. The effect of this on Muslims was to make them feel that they really did not need anything else. Today, there is a widespread apathy among the Muslims with regard to the study of the Bible.

For the Christian worker, the question of Bible or Quran is further complicated by the discrepancies of the Quranic text when compared with the biblical accounts. As pointed out earlier, Muhammad was totally dependent on extra-biblical sources for his information, and these were always oral. Hence, there was no awareness on his part of this wide disparity between his accounts and biblical ones. In fact, it was only somewhere between ninety and a hundred and fifty years later, as the result of debates with Christians who did have the Bible in their hands, that Muslims learned of the serious disagreement in details concerning several stories or accounts common to both. It was at this point that Islam faced its most serious challenge. Either Muhammad was in error or the Bible was. Muslims were unwilling then to consider even the possibility of Muhammad being in error. So, the baseless and false charge was made by Muslims that the Christians and Jews had corrupted their Scriptures (Abdiyah Akbar Abdul-Haqq 1980:38). In dealing with these fabrications, a great deal of patience is required in demonstrating to Muslims the integrity of the Bible from the earliest days until now. (The question of the authenticity of the Bible will be dealt with in a later section of this book.)

In order to more clearly understand the essence of Islam, let us turn now to the subject of Islam defined as Tradition and Law.

CHAPTER 8

ISLAM DEFINED: TRADITION AND LAW

> Ye have indeed in the Apostle of God a beautiful pattern
> (of conduct) for anyone whose hope is in God and the
> Final Day, and who engages much in the praise of God
> (Q. 33:21).

While the armies of Islam were sweeping away all that stood before them during the century following the death of Muhammad (A.D. 632), Muslim scholars were busy collecting, sorting, validating, authenticating, rejecting, and in some cases, inventing a large body of material called "traditions." These traditions were soon canonized into officially approved "Traditions" with a capital "T". In the Arabic language these "Traditions" are called *Hadith*.

Simultaneously, men with a legal bent of mind, the jurisprudents, were using these traditions to derive Islamic laws, which came to be known as the *Shariah*. And so, as the Muslim armies successfully conquered others, they themselves were gradually being conquered by legalists who brought them into bondage to the most exacting kind of law.

Muhammad: The Model Muslim

The primary passion that Muhammad gave to his followers was a concern for law and how to be "rightly guided," a phrase repeated many times in the Quran. They wanted to know the "right way" to do everything. Everything hinged on knowing the will of God because the Muslims' understanding was that keeping the law would ensure them a place in paradise forever. In Arabia, characterized as it is by so much desert land, water is everything. The pathway to water is, literally, the pathway to life. The word for the pathway to water, in Arabic, is *shariah*. That is why the Laws were called *Shariah*. Muhammad and Muslims ever since have thought that the keeping of these laws would lead to life.

However, the phenomenon of the Muslim community patterning its behavior after that of their Prophet was something Muhammad himself cultivated. Muhammad asked all people to follow him. In the text at the head of this chapter, we read the words, "Ye have indeed in the Apostle of God a beautiful pattern…" (Q. 33:21). Since the Quranic recitations came through this one man and he made himself the sole interpreter of these words, it was only natural that the "Traditions" should be rooted in the sayings and doings of Muhammad.

In other ways, Muhammad assumed for himself a position that made his word final on all issues. In the following verses from the Quran, note how Muhammad associated his name with God's, linking them together. This is done repeatedly throughout the Quran.

> He who obeys the Apostle, obeys God (Q. 4:80).
> "O men! I am sent unto you all, as the Apostle of God, to whom belongeth the dominion of the heavens and the earth: there is no god but He: it is He that giveth both life and death. So, believe in God and His Apostle, the unlettered Prophet, who believeth in God and His Words: follow him that (so) ye may be guided" (Q. 7:158).
>
> Say: "If ye do love God, follow me: God will love you and forgive you your sins: for God is Oft-Forgiving, most Merciful."
> Say: "Obey God and His Apostle:" But if they turn back, God loveth not those who reject Faith (Q. 3:31, 32).

In addition to the exhortation to follow him, Muhammad, in the above quotes, even promised the forgiveness of sins to those who did. For those who rejected him, Muhammad stated that God would not love them because they had rejected faith, thus equating real faith with obeying him.

He also attempted to strengthen his claim of superseding Christ in several ways. The following quote illustrates how Muhammad put prophetic words into Jesus' mouth concerning Muhammad's coming.

> And remember, Jesus, the son of Mary [Muhammad's favorite way of referring to Jesus, rather than Son of God], said: "O children of Israel! I am the Apostle of God (sent) to you, confirming the Law (which came) before me, and giving Glad Tidings of an Apostle to come after me, whose name shall be Ahmad." [*Ahmad* is an Arabic word having the meaning "Whose Name is Praised," which is similar to Muhammad, that is, "The Praised One] (Q. 61:6).

Notice in the above quote Muhammad's attempt to capture the expression "Glad Tidings" or "Good News" (The Gospel) and apply it to himself. What we have here is the effort on Muhammad's part to replace Jesus as the central focus of all Scripture, and take that place for himself. This effort is further reinforced by his teaching that he was the Seal of the Prophets (Q. 33:40), meaning the climax of the line of all the prophets. Elsewhere in the Quran, and many times over, Muhammad reduced Jesus to being merely one of the prophets, and by making himself the last and the Seal of the Prophets, gave himself the place of preeminence.

With so much emphasis placed on the speech and behavior of Muhammad, it was only a question of time before the doctrine of his infallibility and sinless character developed (Rahman 1979:69). From this phenomenon, it was not such a long step to gravitate towards the idea that Muhammad was divine (Vander Werff 1977:237). Indeed, in a private interview with one of the prominent bishops of the Church of Pakistan who asked to remain unnamed, I discovered in November 1990 that books at the popular level are now being published ascribing deity to Muhammad. And I myself have collected Urdu and Punjabi devotional music in which Muhammad is worshiped as Lord. Samuel Zwemer's piercing indictment of Islam at this point is just as apropos today as when he first wrote it.

> The sin and guilt of the Mohammedan world is that they give Christ's glory to another, and that for practical purposes Mohammed himself is the Moslem Christ ... Jesus Christ is supplanted by Mohammed not only in Moslem tradition and in the hearts of the common people

> ... He is supplanted in the hearts of all Moslems by Mohammed (Zwemer1924:157, 166).

The irony of Islam is that while a slim minority of Muslim theologians spend their energy denying Christ as Savior and His deity, multitudes of spiritually hungry Muslims, longing to get in touch with the divine, have tragically ascribed to Muhammad those very qualities. And theologians have inevitably reinforced this doctrine of the infallibility of Muhammad to safeguard their doctrines from the charge of error.

Rahman in his valuable work, *Islam*, summarized it well. "Man must discover, formulate and execute that Will of which the final index is the Quran and Muhammad the most perfect commentator" (1979:83). In this schema, Muhammad became the fountainhead of the entire system. All else must be derived in one way or another from the words and doings of this Arabian man.

The Development of Tradition and Law

It was to Muhammad alone that the words of revelation came, which were eventually collected in what is now called the Quran. For those who believed him, these words became "The Word of God."

Muhammad was also the sole interpreter of what these words meant, at least in his own lifetime. So not only did his followers believe everything that he said was given to him at these special occasions of revelation, but they also treasured his "non-inspired" comments about what these words meant, as well as myriads of other matters not taken up in the Quran. In due time, these "non-inspired" sayings, along with Muhammad's model behavior, were held with the same reverence that the Muslims imputed to the Quran.

In the Arabic, there is an expression for the traditions of the elders. It is called *Sunnah*, meaning "the trodden path." Before Muhammad's appearance, there already was a *Sunnah*—a body of traditions that regulated the behavior of the Arabs. But the force of Muhammad's personality and teaching was so great that he permanently altered the lifestyle of his formerly idolatrous kinsmen. In supplanting an already developed idolatry with Arab monotheism, a matrilineal society with a patrilineal one, Christianity and Judaism with Islam, he so closely associated his own name with God's name that for all practical purposes his words, both in the Quran and outside of the Quran, were accepted as God's words. With the inauguration of Islam, Muhammad's exemplary behavior became the new *Sunnah* of the Arab believers. In this way, Muhammad was the sole founder of Islam.

As long as Muhammad was alive, those who believed in him either did what he said, remembered everything he said, or imitated him in all that he did. His life, then, became normative for all who believed in him. The power of his personality was such that he permanently altered the lifestyle of those Arabs who acknowledged him to be a Prophet of God. After his death, his companions perpetuated his *Sunnah* or model behavior. And even after they died, the succeeding generation was able to perpetuate this tradition with great faithfulness.

But a time came when these early generations of believers were no more and men's memories began to fail. And with the military successes of the Muslim armies, vast territories of conquered peoples were swept into the *Dar al-Islam,* "The House of Islam." These new believers needed to be taught the ways of Islam based on the traditions of Muhammad's life. So it was inevitable that the *Sunnah,* or "Living Tradition" of Muhammad would have to be written down in order to preserve the memory of Muhammad's exemplary behavior as the preeminent or "first" Muslim.

The writing down of these traditions was developed into a special "science" and the material written down was called in the Arabic language, *Hadith,* or the "Written Traditions." The *Hadith* then, along with the Quran, became the primary source for all the material that was to mold early Islam.

In gathering these traditions, two major concerns preoccupied the writers. The first was the reliability of the "chain of witnesses" on whose testimony these "sayings" were received. This was called *isnad.* The second was the compatibility of the text with the previous "revelation," meaning the Quran. The word for text in Arabic is *matn.* So, the "science" of preserving the traditions of Muhammad (which eventually included that of his immediate "Companions" and "Successors") had to do with the testing of a chain of witnesses, the *isnad,* and the subject matter of the text, the *matn,* in terms of its authenticity, genuineness, reliability, and trustworthiness.

While writers were formulating the *Hadith*, jurisprudents were busily developing the *Shariah*. Muhammad and Muslims ever since have thought that keeping these laws would lead to life. For the Muslim, since everything is supposedly based on the life of Muhammad, it became extremely important to know how Muhammad handled every situation in his own lifetime, or, by analogical reason and deduction, project how he would have handled a given situation had he been there. Legal scholars sprang up in various parts of the growing Muslim empire. To strengthen their opinions, these jurists searched far and wide for written traditions that supported their conclusions, and other jurists did the same. Consciously or unconsciously, the *Hadith* began to multiply.

Interestingly, the laws were canonized before the *Hadith* were standardized. The result was that instead of having one standardized body of law, four officially recognized schools of law came into being. These schools of law did not differ greatly in the main body of their rules. Today, because of widespread travel, there is a tremendous intermingling of Muslim peoples, and a great level of tolerance among the followers of each of these schools of law.

The dates of these men give us a clue as to how long it took Islam to codify its laws. The first of them died in A.D. 767, about 145 years after the death of Muhammad, and the last of them died in A.D. 855, about 232 years after the death of Muhammad. The names and dates of these founders are as follows:

- Hanifa, died 767, his law is practiced in Western Asia, Lower Egypt and Pakistan.
- Malik, died 795, his law is practiced in Upper Egypt, North and West Africa.
- Shafii, died 819, his law is practiced in Indonesia.
- Hanbal, died 855, his law is practiced in Central and Northern Arabia.

The *Hadith* continued to grow to monstrous proportions during and even after the Law was codified. A little over two hundred years after the death of Muhammad, the *Hadith* had grown to over 500,000 separate sayings attributed to Muhammad. Eventually, six prominent scholars arose to stop this wild proliferation of reputed "traditions." These scholars purged all traditions deemed unacceptable, either because the chain of authority of the witnesses was weak, or the content of the tradition did not coincide with the Quran and other traditions deemed authentic. The names and dates of the six recognized codifiers of these *Hadith* are as follows:

- Bukhari, died 870
- Muslim, died 875
- Ibn Maja, died 886
- Abu Daud, died 888
- Al-Tirmidhi, died 892
- Al-Nasai, died 916

Of these six, Bukhari and Muslim are considered the most authoritative. Bukhari's collection is by far the most voluminous. Of the half million or so "sayings" he sifted through, he retained just a little over 7,000 as authentic. The other collectors agree with Bukhari in the main, but each includes some sayings not found in the others.

This passion to lift up Muhammad as the Model Man for the whole human race is startling. The world is to be won to Islam, according to Muslim teaching, and we are all to conform to the words and doings of this seventh century Arab man. But the point for us, now living more than a thousand years after all this activity came to a close, is that these twin movements of establishing the *Hadith* and deriving the *Shariah* has tended to lock Muslims into a seventh century model based on Muhammad's reputed words and deeds.

It is in the Muslim obsession with guidance, and hence, law and tradition, that Islam's pattern of development differs so radically from that of Christianity. Under the guidance of the living Holy Spirit, the writers of the Gospels refused to go down that kind of road. For example, John wrote: "Jesus did many other things as well. If every one of them were written down, I suppose that even the whole world would not have room for the books that would be written" (John 21:25). Earlier, John had given reasons for why all of this was not written down. The first is that enough was written to engender saving faith in a believer.

> Jesus did many other miraculous signs in the presence of his disciples, which are not recorded in this book. But these are written that you may believe that Jesus is the Christ, the Son of God, and that by believing you may have life in his name (John 20:30, 31).

The second reason, in my opinion, is that God did not want the Gospel or our response to it locked into a first century Jewish traditionalism. Although it is helpful to know Jewish traditions as they do throw light on the Scriptural text, we need not follow all the practices of Jewish culture because so many were culturally specific for that milieu and not to be imitated.

Furthermore, God gave the living Holy Spirit to His church to guide and instruct it in a dynamic, living way, a way that would fit the teaching to each cultural context around the world and down through history. In other words, God, by limiting the material, liberated the Gospel to spread into myriads of cultures and languages. The extraordinary flexibility demonstrated by the multitudinous forms and structures of the Christian Church allowed for the spread of the kingdom of God into all cultures.

By contrast, Islam is committed to a relatively inflexible seventh century Arab model which, in spite of the verse that says, "Let there be no compulsion in religion … " (Q. 2:256), must be imposed on the rest of the world, by persuasion or by force, if necessary (Q. 8:38, 39).

That Islam has not been able to live comfortably with its ancient Laws and Traditions is attested by the deviations, attempted reforms, new innovations, syncretistic compromises, and efforts to accommodate to modernity, resulting in the rise of numerous Muslim sects and trends around the world. Islam lives in a perpetual tension between the ironclad norm established long ago for all time by codifiers of the Traditions and the Law on the one hand, and the unsatisfied hunger of the human spirit for spiritual experiences that satisfy that hunger in culturally appropriate ways today.

In fact, in Islam today, movements are afoot that question the place of the *Hadith* in the modern world. Colonel Muammar Abu Minyar al-Qaddifi of Libya went so far as to abolish all of the *Hadith* and replace them with his own ideas in his famous *Green Book*. On a recent visit to

Egypt, this author learned that many of the *Hadith* are now being ignored as not authentic. However, until drastic reforms overtake the Muslim world, all Muslims are locked into the Quran, the *Hadith*, and the *Shariah*.

Christian workers must necessarily familiarize themselves with Orthodox Islam, not only to understand what this means to those Muslims committed to this way of life, but also to understand how and why non-Orthodox forms of Islam deviate from that norm. Later in this book, we shall look at some of these variant forms of Islam, but before we do, let us become acquainted with the standard reduction of Orthodox Islam into its succinct articles of faith and practice.

CHAPTER 9

ISLAM: ITS CREEDS AND DUTIES

And We will make it easy for thee (to follow) the simple
(path) (Q. 87:8).

As Muslims continued to expand their territory through military
conquest, they overran peoples of other religions. Suddenly, they
found it necessary to define themselves in contrast to followers of these
older religions. Furthermore, "This urgency was sharpened by ... the rise
of dissident groups within Islam itself, for one must know what true Islam
is if one is to distinguish it clearly from what falsely claims to be Islam"
(Jeffrey 1958:71).

Gradually, out of the mass of material, collected in the *Hadith* and
the *Shariah*, a pattern emerged to guide Muslims in their daily lives. It fell
into five categories: "Things enjoined, things commended, things deplored,
things prohibited, and a central area where actions ... may be said to be
neutral" (Cragg 1969:53). Gradually, certain actions and beliefs were owned
by the Muslims as those which distinguished them from their neighbors.

These obligatory expressions of faith and practice have been neatly
subsumed under two key words: *iman and din. Iman* in its larger sense has
been defined as "the conviction and commitment to accept God as the
Lord and submit completely to His Will as revealed in the Law, the *Shariah*"
(Nicholls 1979:155, 156). But in the narrower sense it has been reduced
to six articles of faith:

1. Belief in God.
2. Belief in angels.
3. Belief in the holy books.
4. Belief in prophets.
5. Belief in the day of judgment.
6. Belief in the decrees of God.

Similarly, the distinctive duties of Islam (*din*), sometimes called the "Pillars of Islam," are listed as:

1. Recitation of the creed (*shahadah*).
2. Performance of ritual prayers (*salat*).
3. Giving of alms (*zakat*).
4. Keeping the fast (*sawm*).
5. Going on the pilgrimage (*hajj*).
6. Waging holy war (*jihad*). (Most do not include this.)

Iman

1. Belief in God

Muslims pray in Arabic. The word for God is "Allah." Muhammad taught that God has no partners, no equals. He is one. He is totally different from humans. One cannot say He has a face, or hands, or anything that would compare Him to a man. Daud Rahbar, in his book *God of Justice*, maintains that the essential nature of God in the Quran is that of strict vindictive justice (Rahbar 1979:8).

Muslims make much of the "names" of God. The Quran refers to the beautiful names of God without listing them (Q. 7:180). Muslim *Hadith* say that God has ninety-nine beautiful names. They often use prayer beads in remembering these names. "The Muslim rosary normally consists of thirty-three beads with a tassel, and is run through the fingers three times to complete the ninety-nine names" (Jeffrey 1958:93). Great merit is supposed to accrue from this exercise.

Quran 112 well summarizes Muhammad's concept of God:

Say: He is God, the One and Only;
God, the Eternal, Absolute;
He begetteth not, nor is He begotten;
And there is none like unto Him.

2. Belief in Angels

Angels are created beings who do not have freewill. Four are considered archangels: *Jibrail*, the Angel of Revelation;

Mikail, the patron angel of the Jews; *Israfil*, who shall sound the trumpet that will destroy the world at the end of time; and *Izrail*, the Angel of Death. Satan (*Iblis*) was formerly an angel but he disobeyed God and was turned into a *jinn* (Glasse 1989:42). Other orders of angels exist as God's servants.

Jinn is another order of supernatural beings—demons. Muslims believe they "were created of fire, were male and female [they believe angels are sexless], mortal ... They can possess humans. There are also tales of marriage of *jinn* with humans" (Jeffrey 1958:105). In Folk Islam (this will be taken up later) it is thought that when a human is born, a *jinn* of the opposite sex is born simultaneously (Musk 1989:103).

3. Belief in the Holy Books

Muhammad and his contemporaries held a peculiar view of the inspiration of Scripture, the Quran being their case in point. Etymologically, the term "Quran" simply means "recitation." Theologically, it means the "Word of God." It is eternal and uncreated. The Muslim believes that "the Arabic copy that [he or she] uses today is an exact replica of a heavenly prototype, dictated word by word to the Prophet Muhammad" (Hitti 1970:26).

Muslims believed that there were perhaps 124,000 prophets from Adam to Muhammad, and that each of them was given a book in precisely the same way that Muhammad thought God sent the Quran down to him. All previous books have been lost except the Taurat (Law) given to Moses, the *Zabur* (Psalms) given to David, and the *Injil* (Good News) given to Jesus.

The Muslim belief is that each revelation is divine in its origin and permanently valid in its doctrine. Each contains rules and regulations suitable for its own time and for the people who received it, but later laws and methods of worship and service are improvements on earlier systems of ethics and obedience. Islam is thought to be the best and final revelation, and therefore, it is not only commended but commanded for the followers of the former revelations (Calverley 1958:65).

4. Belief in Prophets

According to Gibb, "The doctrine of Apostles (Prophets) is, as the *shahadah* shows, next to the Unity of God, the central doctrine of the Quran" (1949:39). God has sent prophets to every people of every age to teach them God's way for their age. Even though Muslims are required to believe in all the prophets without distinction, Muhammad emerges as the last and greatest. Muhammad even went so far as to put words in Jesus' mouth to foretell his own coming. Note Ahmad, which means "whose name is praised," is similar in meaning to *Muhammad*, "the praised one," as mentioned earlier.

And remember, Jesus, the son of Mary, said: "O Children of Israel! I am the Apostle of God (sent) to you, confirming the Law (which came) before me, and giving Glad Tidings of an Apostle to come after me, whose name shall be Ahmad" (Q. 61:6).

5. Belief in the Day of Judgment

One of the frequent and thundering themes in Muhammad's preaching was the Day of Judgment, sometimes called the Day of Doom. This particular theme relates also to Muhammad's teaching on the resurrection, paradise and hell. His system was based on the idea that God will:

Judge the deeds of men for the purpose of rewarding the faithful and punishing the guilty. Not only mankind but also the *jinn* and irrational animals will be judged ... A balance will be present to weigh the deeds of all, and sentence will be passed depending on how the scales are tipped. He whose balance is laden with good works will be saved; he whose balance is light will be condemned (Farah 1968:114, 115).

The Quran itself provides the best description of Paradise:

> And those foremost (in faith) [Islam] will be foremost
> (in the hereafter). These will be those nearest to God:
> in Gardens of Bliss ... (They will be) on Thrones
> encrusted (with gold and precious stones), reclining
> on them facing each other. Round about them will
> (serve) youths of perpetual (freshness), with goblets,
> (shining) beakers and cups (filled) out of clear-flowing
> fountains [of wine]: No after-ache [hangover] will they
> receive therefrom, nor will they suffer intoxication: And
> with fruits, any that they may select; and the flesh of
> fowls, any that they may desire. And (there will be)
> [female] companions with beautiful, big and lustrous
> eyes,—like unto pearls well-guarded. A reward for the
> Deeds of the past (Life) (Q. 56:10-12,15-24).

Hell is pictured just as graphically in repulsive images cited
in the two Quranic references below:

> Those who reject our Signs, We shall soon cast into
> the Fire: as often as their skins are roasted through,
> We shall change them for fresh skins, that they may
> taste the Penalty (Q. 4:56).

> In front of such a one is Hell, and he is given, for
> drink, boiling fetid water. In gulps will he sip it, but
> never will he be near swallowing it down his throat:
> Death will come to him from every quarter, yet will he
> not die, and in front of him will be a chastisement
> unrelenting (Q. 14:16, 17).

Again, of special interest to the Christian is the role assigned
to Christ at endtimes.

Jesus, descended from heaven, will appear in the mosque in Damascus ... He will slay *Dajjal* [the Antichrist] at the gates of Lydda, and he will obtain from God the destruction of Gog and Magog. He will marry, have children, and will reign on the earth for forty years, where he will cause peace to prevail among men and beasts (Gaudefroy-Demombynes 1968:52, 53).

6. Belief in the Decrees of God

Perhaps no doctrine of Islam has been more controversial than the one that has given us the word *kismet* or fatalism. Gibb summarizes well the basis for this.

His Decree is inescapable, and all things are determined and disposed by His foreknowledge, pictorially expressed as written on a "Preserved Tablet." Men are his creatures ... and must submit their wills to His ways, however mysterious (1949:38).

Muhammad's words in the Quran are the source of this doctrine: "Thus doth God leave to stray whom He pleaseth, and guide whom He pleaseth: and none can know the forces of thy Lord, except He" (Q. 74:31). Al-Ashari (died A.D. 935), one of the most famous of all Islamic scholastic theologians, commented thus on this topic:

The proof that God is free to do whatever he does is that He is the supreme Lord, subject to no one, with no superior over Him who can permit, command, chide, forbid, or prescribe what he shall do and fix bounds for Him. This being so, nothing can be evil on the part of God ... since the Creator is subject to no one and bound by no command, nothing can be evil on His part (Cragg 1969:12).

Al-Ashari, in this way, sought to avoid the problem of making the Quranic "God" responsible for creating evil. He attempted to do this by putting God above the question of good and evil, thus portraying God as amoral. Cragg tries to mute the seeming harshness of this doctrine, basing his comments on other Quranic references that talk of man's responsibility:

> The wisest course in this vexed theme of Islamic doctrine is not blindly to insist on the centuries old traditions of determinism ... It lies rather in seeing the Islamic view of events and wills as enveloped, positively, in this totality of the Divine rule. All things are to be related directly and, as it were, jealously, to the will of God ... such a zeal ... does not now preclude the vigorous role of human action (Cragg 1969:13).

Such then are the "Articles of Faith" through which Islam in its early centuries attempted to assert its distinctive beliefs upon its neighbors, particularly the Jews and Christians.

Al-Din

Din is often translated as "religion," but it actually means much more than that. If the *Shariah* is the mapping out of all the requirements God has placed upon humankind, then *din* is the human response to those obligations. It is a whole way of life. *Din* encompasses ethics, politics, morality, law, justice and all other aspects of life relating to the thoughts and actions of humankind.

> For the Westerner, used to viewing religion as a matter of private conscience, this is the fundamental point to grasp in trying to understand Islam. It is not that religion dominates the life of a faithful Muslim, but that religion, in this comprehensive sense, is his life (Roberts 1982:35).

So we see that *iman* and *din* developed certain articles of faith and duties that distinguished Islam from other religions. In the case of *din*, these might be called religious obligations. These are supported by one of the early traditions attributed to Ibn Umar (died 634), which states:

Islam is built upon five things: on confessing that there is no deity save Allah [*shahadah*], performing prayers [*salat*], giving the legal alms [*zakat*], going on pilgrimage [*hajj*] to the House [that is, the *Kaaba* at Mecca], and fasting during the month of Ramadan. Thus did the Apostle of Allah hand it on to us, but beyond that there is holy war [*jihad*], which is an excellent thing (Jeffrey 1958:81).

Below are brief comments made on these six practices.

1. The Confession of the Creed (*shahadah*)

The *shahadah* is one of the briefest of all creeds. It states: "There is no God but God, and Muhammad is the Apostle of God." The first part of this is similar to the confession found in Moses' Book of Deuteronomy: "Hear, O Israel: The Lord our God, the Lord is one" (Deut. 6:4), which was affirmed by Jesus. The latter part of the *shahadah* was Muhammad's own invention.

To recite this with intention makes one a Muslim. These words are the first words that every newborn Muslim baby hears and the last to be recited in the ears of the dying:

It is the commonest utterance of the individual believer and is the chant of dervishes [Muslim mystics] at the meetings of their orders. It is on the official flag of one Muslim nation [Saudi Arabia]. The psychological and religious influence and value of this brief Creed has been incalculable for Islam (Calverley 1958:56).

2. The Performance of Ritual Prayer (*salat*)

The following discussion of *salat* is based on the excellent research of John C. Blair in his book, *The Sources of Islam*, (1925:118-135).

Muhammad, we know, had early and friendly contacts with Jews and Christians, especially when he was trying to win them to become his followers. The Jews had three appointed times of daily prayer. Muhammad's borrowing of this is reflected in the Quran: "And establish regular prayers at the two ends of the day [early morning and close of day] and at the approaches of the night" (Q. 11:114).

Later, after Muhammad's purported night journey to heaven, he felt God was telling him to observe prayer five times a day. Unfortunately, this is not found in the Quran; but there is a passage that mentions prayer four times a day: "So (give) glory to God, when ye reach eventide and when ye rise in the morning; Yea, To Him be praise, in the heavens and on earth; and in the late afternoon and when the day begins to decline" (Q. 30:17, 18).

Muslim commentators claim the last mentioned one actually covers the last two of the five required times of prayer. These five obligatory times of prayer are:

Early morning before sunrise (*fajr*)
Just past noon (*zuhr*)
In the afternoon (*asr*)
Just after sunset (*maghrib*)
After evening twilight has faded (*isha*)
(Ali 1977:1054)

On the human level, we know that Muhammad borrowed segments of his religious practice from a semi-Christian group of monotheists living in southern Arabia, called Sabians. Trimingham gives a brief and interesting description of who these people were in his book, *Christianity among the Arabs in Pre-Islamic Times* (1979:296-301). The Sabians observed seven times of daily prayer, five of which coincided with those eventually established by Muhammad. Blair digs deeper in his research, though, to point out that it was the people of ancient Persia, the Zoroastrians, who first established this practice. Some scholars believe that Muhammad chose the five appointed times of prayer as a middle way between the Jews (three times) and the Sabians (Goitein 1968:84, 85).

These stated times of prayer are more like formal worship, with the recitation of memorized Arabic lines and portions of the Quran. There is allowance in the ritual for spontaneous personal requests. The question of ritual purity is also extremely important when a Muslim prepares for prayer. Strong evidence exists that Muhammad obtained this idea from the Jews.

Historically, we know that Muhammad and his followers first faced Jerusalem when reciting their prayers. Then after a most unhappy confrontation with the Jewish tribes of Medina, Muhammad changed the direction of prayer to Mecca (Q. 2:142-145). Prayer is made with the eyes open. The postures adopted by the one praying scrupulously imitate the example of Muhammad. Prayers may be shortened in time of battle or danger and traveling.

3. Giving of Alms (*zakat*)

Islam did not emerge with all of Muhammad's beliefs complete. Even in his lifetime, many practices underwent modifications. *Zakat* is a case in point.

The caliph Umar (the second successor of Muhammad, 634-644) perfectly reflects the "salvation by works" assumptions taught by Muhammad. He said: "Prayer carries us half-way to God, fasting brings us to the door of His palace, alms procures us admission" (Blair 1925:145). Hitti explains the distinction between obligatory and voluntary giving:

> Almsgiving ... falls into two categories: voluntary, practiced as an act of love and piety [*sadaqat*], and obligatory or legal [*zakat*] ... It is stressed not only as a social obligation but also as a means of self-purification ... the exact amount of *zakat* varied but was later fixed by canon law at one-fortieth of the individual's income (1970:35).

> Gibb provides further details for us:
> It [*zakat*] is to be exacted from all who, whether voluntarily or under constraint, enter the brotherhood

of Islam; but it is not a tax. Rather is it to be regarded as a loan made to God, which he will repay many-fold. Free-will offerings [*sadaqat*] are also a means of expiating offences, and are to be given to relatives, orphans, the needy and travelers. The objects upon which the revenue from *zakat* is to be spent are defined as: the poor, the needy, those employed in its collection, those who are to be conciliated [enticed to Islam or held to Islam], slaves, prisoners, debtors, wayfarers, and the "Way of God." ["The Way of God" refers to *jihad,* according to Gibb] (1949:44, 45).

Today, only a few governments of Muslim countries arrange for the collection of *zakat,* with the notable exception of Iran. It is significant that by controlling the collection of *zakat* in Iran, the clergy won control of the government. And where the clergy do not control these funds, they do not control the government.

4. Keeping the Fast (*sawm*)

The fast is approximately thirty days and takes place during the Muslim month of Ramadan. Since the Muslim calendar is based on the moon rather than the sun, their year is approximately eleven days shorter than the solar year. Hence, this month begins eleven days earlier each year. The fast is to be kept from sunrise to sunset each day of Ramadan.

During the fast the Muslims may not partake of any food or drink; nor may he smoke, or have sexual intercourse with the opposite sex, from the time when a white thread may be distinguished from a black one before sunrise until sunset ... Mosques are well attended during Ramadan, and the *rakah* (full cycles of prayer) accompanied by recitations from the Quran and interspersed after each four by meals may well last the whole night. The fast is broken immediately after sunset with a light meal ... The fast ends on the first day of the month of *Shawwal* with a great feast termed *Id al-Fitra* ... On this day the statutory alms marking the end of the fast are given and the head of each household gives to the poor a prescribed quantity of the customary food of the country as an act of piety. The feast is an occasion for festivities lasting three full days during which time Muslims rejoice and exhibit their new clothes and exchange embraces (Farah 1968:144, 145).

5. Going on the Pilgrimage (*hajj*)

The crowning act of the Muslim religion is the pilgrimage to Mecca. Muhammad made it obligatory once in a lifetime for those who were healthy and could afford it. "Pilgrimage thereto is a duty men owe to God ..." (Q. 3:97). Formerly, that is, before Muhammad established Mecca as the pilgrim center for all Muslims, the pagan Arabs had established a shrine there—a cubical house called the *Kaaba*. Local deities were placed in it. And four of the lunar months were established as sacred for the Arab tribes to make their way to Mecca. There was to be no war during those months.

When Muhammad, with a force of ten thousand Muslims, captured Mecca, he set about cleansing the *Kaaba* of its idols and called the *Kaaba* "The House of God." It is considered by Muslims to be the navel of the earth.

It was created first, and round it the world spread out. The site of the Kaaba is the central point of the whole universe ... it stands squarely on an axis joining earth to heaven ... The earthly Mecca knows a celestial counter-part, where angels congregate in their millions to worship (Musk 1989:163).

Due to the transmigration of Jewish tribes from the Middle East into the environs of Mecca, bringing with them the stories of Abraham, Ishmael and Isaac, legends based on old biblical accounts existed in Mecca long before the days of Muhammad. Blair's description captures the pilgrim rites so well:

> The precincts of the Kaaba were hallowed as the scene of Hagar's distress, and the sacred well Zamzam as the source of her relief. The pilgrims hastened to and from between Safa and Marwa, in memory of her hurried steps in search of water. It was Abraham and Ishmael who built the Temple [*Kaaba*], embedded in it the black stone and established for all Arabia the pilgrimage to Arafat. In imitation of him it was that stones were flung by the pilgrims as if at Satan, and sacrifices offered at Mina in remembrance of the vicarious sacrifice by Abraham (Blair 1925:169, 170).

The traditional days of the *hajj* take place from the seventh to the tenth day of the twelfth lunar month, *Dhu'l-Hijjah*. In a later chapter, we shall call attention to Folk-Islamic practices attached to various places and behavior connected with the pilgrimage in Mecca.

Before leaving this subject, I would like to draw attention to the significance given to Abraham, Hagar and Ishmael in the ceremonies of the pilgrimage. Here, so poignantly expressed, we find the hunger of the Muslim heart powerfully exercised in this effort to identify with Abraham, "The Friend of God," through Ishmael and Hagar.

6. The Duty of Holy War (*jihad*)

Undoubtedly, this is the most controversial of the pillars of Islamic duty. Muslims seldom include it in their list, and for good reason. In trying to put a good face on Islam to non-Islamic peoples, it would be too unnerving to learn that the Muslims are committed to conquering the world for Islam, either by preaching, by persuasion, or by the sword. The only exceptions to this are the Christians and Jews, that is, "The People of the Book." Christians and Jews, if they come under

Islamic rule, are subjected to a humiliating tax, denied full status as citizens and the right to compete for the highest public offices. Other peoples are either forcibly converted or put to the sword.

Here in the West, Muslims are strenuously trying to downplay this aspect of Islam. For example, the literal meaning of *jihad* is "striving." In the Islamic context, it means "striving in the way of God." This could mean educational, intellectual, or moral improvement, or striving for technological advancement, or seeking to promote Islam by non-violent means. This all fits under the rubric of *jihad*. Moreover, some modern-day propagators of Islam would call our attention to Quran 2:256, which says: "Let there be no compulsion in religion ... " Unfortunately, the burden of Islamic history bears witness that this verse has not been an adequate counter-balance to the more than fifty references to *jihad* in the Quran. *Jihad* as commonly understood means "holy war," militarily prosecuted against the enemies of Islam. For example, Saudi Arabia lives in a perpetual state of holy war with Israel. Iran proclaimed its war against Iraq as a *jihad*. Iraq insisted that its war against Kuwait and its allies was a *jihad*. Muammer Gaddafi was quoted by the Islamic News Service in November 1989, as saying, "The global expansion of Islam has entered a new stage ... the Islamic holy war will now be carried out by an International Islamic People's Commando charged with the task of conducting Islamic mass activities" (News Network International, 12/13/89, p.18).

Where does this spirit come from? What is there in Islam that inspires such men to have these expansionist dreams? The root is found in the life and teaching of Muhammad. Let us look at some of his instructions in the Quran.

> But when the forbidden months are past, then fight and slay the Pagans wherever ye find them, and seize them, beleaguer them, and lie in wait for them in every stratagem (of war); but if they repent, and establish regular prayers and practice regular charity, then open the way for them: for God is oft-forgiving, most Merciful (Q. 9:5).

In the following passage, we learn that Muhammad viewed all non-Muslims as on Satan's side, even though other passages make special exceptions for Jews and Christians.

Those who believe [in Muhammad and Islam] fight in the cause of God [Islam], and those who reject Faith [Islam] fight in the cause of evil: so fight ye against the friends of Satan: feeble indeed is the cunning of Satan (Q. 4:76).

In the end, other verses giving preferential treatment to Jews and Christians notwithstanding, this kind of spirit has colored Muslim attitudes towards Christians and Jews for hundreds of years. In the following passage, I would like to call attention to the word "prescribed." "Fighting is prescribed for you, and ye dislike it. But it is possible that ye dislike a thing which is good for you, and ye love a thing which is bad for you. But God knoweth, and ye know not" (Q. 2:216). In other words, Muhammad made fighting (holy war) mandatory for all Muslims. It is a way of life. The next quote lends itself easily to the dream of world conquest. It is all encompassing.

Say to the Unbelievers [in Islam], if (now) they desist (from unbelief) [in Islam], their past would be forgiven them; but if they persist, the punishment of those before them is already (a matter of warning for them). And fight them on until there is no more tumult or oppression, and there prevail [Islamic] justice and faith in God [Islam] altogether and everywhere (Q. 8:38, 39)...

In recent times, some Muslim fundamentalists in areas such as Pakistan, Bangladesh, Sudan, and Malaysia have forced Islamic Law on non-Muslim citizens. In others, they have declared *jihad* against an occupying power to set Muslims free (versus the Soviet Union over Afghanistan, versus Israel over the Palestinians). The late Maududi of Pakistan talked of "the imposition of Islamic Law on the whole world." Qaddafi spoke of "the global expansion of Islam."

Yes, *jihad* is part of the warp and woof of Islam. It is rooted in the behavior of Muhammad, the Founder of Islam, and permanently enshrined in his teaching in the Quran. *Jihad* easily qualifies as the sixth pillar of Islam.

In this chapter we have covered the material which pertains to Orthodox Islam. These are the standard beliefs and practices as prescribed by Tradition and Law. These basic beliefs and duties have had an enormous influence in molding Muslim minds everywhere. And yet, vast segments of the Muslim community worldwide do not strictly adhere to these basic tenets. In the next section we will comment on these "other Islams."

PART THREE

VARIETIES OF ISLAM

CHAPTER 10

ETHNICITY AND POLITICS IN ISLAM

The main part of the Muslim world, stretching as it does from the Atlantic Coast of Africa to the islands of the Philippines, covers a vast melange of races, peoples, ethnolinguistic groups, political ideologies, various levels of technological development, literacy, social conditions and differing religious propensities.

Since Islam traditionally makes no distinctions between religion and politics, political issues, power struggles and economic unrest set the tone for what is going on in the Muslim world. They also, I might add, keep Islam in a perpetual state of turmoil.

For the Christian worker, it is important to avoid stereotypes and to understand just what kind of people your Muslim neighbors are. We want to meet them where they are. We want to know how to relate the Gospel of Jesus Christ, wherever possible, to the points of greatest perceived need. Therefore, without going to encyclopedic dimensions, some of the major variations of Islam will be set forth in part three.

Political Boundaries

Theoretically, no separate countries should insist within Islam; there should only be *Dar al-Islam*, "The House of Islam," one worldwide monolithic block of Muslims, pitted against *Dar al-Harb*, "The House of War." Inside the *Dar al-Harb*, there is a place for the Jews and Christians. The Arabic word used to describe them is *dhimmis*. They are tolerated, but not allowed to propagate their faith among Muslims, or hold high office, and they must pay a special punitive tax for being non-Muslims.

In actuality, at the time of the writing of this book, forty-nine nations have either Muslim majority populations or a Muslim plurality, and scores contain significant Muslim minorities. A list of all Muslim populations is found in appendix A. A list of the forty-nine Muslim countries is found in appendix B. These political divisions are considered an abnormality by Muslim idealists, who blame the division of the Muslim world into these separate countries on the West when it withdrew colonial rule.

A further contributor to lack of political unity among Muslims is that when Muhammad died unexpectedly at the age of sixty-two, he had made no arrangement for a successor, a caliph. At first by common consent, later by violent power struggles, Muslims have had sometimes two or three rival caliphs ruling simultaneously. For example, the caliphates of the Umayyads in Cordova (930-1030), the Fatimids in Egypt (969-1171), and the Abbasids in Baghdad (750-1258) overlapped from the years 969 to 1030. Since 1924, when Kemal Ataturk abolished the caliphate, Islam has been a headless tangle of endless political intrigue, especially in the Middle East. What David Pryce-Jones wrote of the Arabs might well apply to large parts of the Muslim world: "Apparently busy as sponsors and clients, the Arabs are in reality stalemated in intentions and ambitions and rivalries that duplicate, neutralize, and finally oppose one another" (1989:406).

Surely, out of this ceaseless turmoil of violence and oppression, there is a hunger in the hearts of millions of Ishmael's children for righteousness. I believe that because Islam has failed to bring righteousness, justice, and (with the exception of the oil states) prosperity to its peoples, individual Muslims are hungering by the millions for the good news of the kingdom of God as preached and taught by Jesus Christ.

Ethnicity

Although not as widespread as Christianity, or as numerous, Islam has swept into its fold peoples from hundreds of different ethnic groups. How Islam has tended to cope with this is a mirror image of how early Christianity attempted to strive for uniformity. The attempt to enforce uniformity has not worked in either case. The Christian Church first split between its Eastern and Western power bases. Then the Reformation unleashed trends that liberated the church to spread into every conceivable ethnic group in the world without having to belong to one monolithic cultural expression of Christianity derived from just one ethnic base. Islam has not been so fortunate.

The reasons are not hard to find. Muhammad first perceived himself as an Arab prophet for the Arab people (Q. 14:4), then as a prophet for all people (Q. 25:1), who brought to the world a clear Arabic Quran (Q. 12:2) that came from the purest source in heaven (Q. 43:3). He perceived his hometown, Mecca, as the "Mother of Cities," veritably, the center of the world (Q. 2:142). Moreover, Muhammad enjoined the memorization of the Arabic Quran and demanded total loyalty to his every word, thus making himself the measure of a true and perfect Muslim for all time. In this way, Islam became totally locked into a seventh century Arabic book with an Arab prophet, forever bound to practice religion in Muhammad's seventh century Arabic style in the Arabic language.

Herein lies the undoing of Islam. It did not take long for the Muslim empire to fall apart. Just as in early Christianity, the seat of empire moved from Jerusalem to Antioch to Alexandria to Rome to Constantinople, and finally back to Rome; so in Islam, the seat of empire shifted from Medina to Damascus to Baghdad. After the Mongol invasions, Arabic, Persian and Turkish empires sprung up along with sultanates and kingdoms in the wake of Muslim expansion.

Commenting on some aspects of this ethnic and racial rivalry, Bernard Lewis, in his book, *Race and Color in Islam*, points out how the early conquering Arabs felt about those who were fairer than themselves as well as those who were darker (1971). He also documents the prejudices that exist between Arabs, Persians and Turks.

Anthropologists call this problem "ethnocentrism," the belief that the ethnic group to which one belongs is superior to all other groups. For example, the Arab Muslims insist that the Quran is untranslatable and is the standard for all time and peoples. In this way they have created an atmosphere of widespread disenchantment among the hundreds of non-Arab Muslim societies around the world (four out of every five Muslims are not Arab).

A classic illustration of wide ethnic diversity within Islam lies in the contrast between Morocco and Indonesia. In *Islam Observed*, Clifford Geertz points out just how radically different Islam is in these two societies.

> They both incline toward Mecca, but, the antipodes of
> the Muslim world, they bow in opposite directions. In

Morocco, Islam is that of saint worship and moral severity, magical power and aggressive piety ... In Indonesia, however, the peasantry absorbed Islamic concepts and practices, so far as it understood them, into the same general Southeast Asian folk religion into which it had previously absorbed Indian ones, locking ghosts, gods, *jinns*, and prophets together into a strikingly contemplative, even philosophical animism (1968:13).

The above illustration only paints in broad brush strokes two vastly different cultures. Inside Morocco and Indonesia there are further subdivisions of peoples. In Morocco, you will find Arabs and several distinct kinds of Berbers. In Indonesia, the Malays subdivide into the major ethnic groups of Javanese, Sundanese, Madurese, Minangkabau, Batak, Sumatrans, Bugis and Balinese, as well as hundreds of minor groups.

The Islam one finds in each group differs perceptively from group to group. In Christian work, it pays to come to terms with these ethnic realities. In fact, Donald McGavran, in his book, *Ethnic Realities and the Church: Lessons from India* (1979), argues convincingly that when the Christian worker accepts these "ethnic realities," there is apt to be significant church growth, and when one ignores them by attempting to mix all peoples together, there is apt to be no growth. Richard Weekes in his two-volume work, *Muslim Peoples*, lists 408 major ethnic groups of Muslims (1984:913-926). More recently, the Joshua Project of the A.D. 2000 movement lists 1871 identifiable Muslim people groups. In Muslim work, as in any other, our goal is to plant churches in every ethnic group of people. Coming to terms with Muslim ethnicity, therefore, is a must.

CHAPTER 11

THE GREAT SCHISM: SUNNIS AND SHIAS

Just as we have recognized nationality as a way people perceive themselves in terms of belonging to a political nation-state, and ethnicity as a way in which people share a common identity on the basis of race and often language, we also know that Muslims are distinguished from one another on the basis of their allegiance to a particular theological persuasion. Some of these may have their roots in political issues and power struggles, some may be rooted in ethnicity, and some may simply be the result of different ways of perceiving God, the Prophet, Revelation and Tradition. Or they may be the result of a combination of any of the above. In any case, there are many well-defined kinds of Islam, and we are going to take a brief look at two of them in this chapter.

The Sunnis

One often hears that Islam imitated Christianity in all of its multitudinous varieties. In a general way, I think this is true. Just as we have a major division between Protestants and Roman Catholics, with numerous subdivisions in both, so Islam has two major branches: the Sunnis and the Shias.

The Sunnis correspond to the Protestants in that their final authority is vested in authoritative written material—first the Quran, and then the formal collections of the *Sunnah*, called *Hadith*. It is from the word *Sunnah* ("The Trodden Path") that these people got the nickname "Sunnis."

Behind these written materials, of course, is the commanding figure of Muhammad. Sunnis, and up to a point, Shias, seek to follow the teaching of Muhammad in the Quran and his exemplary model of behavior recorded in the *Hadith*, the written form of the *Sunnah*. While the Quran is the final authority on all matters, the *Sunnah* spells out in practical detail how

Muhammad did things. Hence, the *Sunnah* is extremely important in instructing Sunnis on how to pattern their lives after that of Muhammad.

The importance of the *Sunnah* arises from the function of the Prophet as the founder of the religion, and hence the inspired and provident nature of his acts, and the Koran's injunction to pattern oneself after him: "You have a good example in God's Messenger" (Quran 33:21). It includes what he approved, allowed, or condoned ... and what he himself refrained from and disapproved of (Glasse 1989:381).

There are many varieties of Sunni Islam as a result of rivalries, degrees of nominalism and syncretism. Both the Sunnis (80-90% of the Muslim world) and the Shias (10-20% of the Muslim world) follow their own *shariahs*, which are rival versions of Islamic law.

The Shias

The Shias, like the Roman Catholics, are distinguished from others on the basis of their concern over apostolic succession. Unlike the Sunnis, the Shias feel the leader of the worldwide community of Islam should come from the family of the Prophet.

The word *shia* literally means "faction," or "party." By common understanding, it is applied to those people who believe that the first three democratically elected successors to Muhammad (caliphs) were illegitimate, and that Ali, who was a cousin of the Prophet as well as his son-in-law, was the true successor to Muhammad. *Shia* thus means "The Party of Ali." All branches of Shia Islam trace their roots back to Muhammad through Ali.

Martyrdom is one of the key themes of Shia Islam. It is rooted in the events attending the fate of Ali and his two sons, Hasan and Husayn. When Ali was the caliph, his authority was challenged by Muawiyah, the governor of Syria. When Ali did not prosecute the war with Muawiyah as vigorously as some of his followers wanted, he was assassinated by a group that became known as the Kharijites.

Ali's son Hasan succeeded him but he capitulated to Muawiyah and was killed. Ali's surviving son Husayn then assumed the caliphate. Husayn, hopelessly outnumbered in the Battle of Karbala, was martyred in A.D. 680 by the forces of Muawiyah's son Yazid. This martyrdom of Husayn, according to Glasse:

Is the central event of Persian-inspired Twelve-Imam Shiism, comparable to Christ's crucifixion in the powerful emotions it evokes. It becomes the focus of profound themes of guilt for betrayal, of the expectation of vengeance and justification, and, with messianic overtones quite alien to Sunni Islam, of the chosen one's death as a sacrifice in expiation for the sins of others. The anniversary of the event, the tenth of Muharram, which coincides with an auspicious holiday [a special day of blessing] observed in the Sunni calendar since the Prophet's times, is for Twelve-Imam Shiites the culmination of a turbulent ten-day period of mourning (1989:365).

The men who succeeded Ali and Husayn in leading the Shia community were called *imams*. In Sunni Islam that word simply means one who leads in the congregational prayers. In Shia Islam, the *imams* hold:

Spiritual and political preeminence and possess special graces, miraculous powers, secret knowledge and favor which God has bestowed on no one else. The *imams* channel a Divine Light and are also considered to be sinless (Glasse 1989:366).

So in Shia Islam, we find that scholars are reputed to have divine power to work miracles and divine wisdom to bring out the hidden meanings of verses in the Quran. Indwelt by Divine Light, they are qualified to be leaders of the Shia community. There are also hierarchies of qualified scholars rated according to their wisdom, power and piety. The higher *echelons* of these scholars are called *ayatollahs* (Signs of God) in Shia Islam. Usually, one of them is chosen by his peers to be the supreme leader or chief *ayatollah* of the Shia community. Such a man was the late Ayatollah Ruhullah Khomeini. Today, Iran is the only Muslim country in the world with a Shia government.

In its early days, the succession of leadership was passed on from one chief *imam* to the next. Unfortunately, this line of succession was interrupted by the death and disappearance of either the fifth, seventh, or twelfth imam, depending on which branch of the Shia faith one belongs to. The "fivers" are called *Zaydis*, and the "seveners" are called *Ismailis* after the name of their disappeared *imam*. The "twelvers" are simply called "twelvers," or "*imamis.*"

The Zaydis do not insist on any special sanctity for their *imams*. The *Ismailis* believe in a form of dualism between good and evil, obviously an idea borrowed from Persian Zoroastrianism. They resemble early Gnostics in this doctrine and are also very secretive about their religious practices. The "twelvers" hold to the idea that their *imam* is an intermediary between God and humans. The "twelvers" also believe that their *imam* is occulted or suspended alive somewhere between heaven and earth, is invisible, and will return at the end of the age. In the meantime, the leading ayatollah is supposed to be in direct touch with this occulted *imam*. There are other minor offshoots of Shiism which we will not take up here.

Common to both Sunni and Shia Islam is the related idea that a *Mahdi*, meaning "rightly guided one," will appear at the end of the age, an idea that possibly grew out of interaction of Islam with Christian doctrine of the return of Christ. The "twelver" Shias believe their occulted *imam* will be the *Mahdi*. The other branches of Shiism have their own ideas of who the *Mahdi* will be. Some Sunni Muslims believe that the *Mahdi* will return with Christ at the end of the age.

CHAPTER 12

MYSTICISM: ESCAPE FROM LAW

Sufism is the English word derived from the Arabic word for mysticism. The word has an interesting history. Most scholars agree that "Sufi" came from the Arabic word "*suf*" for wool. Sufis were ascetics who adopted a simple lifestyle in protest against the opulence of their godless Muslim rulers. In a sense, they renounced the world and went seeking God. They wore rough woolen garments from which they got their nickname "wooleys" or Sufis.

The Development of Sufism

There were several reasons for the birth of this movement. Muslim caliphs were no exception to the rule that "power corrupts, and absolute power corrupts absolutely." Following the great success of the Muslim armies in the early centuries of Islam, a great gap developed between the rulers who became corrupt and the pious scholars who were powerless against them. Among the pious scholars there was a division between those who thought they could own property and lead normal lives and those who wanted to renounce the world, follow a path of physical self-denial, and seek God. The Sufis were those who renounced the world and became "seekers."

Sufism received a further impetus from the bitter wars over orthodoxy and law. These endless controversies led to a great sterility of the spirit. In reaction to this, many pious Muslims sought to have experiences with God rather than debates about Him. Sufism was further stimulated by the daring thought that if Muhammad could receive revelations from God, so could others. Without creating new scriptures, they wanted to replicate Muhammad's experiences of direct contact with God. In addition, Nazir-Ali points out, "Sufism developed as a result of stimulus which Muslims received from the Christian monasticism of the Middle East" (1987:22).

Islamic mysticism, at its best, could be represented by the sayings of Rabiah al-Adawiyya (713-801) of Basra:

I exist in God and am altogether His. I live in the shadow of His command....To a royal Husband am I betrothed, and to Him do I minister; and if I leave His ministry, my Betrothed will be wroth with me and will write me a letter of divorce and will dismiss me from His house (Smith 1995:186).

I have loved Thee with two loves, a selfish love and a love that is worthy of Thee. As for the love which is selfish, therein I occupy myself with Thee, to the exclusion of all others. But in the love which is worthy of Thee, Thou dost raise the veil that I may see Thee. Yet is the praise not mine in this or that, but the praise is to Thee, in both that and this (Smith 1995:223).

Sufi Beliefs
Gradually, Sufism developed both structurally and metaphysically. What was at first a form of religion adopted by individuals and communicated to a small circle of companions gradually became a monastic system, a school of saints, with rules of discipline and devotion. Sufi novices (*murid*) learned these from spiritual directors (*pir or ustad*), to whose guidance they submitted themselves absolutely (Nicholson 1907:392).

The development of theosophical thought in the movement is most noteworthy. Theosophy is any of various forms of philosophical or religious thought based on supposed insights into the divine nature. Fazlur Rahman explains:

The early ascetic piety, with its emphasis on the interiorization of the motive, was a reaction to the external development of the law. During the 9th and 10th centuries Sufism developed a doctrine of "gnosis" (*marifa*), of an inner experiential knowledge which it progressively came to oppose to the intellectual knowledge (*ilm*) of theology which developed during the same period (Rahman 1979:141).

Thus, in the course of a century, Sufism, which was initially little more than asceticism, became first mystical and then theosophical, and even ran the risk of being confused with pantheism (Nicholson 1907:391).

Still later, Sufism bred all kinds of disorderly and frenzied rituals involving self-inflicted wounds, swaying chanters falling unconscious to the floor, or members whirling themselves into religious ecstasy, only to be hung up by their feet until they returned to their senses. Such scenes were graphically described by eyewitness John A. Subhan (1938:1-4).

All of the orders of Sufism do not follow the same stages of discipline. Each order sets its own rules. Below, Subhan describes the steps or stages of the mystic journey laid out for the disciple in the Sufi Order to which he formerly belonged (1938:68-72).

1. Repentance: awakening from indifference to evil and developing a sense of contrition for sin.

2. Love: the adept gives himself to remembrances of the names of God and seeks to exclude all thoughts except of God.

3. Renunciation: the aspirant is urged to observe poverty and renounce all worldly desires. Ultimately, he renounces all but God Himself.

4. Knowledge: the aspirant contemplates the nature, attributes and works of God until God is all he thinks about.

5. Ecstasy: By remembering and reciting the names and attributes of God, a state of mental excitement or ecstasy is induced.

6. Reality: The heart is now supposed to be illuminated with the true nature of God. At this point, the aspirant is to seek to be utterly dependent on God—to trust Him.

7. Union: At this stage, the mystic believes he "sees" God face-to-face. The mystic believes his old self is annihilated and he is utterly satisfied with God and God is utterly satisfied with him.

The Sufi emphasis on the inner experience was coupled with the deep desire to escape from one's self, or as the Sufi would put it, the annihilation of self, thus making possible one's absorption into God. In addition to offering a supposed "seeing" of God, or union with God, Sufism was characterized by the spontaneity with which local groups could spring up around an itinerant preacher or a homegrown mystic of great piety. In the course of its development, the heads of these orders (or their followers) felt it necessary to trace the divine light resident in their leader (*pir or shaykh*) back to Muhammad himself (Parshall 1983:57).

Sufis meet either in established meeting houses, or informally wherever it is convenient. Natural groupings of people can voluntarily come together. For example, farmer types in rural communities, men gathered together in military units, men of similar professions and trades, women in local neighborhoods, and units of like-minded people within a city. In short, any natural grouping of people could unite anywhere around a pious leader.

Sufi orders encouraged the use of poetry and music. Talented composers wrote beautiful music for their love songs to God. Some brotherhoods encouraged dancing as part of worship. Since music and dancing were never permitted in the mosque, Sufis built their own lodges or met outdoors.

The Recovery of Music

It was Zephaniah, the Prophet, inspired by God's Spirit, who has revealed to us that God sings! "The Lord your God is with you, He is mighty to save. He will take great delight in you, He will quiet you with His love, He will rejoice over you with singing" (Zeph. 3:17). And why wouldn't he? After all, we are made in His image and we sing. He loves to hear us sing. And He has given us His Spirit to assist us in singing: "be filled with the Spirit. Speak to one another with psalms, hymns and spiritual songs. Sing and make music in your heart to the Lord, always giving thanks to God the Father for everything, in the name of our Lord Jesus Christ" (Eph. 5:18–20). Muslims therefore, have turned to romantic and folkloric music. The Sufis could not help but "borrow" religious music from their neighbors—God made us musical. We Christians have so much to offer Sufis in our rich tradition of music.

It was the "singing Sufis" who led so many pagans into the folds of Islam. Now it is our turn to lead the Sufis into the arms of Jesus with music and song. "Let us come before Him with thanksgiving and extol Him with music and song" (Ps. 95:2). Dancing, too, to the music of many instruments, is to have its place in the winning of the Sufis, for some Sufi orders dance in search of ecstasy. The Psalmist writes:

> Let them praise his name with dancing and make music to him with tambourine and harp. For the Lord takes delight in his people; he crowns the humble with salvation (Ps. 149:3, 4).

> Praise him with the sounding of the trumpet, praise him with the harp and lyre, praise him with tambourine and dancing, praise Him with the strings and flute, praise him with the clash of cymbals, praise him with resounding cymbals. Let everything that has breath praise the Lord. Praise the Lord (Ps. 150:3-6).

Let's help the Sufis discover their real roots in Jesus. Let's use their very strength in music and song to woo them to the True God.

The Spread of Sufism

From humble beginnings in the eighth and ninth centuries, these Sufi orders swept the Muslim world and constituted a highly successful missionary movement in the centuries that followed. It is generally conceded that the "singing Sufis" did as much to convert pagans to Islam as did the Muslim armies. Sufism could exist as a highly organized secret order, or individuals could meet in loose, unorganized associations. A member could be residential or attend as a volunteer.

Along with all the strengths and advantages that this movement offered its members, Sufi suffered many weaknesses. By offering the devotee supposed direct access to God, it weakened the place of the law, weakened the position of the Quran and the *Hadith*, and led to a great deal of nominalism and in many cases, moral laxity.

One of the unusual things one will notice about Sufism is that it is so pervasive. In one variety or another it is found throughout the Muslim world. Theoretically, one can be a member of most Muslim sects and still be a member of a Sufi order, although offering a "seeker" "direct access to God" renders the need of a Shiite-type *imam* or ayatollah unnecessary. This belief in direct access to God, by the way, allowed many Shias (discussed earlier) to defect to Sufism and the Sunni branch of Islam.

Because of its ready accommodation to local religious practices, Sufism opened the door to many kinds of syncretism. Let us now turn to the syncretistic accommodations that Sufism allows, giving birth to that hybrid form of Islam we tend to call Folk Islam.

CHAPTER 13

FOLK MUSLIMS: ISLAM AND THE POWERS

Folk Islam is a broad, catch-all phrase that describes a syncretized form of Islam. In this phenomenon, Islam of several varieties mixes with animistic religion. Animism is the belief that spiritual beings or spiritual power reside in all kinds of animate and inanimate objects, such as other people, animals, reptiles, birds, insects, fish, stones, trees, lakes, mountains, caves, heavenly bodies, places, buildings and various kinds of paraphernalia used by witches, sorcerers, diviners and necromancers. The latter would naturally involve the devotee in practices aimed at the appeasement of demons.

The people who live in the world of Folk Islam are concerned with manipulating these spiritual beings and powers for their own good. Usually this takes the form of efforts to either appease these spirits or to neutralize them, as well as use them to bring blessings to themselves or even curses on their enemies.

Sufism, with its ready acceptance of pre-Islamic, local religious practices, opened the door wide for these spiritual beings and powers. At the surface level, there is a tacit acknowledgment of some form of Islam. But in daily life, the traffic is with the spirits and spiritual powers that one encounters at every turn. Paul Hiebert comments: "Folk religion focuses on problem-solving in everyday life." He goes on to list the kind of questions that Folk Islam tends to deal with:

- The meaning of everyday life and of death.
- The well-being of a person or group, and the threat of misfortune.
- The question of success or failure.

- The need to plan one's life and to know the unknown, past, present and future.
- Human relationships, and relationships to ancestors, spirits, gods, demons, animals and plants (Hiebert 1989:47, 49).

Orthodox Islam tends to focus on ultimate reality, the questions of the origin of things, meanings and final destiny. Folk Islam provides the immediate answers to the questions one faces at every stage of life. Orthodox Islam tends to deal with ultimate truth in theological terms. Folk Islam tends to deal with power, whether in persons, visible and invisible, or with power resident in things.

It is not surprising, then, to discover in the world of Folk Islam such practitioners as saints, holy men or women, sorcerers, witches and shamans. These practitioners will either attempt to perform exorcisms, or invite evil spirits to come and live in a person. There will be sacred places, buildings, shrines, stones, mountains, lakes and animals where one is supposed to go to obtain blessing. There will be places haunted by evil powers, places to be avoided at all costs.

Throughout the Muslim world, one finds the almost universal fear of the "evil eye." The evil eye is a form of curse. The one who has the evil eye, motivated by envy or jealousy, wishes evil for his or her neighbors, family members or other people's possessions.

Rituals and ceremonies have been locally developed to attempt to control or appease these beings and forces. In large parts of the Islamic world, Muslims practice magical incantations, amulets, animal sacrifices, vows to be paid, annual pilgrimages to local shrines, touching and kissing tombs thought to contain blessing (baraka), and tying prayer requests in the form of colored cloth to the branches of trees near the burial places of holy men.

The Christian worker cannot treat these matters lightly or even try to ignore them. Charles Kraft learned this lesson in his experiences among the Higi of Nigeria. Because of his set of assumptions, attitudes characteristic of his Western secular worldview, he was unable to comprehend the spiritual realities with which his Higi friends were contending.

Time after time Nigerians would turn our discussions to
the disruption in their lives they claimed were caused by
evil spirits. Such things as disease, accidents, death, the
infertility of humans, animals, fields, drought, and the
disruption of relationships were all seen as the work of
these evil entities (Kraft 1989:4).

In brilliant and lucid detail, Kraft goes on to explain the "paradigm
shift" he underwent as his worldview shifted from a Western secular one
to that of the Scriptures. From being ineffective in the face of evil spiritual
phenomena, he learned how to deal with them on the basis of his newly
discovered biblical worldview, through the power of the Spirit of God
(1989:117-132).

Many of us who have ministered extensively in different parts of the
Muslim world have concluded that about eighty-five percent of all Muslims
traffic in the spirit-world through one or more of these Folk Islamic
practices.

In a later section we will suggest approaches for the Christian worker
in dealing with these phenomena.

CHAPTER 14

MILITANT ISLAM: A RETURN TO ROOTS

Religion encompasses all of life for a Muslim. In the West, we are accustomed to the reality of the separation of Church and State. In Orthodox Islam, there is no equivalent to this idea. Along with everything else, religion is politics. Conversely, all politics are practiced in the name of religion, with the exception of those Muslim countries which have adopted some secular form of government. Muslims must strive (*jihad*) in "the way of God" in every area of life, including the political arena. For the Muslim who is true to the Quranic teaching, there is no rest until the whole world is brought under the rule of Islamic Law (*Shariah*).

According to this precept, the world is divided into the "House of Islam" (*Dar al-Islam*) and the "House of the Resisters," or the "House of War" (*Dar al-Harb*). Islam is committed to a ceaseless effort to impose itself on the rest of the world.

In actuality, this is not the way it has worked out. Islam's early efforts at world domination were stymied, usually by successful military resistance. Also the problem of "worldliness" afflicted the early Muslim rulers (caliphs and Sultans). Both the Umayyads (661-750) and the Abbasids (750-1258) were plagued by decadence in their rulers. The latter came to an end due to the Mongol invasions. This was followed by the rise of local rulers throughout the Muslim world, the most prominent being the Ottoman Empire (1342-1918). Since the abolishment of the Caliphate in 1924, Islam has not had a caliph to rally around and help its followers realize their dream of world conquest.

With the rise of Western colonialism and the subjugation of about ninety percent of the Muslim world by Western powers, the Muslim political self-image suffered a devastating blow. The West ultimately dismembered the Ottoman Empire, and divided it into several Muslim States, the countries of the Middle East as we know them today.

Starting in the last century with the preaching of Jamal ad-Din al-Afghani (1838-1897), an awakening of pan-Islamic sentiments occurred among the Sunnis. He was not the first to preach a revival of Islam, but he may mark the beginning of that militant Islamic thinking which has carried on into this century. The great Indian Muslim theologian, Abul Ala Mawdudi, initially disagreed with the formation of Pakistan because he felt nationalism was the invention of the colonialists. He insisted that there should only be one country for all the Muslims of the world and that no Muslim should live anywhere under non-Muslim rule. In the absence of such a universal Muslim state, he later migrated to Pakistan to help create a true Muslim state, rather than live under non-Muslim rule in India.

In Egypt, the most eloquent and prolific writer to come out of the Muslim Brotherhood Movement, founded in 1927 by Hasan al-Banna, was Sayyid Qutb. For him:

> Islam presents to mankind a perfectly integrated
> exemplary system the like of which the earth has not
> known either prior to Islam or since ... It has offered to
> humanity a wholly integrated treatment of all human
> issues (Cragg 1985:55).

Qutb expressed his convictions very courageously in political agitation against the regime of Gamal Abd al-Nasir. He was executed by Nasir in 1966.

On the Shia side, before Khomeini came to power, there was Ali Shariati of Tehran. For him:

> Life is conviction and struggle and nothing more ... Look
> at the companions of the Prophet: they were all men of
> the sword, concerned with improving their society, men
> of justice ... Among the companions of the Prophet and
> the *mujahidin* in the early days of Islam, who is the
> intellectual, who the activist, who the cleric? Absolutely
> no such classifications exist. Everyone promulgates Islam,
> fights, and also farms, cultivates dates, or herds camels.

Each person is simultaneously worker, warrior and intellectual (Cragg 1985:76, 84).

For this thoroughly courageous Iranian intellectual, often called an "Islamic Liberation Theologue," living in exile, the only path was one of persistent action until Islam was in control and busily involved in changing the world for good (as understood by him). Shariati, like Sayyid Qutb before him, was martyred (1977) for his activist convictions, probably by the late Shah of Iran's dreaded Savak police.

Undoubtedly, the most well known Shia activist in our era was the late Ayatollah Ruhollah Khomeini (died June 3, 1989). He had an unbelievably strong conviction that Islam was of God and was destined to conquer the world. On his return from exile to Iran, he said:

> We must settle our accounts with the great super powers and show them that we can take on the whole world ideologically, despite all the painful problems that face us ... We shall export our revolution to the whole world. Until the cry, "There is no God but God" resounds over the whole world, there will be struggle (Wright 1989:27, 108).

When exported to Lebanon, this revolution gave birth to an indeterminate number of groups and movements, the better known of which are Hizbollah and Islamic *jihad*. Today, there is a kind of "spontaneous combustion" going on in some of the world's hot spots, like Lebanon, where many groups have sprung up and each is a law unto itself, with a militant Islamic ideology.

Elsewhere among Muslims in the Middle East, South Asia, Southeast Asia, and the newly independent countries of Central Asia, Islam is awakening. In the case of the Kazakhs, Chechens, Tatars, Azerbaijanis, Kyrgyz, Uzbeks, Turkmens and Tajiks, there are ethnic overtones to these freedom movements. In Turkey, frustration with the status quo, blamed on secularism, is the driving force. In Pakistan and Bangladesh, the imposition of Islamic Law is supposed to solve the all too obvious ills of society. In the Philippines, it is the cry for autonomy from the so-called

Christian rule of the majority of people. In the Sudan, civil war is again raging because the Islamic majority is seeking to impose *Shariah* Law on the Tribal and Christian minorities. In Nigeria and Malaysia there is terrific tension for the same reason. In Afghanistan, with the rise of the Taliban movement, we are witnessing the most ruthless effort yet seen in the world to take Muslims back to the "pure" Islam practiced in Muhammad's time.

Here in the West, *jihad* is taking a different form. But the spirit is the same: competition and striving for ascendancy. Abandoned churches in the ghettos of our cities bought by Muslims and turned into mosques. Beautiful new mosques are built in prominent places. Chapters of Muslim student associations are forming on hundreds of college and university campuses. Arabic and English language programs are appearing on television, promoting Islam. Attractive literature is being published that portrays Islam in a very favorable light. The mood among Muslims is definitely upbeat. Recently, I had a phone conversation with a prominent political exile from a Muslim state who said, "Now that Communism has collapsed, the real struggle begins. It's between Islam and Christianity." I detected a note of triumph in his voice.

These things should not surprise us for two reasons. The first is that if one is going to be a consistent Muslim, he should be a militant one. That is the nature of Islam. As the late Dr. Fazlur Rahman has reminded us, it is part of the warp and woof of Islam, rooted in the behavior and teaching of Muhammad (1979:211). The second reason is that the Quran teaches that Muhammad was supposedly the last of the prophetic line (Seal of the Prophets). If Islam were just a localized religion, it would have collapsed. But since it claims to be a world-wide religion, it is therefore driven to seek world domination.

CHAPTER 15

ISLAM AND SECULARISM

Secularism is a broad term, sometimes used interchangeably with the West, or Western Culture. It has been variously described as the scientific approach to life, as a form of anti-supernaturalism where humankind attempts to solve all its problems without divine help, or as an agnostic or even atheistic type of materialism, whether of the capitalistic, socialistic or communistic varieties. Its net effect is to downplay religion and exalt the human race's ability to get along without God. Implicit in this sense of self-sufficiency is the idea that there is nothing "out there," or that if there is a God, no one knows much about Him. And along with this comes even less inclination to believe in a devil, or fallen angels or demons.

There is no doubt that this "scientific attitude" and "can-do" mentality have released tremendous creative energy into Western culture, resulting in unprecedented technological achievements. This has been accompanied by the West's almost total domination of world economies, with the exception of the "oil countries." Due to the astonishing technological achievements and economic dominance of the West, the assumptions behind this secular worldview have become widely pervasive.

Islam and Colonialism
The subjugation of ninety percent of the Muslim world by Western colonial rule in the early part of this century—up to the period of the Second World War—has left an indelible imprint on the minds of Muslim peoples. Today the Muslim world struggles with the question of how to acquire Western technology without accepting the philosophical assumptions behind it. This interaction of Western cultural values with Islamic values has given birth to a wide variety of Muslim responses which stretch across a spectrum from extreme accommodation to total rejection.

Militant Islam, as mentioned previously, responded with rejection. It is the accommodative responses which occupy us here.

The Problems of Accommodation

The West's technological achievements bring with them a worldview, a set of assumptions about reality, vastly different from that of seventh century Islam. The dilemma Muslims find themselves in is that the teaching and model behavior of Muhammad are supposed to be normative; that is, the final rule of faith and practice. Since Muhammad, even in his most brilliant moments, could not have imagined the technological achievements of the West or the worldview that gave rise to them, Muslims are at a loss to explain how they could have happened outside of Islam. By absolutizing Muhammad's Quran and his model behavior as preserved in the *Hadith*, along with his perceptions of reality, good Muslims are locked into a system that neither fits the twentieth century nor explains how something other than Islam could achieve so much. Islam is supposed to be the quintessential faith with an answer for everything.

Christians, we might add, are in a much happier situation, for Jesus introduced a spiritual kingdom that was distinct from the kingdoms of this world. Although Jesus' teaching on spiritual values acted as a leavening agent in other cultures so that Christianity always had a cultural form, that form was never absolutized. Christianity was able to develop in culturally appropriate ways among the many cultures where it took root.

Under these circumstances, Islam has two courses of action open before it. The first is to attempt to read into the Quran and the *Hadith* meanings that are not there, that would show that the Quran anticipated all that we see today. The other choice is to admit that the Quran and Muhammad's teaching and model behavior were inadequate for developing an enduring worldview that would weather the unfolding developments of subsequent centuries, particularly this one we call the "Technological Age."

Any effort which Islam may make to break out of Muhammad's narrow confines will tend to cast doubt on the adequacy of the Quran or diminish the credibility of Muhammad. To date, Islam has been unwilling to take this drastic step. Once the gate to radical innovation opens, the movement away from the Quran and *Hadith* might gain enough strength to discredit Islam and cause it to collapse as a system.

Islam's Early Attempts at Accommodation

Perhaps the earliest and most dramatic illustration of radical accommodation in this century is that of Turkey. In 1924, Kemal Ataturk, from his role as a hero-general of the army, assumed the position of president of his newly-founded Republic of Turkey. He moved quickly to declare Turkey a secular state, drafted a constitution guaranteeing religious freedom, changed the written script from Arabic to Roman, closed the Islamic religious schools, removed the veil from women, forbade the Sufi brotherhoods from meeting and enacted many other changes in an effort to make religion a private matter. This experiment met little resistance in its early decades.

Only recently has a fundamentalist revival movement begun to gain strength. In spite of drastic secular laws, the Turkish people equate their ethnicity with being Muslim ("To be a Turk is to be a Muslim"). Kenneth Cragg's assessment of Turkey is just as valid today as when he wrote it over thirty years ago:

> One thing is clear, namely, that Islam in Turkey is far too virile for secularism to ignore and too unpredictable to hold free rein. The fact of its survival is undoubted, the temper still in doubt. It has outlived Ataturk but is yet in the toils of his legacy (Cragg 1965:154).

The story of Arab interaction with the West is further mirrored in developments in Egypt. Muhammad Abduh (1849-1905), a Muslim reformer in Egypt was highly stimulated by the ideas of his hero reformer, Jamal ad-Din al-Afghani (1839-1897). However, Abduh adapted them according to his own genius in his formative influence on events in Egypt. "His essential thesis was that a true Islam, freed from un-Islamic accretions, was perfectly reconcilable with modern thought and conditions" (Cragg 1965:36). The key to Abduh's thinking was the expression "true Islam." He held to the fundamentals of Orthodox Islam by sheer faith. He would not allow them to be tampered with or brought under scrutiny. In considering Muhammad infallible, he was forced to contend that all modern developments were anticipated by Muhammad and evidences of such can be found in the Quran and *Hadith*. In other words, Abduh kept religion and science in separate compartments within his own thinking. He would not allow rationalistic investigations to be used on his religious beliefs. Having secured his faith by placing it beyond scrutiny, and having found the justification for scientific development incipiently indicated in Muhammad's teaching, he blithely appropriated scientific achievements as Islam's own. His disciples have followed in this vein, to the present time.

Current Attempts at Accommodation

Egypt today reflects the unresolved tension between Western values and accomplishments, and traditional Islam's virtual deification of Muhammad and enshrinement of *Shariah* Law derived from his sayings and behavior. The present government has not yet succumbed to the pressure to impose *Shariah* Law, and hence is perceived as un-Islamic or secular by the Orthodox. Assassination attempts have been made by Muslim militants against each Egyptian president from Abd al-Nasir to the present incumbent, Hosni Mubarak. Egypt might be considered a "middle position" case study.

On the far right, Saudi Arabia uses the Quran as its constitution. While this guarantees an outward appearance of conformism at home, the un-Islamic behavior of thousands of Saudis abroad is legendary. As mentioned before, in both Pakistan and Bangladesh military dictators imposed *Shariah* Law on the people. It has yet to be fully implemented against its largely unwilling subjects. The Sudan has moved from one long civil war to another over this issue of imposing *Shariah* Law on its non-Muslim citizens.

Qaddafi, the leader of Libya, presents a unique aberration in the Islamic renewal movement. He has neither a place for the traditional legal scholars of Islam on the one hand, nor a place for the leaders of the Sufi-type brotherhoods on the other. Rather than trying to reform the law, he simply replaced it. He has supplanted *Shariah* Law with his own concepts of a new order in his three-volume writings, known familiarly as *The Green Book*. He explained to Oriana Fallaci in a *New York Times Magazine* interview, December 16, 1979: "*The Green Book* is the guide to the emancipation of man ... the new gospel. The gospel of the new era, the era of the masses."

Commenting on this, John L. Esposito has written:
The Green Book has displaced the Shariah's governance of the political and social order. Mixing populist ideological statements with a broad range of political, social, and economic experimentation, Qaddafi has undertaken nothing less than his own cultural revolution, based not on the divine guidance of the Quran or the example of the Prophet but upon the thought of Qaddafi (Esposito 1984:159, 160).

No doubt, Qaddafi sees himself as a Muslim and as a defender of Islam, as evidenced by an interview with a reporter of *al-Maukif al-Arabi* in Cyprus. He indicated that peace would not come in Lebanon until all the Christians were conquered and forcibly converted to Islam. He said: "The mistake is due to the presence of Arab Christians. An Arab must not be a Christian" (Abd-al-Fadi, in *Al-Nour*, Vol. 2, No. 1, p.2). Aside from the obvious danger of such a doctrine to Christians, it is of interest to us that Qaddafi is not considered a good Muslim by Muslims, especially the Traditionalists. *The Green Book* represents a radical departure from Islam, and in this author's view, the introduction of a pseudo-Marxist ideology under an Islamic facade. When Qaddafi goes, it will be interesting to see if the people return to Traditional Islam or if *The Green Book* has been used to loosen religious ties and move the populace toward a more secular approach to government.

Islam's Flirtation with Communism

Perhaps strangest of all in the Muslim scene is the flirtation of certain Muslim countries with Communism. Ties between the former Soviet Union and Libya, Syria, Iraq and the former Democratic Republic of South Yemen have been the most prominent examples. Among them all (and as a fallout from the rivalry between Egypt and Saudi Arabia over the Civil War in Yemen), South Yemen, for a while, became Marxist. Saudi Arabia, with its vast oil wealth, made North Yemen its virtual economic ward, and then effected a restoration of relations with the Democratic Republic of South Yemen (Pipes 1983:313). Eventually, the Marxist government gave way in the remarkable union of the two Yemens.

The above are just a few examples of the kinds of struggles underway in the Muslim world as it seeks to either adjust to or reject the worldview of the twentieth century secular, technological society. The illustrations cited occurred at the national level. But what about individuals or minority segments within Muslim societies as they respond to the impact of the West and the secular ideas behind it? In my own travels and experiences in many Muslim countries, I have seen individuals and small groups who represent every level of response to this worldwide phenomenon of Western secularism.

CHAPTER 16

A RIVAL PROPHET: MIRZA GHULAM AHMAD

Islam, like Christianity, is beset with heresies and myriads of sects. The Ahmadi sect is pervasive enough to merit comment.

Mirza Ghulam Ahmad (1835-1908) was an Indian Muslim scholar of some repute who engaged both Hindus and Christians in debate. He was particularly nettled by Christian attacks on Islam and Muhammad. He burned with the indignities of Indian Muslims living under British rule. And he was further provoked by the Ulema's (Orthodox Muslim scholars) bafflement and hostility towards scientific inventions. He concluded that Islam needed a new interpreter, a reforming prophet (Mujeeb 1967:543).

Mirza Ghulam Ahmad: The Messiah

In March 1889, Ahmad claimed he was having revelations from God. He also claimed to be the Messiah and a *Zilli* prophet, one sent to interpret the law and clean up corruption. On the dark side, he claimed that he could cause his opponents to die by the miraculous power of his prayer (Hardy 1972:172). His claim to prophethood, naturally, alienated him from the Orthodox Muslim community which believes Muhammad was the Seal of the Prophets, meaning the end of the line. None were to come after him.

Orthodox Islam, in its early years, developed the idea that Jesus would return from heaven, subdue the anti-Christ, and through his preaching usher in the golden age of Islam. Ahmad felt this was not Quranic. He envisioned an Islam freed from this kind of teaching. Again contrary to traditional Islamic belief, Ahmad taught that Jesus was actually nailed to the cross, was taken down while still alive, escaped the tomb and migrated to Kashmir, where he died at a great age. Ahmadis will show you Jesus' tomb there today (Cragg 1956:250).

In addition to claiming to be the Messiah, Ahmad also claimed to be the *Mahdi*, the "rightly guided one," who would appear at the end of the age to restore righteousness before the end of the world. He claimed that this *Mahdi*, rather than Jesus, would appear and reinstate the purity of Muhammad's rule and unite all the schools of law (Glasse 1989:246-247).

Ahmad further alienated the Muslim community by declaring that:

> *Jihad* as a violent struggle for extending the religion was no longer operative and was limited to self-defense only … He declared that coercion in religion was wrong and the punishment by stoning to death for the offense of apostasy was to be condemned … (Karandikar 1968:102).

After the formation of Pakistan, the issue of whether or not Ahmadis were true Muslims provoked two major crises. The first was connected with the Islamic identity and character of the state. The Ahmadis' claim that their founder was a prophet, thus denying the finality of Muhammad's prophethood, provoked rioting and widespread killing of Ahmadis in March and April of 1953. In due time, the question was settled in the High Court of Pakistan (1974) which declared Ahmadis a non-Muslim minority (Esposito 1984:113). Rioting, killing and torching of Ahmadi property followed.

To propagate their faith, the Ahmadis have undertaken fresh translations of the Quran, have developed a great body of attractive literature, are given to open-air preaching, and are excellent debaters. They have been stoutly resisted in the Arab heartland of Islam, but continue to have success in the more peripheral areas, especially in West Africa, East Africa, Southeast Asia and Europe. They have an influence, thanks to their propaganda, far beyond their numbers. There may be no more than 500,000 in the world (Glasse 1989:28).

CHAPTER 17

RACIST ISLAM: AFRICAN-AMERICAN MUSLIMS

The phenomenon of the rise of groups calling themselves "African-American Muslims" is unique to the United States. This chapter, then, is primarily for the American reader, or any others interested in this movement.

Roots of the African-American Muslim Movement

Imagine if the Spirit of Jesus had indwelt those wretched people who, bereft of any light, invented the slave trade. History might have been different if Jesus had had His way. But it wasn't to be. The story of Muslim Arab slave traders finding ready buyers among the white colonizers of the Western world is one of the saddest chapters in the annals of the human race. The rise of the African-American Muslim phenomenon is an outgrowth of that human tragedy.

The "Muslim" part of this movement goes back to the tragic story of the deportation of millions of West African citizens to the "New World" as slaves. Based on knowledge of the slave routes, we know that some Africans were taken from Muslim areas of West Africa (Ajayi and Crowder 1985:33,35), and some were unquestionably from Muslim background. We know this because interviews with African-Americans whose ancestors were slaves indicate that Muslim practices, words, names and ideas were passed down from generation to generation in a few of these families (Berger 1964:49-64). Alex Haley's book, *Roots*, substantiates this idea rather strongly. Even though a large percentage of African-American slaves became Christians (a higher percentage of them are Christians than are white Christians here in the United States), not all went that way. Islam, portrayed as African, became a natural rallying point for a people looking for their roots and their identity.

On the racial side, Eric Lincoln writes that "The Black Muslims" are a symbol and a product of social conflict. They represent a point at the extreme edge of a spectrum of protest" (Lincoln 1973:xx). He documents at least 109 slave revolts among the slaves in the continental United States in the period of slavery between 1664 and 1864. These were a people seeking to be free—understandably—and seeking a place of their own (1973:xx).

The Development of Black Islam

African-Americans began to form organizations for their own betterment and as vehicles of social protest. In this milieu, Timothy Drew, an African American (1886-1929) with some knowledge of Islam, founded the first Moorish Science Temple in Newark, New Jersey in 1913. He took the name Noble Drew Ali. He was succeeded in 1930 by a man named W. D. Fard. No one knows his origins, only that he described himself to the Detroit police as "The Supreme Ruler of the Universe" (Lincoln 1973:14).

W. D. Fard's chief disciple was Elijah Poole, renamed by Fard as Elijah Muhammad. When Fard disappeared in 1934, Elijah Muhammad assumed leadership of the movement. One of his first acts was to deify Fard as the incarnation of Allah, a teaching that was anathema to Orthodox Islam.

Elijah Muhammad's chief spokesperson was Malcolm Little, the son of a Baptist minister who had been greatly discriminated against and was finally murdered by whites. His mother, unable to cope with eight children, went insane and the children were cast upon the state. Malcolm entered into a life of crime, was jailed, and converted to Islam in jail. He took the name Malcolm X, joined Elijah Muhammad and recruited thousands of African Americans to the Black Muslim Movement. Malcolm X was an idealist looking for pure Islam.

Beliefs

Glasse, the compiler of the Concise Encyclopedia of Islam, is convinced that Ahmadi missionaries with their virulent anti-Christian teaching fed the racist side—the "hate the white man" side—of the African-American Muslim movement (1989:71). The founder of the Ahmadis claimed that the white man was the *Dajjal* (the Antichrist, the Devil). Undoubtedly,

Ahmadi missionaries met W. D. Fard and gave him justification for what he already believed about the white man (Glasse 1989:76). To this poisonous anti-white, anti-Christian teaching from Ahmadi missionaries here in the States, Fard added his own interpretation of both biblical and human history.

One of Fard's fanciful interpretations of scriptural ideas was that the real "Armageddon" would be in America between whites and African-Americans. He also taught that primordial humans were Black and that all other races were descended from them (Lincoln 1973:77). This was accompanied by many other fictions eulogizing the Black race and denigrating the White race. W. D. Fard diverted the aching spirit of Black Nationalism from a "Back-to-Africa Movement," as espoused by such men as Marcus Garvey, who was expelled from this country in 1926, to a policy of separatism and agitation for a separate country for Blacks within the territorial United States.

Crisis in the Movement

When Malcolm X exposed an immoral relationship Elijah Muhammad had with two young Muslim women, he was suspended from the movement that had become known as the "Nation of Islam." Louis Farrakhan succeeded Malcolm as the official spokesman for the Nation of Islam. In 1965, Malcolm X was assassinated.

The death of Elijah Muhammad in 1975 precipitated a great crisis in the movement. Elijah's son, Wallace D. Muhammad, new leader of the Nation of Islam, introduced many reforms and moved the organization into the fold of Orthodox Islam. He de-emphasized the race issue and dropped the idea of a separate state for Black Americans.

In 1976, the Nation of Islam changed its name to "The World Community of al-Islam." In 1980 it metamorphosed into "The American Muslim Mission." And in 1985, it took its present name "al-Islam in America." In the same year, Wallace Muhammad acceded to the Orthodox teaching that being the *imam* of a movement was a matter of individual choice and he stepped down as the leader (Battle 1988:37). These reforms precipitated a crisis for those who wanted to remain racist. Estimates for this group, al-Islam in America, range from one-hundred and fifty thousand to almost a million (Glasse 1989:77).

But we have gotten ahead of another development in the movement. In 1977, Louis Farrakhan formed a splinter organization under the old name of "The Nation of Islam." This group is more racist than it is Islamic. He continues to call for a separate territory for African-Americans, maintains that W. D. Fard was Allah and that Elijah Muhammad was the Messenger of God. In doing this, Farrakhan ignored the charges of immorality brought against Elijah Muhammad by Malcolm X. In fact, rumors abound that it was Louis Farrakhan who had Malcolm X assassinated. The highest estimates for the strength of Farrakhan's group is no more than 50,000 (Glasse 1989:77).

There is one other breakaway group called "Hanafi Muslims," so named because they follow Orthodox Islam's Hanafi School of Law. There are no figures on their membership—all that is known is that about a hundred mosques are associated with this 1958 split-away group.

PART FOUR

MINISTERING TO MUSLIMS: THE QUESTION OF ATTITUDE

INTRODUCTION

The previous three parts of the book have covered the unique developments in the life of Abraham which led to the tragic eviction of Hagar and Ishmael from his household; a detailed review of the life and teaching of Ishmael's most illustrious descendant, Muhammad; and the development of several significant sects within Islam.

We begin this section on "Ministering to Muslims" with certain assumptions drawn from the Scriptures. First, we believe that God, who had compassion on Hagar and Ishmael so long ago, would show the same compassion to those who claim affinity with them.

Jesus' great redemptive work on the cross is for all who will believe in Him (John 3:16). God's desire is to see all people saved and come to the knowledge of the truth (1 Tim. 2:4). God is not willing that any should perish but that all should come to repentance (2 Peter 3:9). We believe that these Scriptures should be fundamental principles in molding our attitude toward Muslims: the desire to see all of them saved; not willing to see any of them perish; all coming to the knowledge of the truth; all coming to repentance.

Furthermore, implicit in the great hymns of victory in the Book of Revelation, we read that believers are going to come from "every tribe and language and people and nation" (Rev. 5:9). This, of course, includes Muslims of every ethnic background. Our first challenge in ministering to Muslims is to allow the Word of God to mold our worldview, to believe that God has a mighty harvest among them. Even Old Testament prophecy reinforces the idea that there will be a harvest among the sons of Ishmael. Many scholars consider Isaiah 60 the climax of messianic prophecy. In it we read that Nebaioth and Kedar, Ishmael's two oldest sons, will be part of that wonderful procession of Gentiles who will come with acceptance to the Messiah, offering their wealth freely to Him (Isa. 60:7). Since these men had been dead at least one thousand years at the time this prophecy was given, it obviously means Ishmael's descendants. This certainly would include some Arabs today. We read in Isaiah 21 (700 B.C.) that the Kedar tribal name was linked with the Arabs. Since all Muslims claim identity with Abraham through Ishmael and his descendants, we believe that these ancient prophecies give us hope for seeing a harvest among Muslims.

We, too, like our Heavenly Father, can hear the cry of Ishmael coming through the voices of his descendants, whether they be physically descended or spiritually affiliated with him through Islam. Beneath the veneer of Islamic pride, we see these multitudes as Jesus did, "harassed and helpless, like sheep without a shepherd" (Matt. 9:36). And like the searching shepherd in Jesus' memorable parable, we intend to search for them and find them and bring them into the sheepfold of Jesus, the Good Shepherd.

CHAPTER 18

JESUS' WAY

Jesus said, "My kingdom is not of this world. If it were, my servants would fight …" (John 18:36).

Although prophecy hailed Jesus as "a Lion from the tribe of Judah" (Gen. 49:9; Rev. 5:5), He came as the "Lamb of God, who takes away the sin of the world" (John 1:29)! The apostle John saw Him as "a Lamb looking as if it had been slain, standing in the center of the throne …" (Rev. 5:6). Jesus chose to come as a Lamb. He refused to establish His kingdom with force (John 18:36). Napoleon Bonaparte said of Him:

> Alexander, Caesar, Charlemagne and myself founded empires. But on what did we rest the creations of our genius? Upon force. Jesus Christ alone founded His empire upon love, and millions of men would die for Him. Christ proved that He was the Son of the Eternal (Vollmer 1912:332).

Jesus' Way

Jesus, at every opportunity, shunned the use of coercive power. At His temptation, He could not be baited by Satan to employ the power of God to gratify Himself, dazzle the world with angelic rescuers, or compromise His purity to obtain His goal. He chose to win His right to become the Sovereign Ruler of all mankind by way of the cross, not the sword. It was not that He did not have access to power. He could still storms, command the wind, quiet the waves, multiply food to feed thousands, turn water to wine, heal the sick, rebuke demons, raise the dead: He could have called legions of angels to aid Him, if He had wanted.

Jesus came to establish not a worldly empire, but a spiritual kingdom. He came to deliver from demonic power, to release from spiritual oppression, to heal, to forgive, and to show His power over death itself. He wanted mankind to recognize Him for His goodness and follow Him as the true Son of God. He would build His kingdom on self-sacrificing love, not force. He would give His life as a ransom for many; He would not take life by violence.

The only seemingly apparent exceptions to Jesus' nonviolent life are cited below and neither, on closer examination, could ever really be illustrations for the use of force to win converts or a kingdom. Twice He cleansed the Court of the Gentiles in the Jerusalem Temple to tell the Jews that God's House was a place of prayer for all people (John 2:16; Mark 11:17). These actions were in reality more a demonstration of moral indignation. Only once did Jesus ever use power destructively, and that was to curse a barren fig tree, a terrifying metaphor of the judgment to come for all who repudiate the stewardship of living a fruitful life in God (Matt. 21:19).

Jesus came as the Lamb of God, a sacrificial lamb, to take away the sins of the world. And when Jesus walked among the crowds of common people, He was moved with compassion because He saw them as "harassed and helpless, like sheep without a shepherd" (Matt. 9:36). He told His disciples that He was sending them forth as lambs among wolves (Luke 10:3). Thank God for His precious servants who understood this and lived it. But not all who proclaimed His name followed the spirit of this teaching. Rather than learning from our Lord, some who bear the name of Christian and others who are perceived as Christians, but are not, have gone forth as wolves. And they are perceived as wolves. Both our forebears and peers have stumbled over the issue of power and empire.

Judaism, in turning away from their Messiah, also refused Jesus' teaching about war. In the First Jewish Revolt (A.D. 66-73), the Roman General Titus captured Jerusalem, destroyed the Temple, killed thousands of Jews, and took the Golden Menorah to Rome (Wilson 1989:75). In the Second Jewish Revolt (A.D. 132-135), Rabbi Akiba went so far as to proclaim Simon, a Zealot, the Messiah (*Bar Kokhba*). This time, the Roman General Hadrian leveled Jerusalem, killed about 500,000 Jews throughout Palestine, renamed the city after himself and forbade Jews to even enter the city (Wilson 1989:82). This should have afforded a tremendous object lesson to the Church for all time, but it did not.

Christian Militarism and the Development of Islam

For the first three centuries of its history, the Church kept itself separate from secular power. That changed with Constantine, the Roman Emperor who, after his victories in the civil wars that wracked the empire, embraced Christianity and then declared it the official religion of the empire. Around A.D. 312 Constantine, as a Christian Emperor, went forth to conquer using the symbol of the cross on the shields of his warriors. From that time forward, Christianity has been compromised with various levels of entanglement with empire and plagued by those who have failed to distinguish the secular realm from the spiritual, who have used force to defend their faith, or promote it, as a banner under which to wage its unholy wars.

It is not my intention to get into a long discussion on the question of the separation of church and state. But I do embrace the idea, and believe that those who have sought to advance the gospel of Christ by military means, for example, the Spanish Conquistadors, have done tremendous harm to the cause and the name of Christ. Nowhere has this been more apparent than in the fourteen centuries of Christianity's interaction with Islam.

Muhammad (A.D. 570-632) was aware throughout his lifetime of the long struggle between the Persians and the Christians. The latter was called the Eastern Roman Empire or Byzantine by their foes. In the year that Muhammad made his fateful emigration from Mecca to Medina (A.D. 622), the Byzantine Emperor Heraclius launched a seven-year "holy war" against the Persians. Instead of serving as a check and balance to the Byzantines' militaristic excesses, the Church joined with it, thus weakening the effectiveness of the spirit and teaching with which Christ wanted to establish His kingdom.

How tragic that Muhammad, watching a Christian empire in action, drew the conclusion that one's faith should be wed to the sword. In the most vivid way, Muhammad saw in the example of the Byzantines a model for wedding the sword to the faith. It only took his inventive mind to appropriate the ancient Bedouin tribal tradition of *razzia*, that is, raiding one another's caravans, and rename it *jihad*, that is, striving in the way of God (Watt 1974:108).

The period of the Crusades (A.D. 1095-1291), those Christian military expeditions commissioned by the Church to wrest the "Holy Land" out of the hands of the Muslims, were not an exception to wars fought in the name of and with the blessing of the Church. Rather, they were in keeping with the unbroken tradition of Christian militarism introduced by Constantine in the early fourth century.

Muslims gradually came to learn that Christians were dangerous. If ever that was in question, the colonial period (roughly A.D. 1450-1970) laid that doubt to rest forever. Spain and Portugal led the way in the sixteenth century with their warrior-missionary adventures. The next century saw Dutch, French and English enter the field in a mad race to build empires. Before it was over, Belgium, Germany, Italy and Russia had jumped into the game. Of them, only France is still at it, occupying the island of Mayotte and French Guyana. The six Central Asian Muslim Republics, which formerly belonged to the recently dissolved Soviet Union (Azerbaijan, Tajikistan, Uzbekistan, Turkmenistan, Kyrgyzstan and Kazakhstan), have only recently become free (December 1991). To this could be added the ill-fated Russian invasion of Afghanistan (1979-1988).

To be fair, by the latter end of the colonial period, many of these Western powers no longer went forth in the name of God and their countries, for in several of them the idea of separation of church and state had taken hold. But missionaries, often of the same nationality as that of the occupying colonial power, followed quickly in their wake. Even though these were technically not religio-military incursions, they were perceived as such by the Muslims. Since Muslims make no distinction between religion and state, they tend to see others the same way. That is, they assume there is an implicit link between our governments and our missionaries.

When one marks on a world map the extent of the colonial powers' occupation of the Muslim world, it comes to about ninety percent. In appendix C, the reader will see just how recent the relinquishment is of these occupied Muslim lands and how fresh the wounds are which Western powers inflicted on Muslims. If only we could go into the Muslim world clean! But it is not to be, especially if we happen to have been born a Westerner. It is easier for missionaries who go forth from countries that were never colonial powers. Even so, Islam contains an inherent animus toward Christianity that must be overcome.

Islam and American Militarism

American readers may need to remind themselves that their country, too, has stained its hands with Muslim blood, beginning in 1898 when America defeated Spain and took over the Philippines. Spain had been trying for centuries to rule the Muslim peoples of Mindanao and the islands of the Sulu Archipelago. They had been at war intermittently with these Muslims for almost four hundred years. America stepped in where Spain left off, and fought the Muslims of the Philippines.

In more recent times, America has exhibited a strange ambivalence in its relations to Muslim countries. She invaded Lebanon in 1956. She bombarded it from the sea in 1986. America is the chief supporter of the modern state of Israel since 1948, and yet she stepped in and forced France, Britain and Israel to back off from their attempted seizure of the Suez Canal in 1956. In the Iran-Iraq War (1979 to 1988), the United States assumed the responsibility of defending Kuwaiti ships, and later all ships under attack by Iran, thus tilting toward Iraq. Yet later (1991), the United States went to war with Iraq to expel Iraqis from Kuwait. The United States' quarrel with Libya is well known. We could say more of our armament deals with several Muslim countries, beginning with Saudi Arabia, and others such as Egypt, Jordan, Pakistan and the Afghan Resistance Movement.

But the most painful thorn in the side of Islam is what the West and its friends did to bring into being the modern state of Israel. America was the first country to recognize the state of Israel following the United Nations Resolution of 1948. Ever since then, in the eyes of Muslims not only in the Middle East, but around the world, Americans have been perceived as the power behind Israel, and hence the real enemy of Islam. Muslims ever since the Jewish victory in the War of 1967 feel they have been deprived of one of their most treasured possessions: Jerusalem. Muslims consider Jerusalem their third holiest city, after Mecca and Medina. The Dome of the Rock and al-Aksa Mosque, both in Jerusalem, are sought out by pilgrims from all over the Muslim world. In addition, Palestinians were driven out of their land by the Jews in 1948, forced to leave their farms, orchards, businesses, and homes. Palestinian refugee camps can still be found today in Lebanon and Jordan.

When the pain of losing these sacred places, which Muslims had controlled for almost thirteen hundred years, is compounded with the pain of what the Jews have done to the Palestinians, it becomes the most inflammatory issue between Islam and the West—and in line with the way they perceive Westerners. We are considered guilty because of our blind support of Israel. It's as though all of our vaunted espousal of democracy and the rights of individuals, our well publicized stance on "human rights" has washed away in the flood of our unquestioning support for political Israel, right or wrong.

One modern day writer, Barbara Tuchman, has tackled this inexplicable blind spot in our uneven treatment of Jews and Palestinians in her book, *Bible and Sword* (1956). Tuchman, who only traces the history of this issue up to the time of the Balfour Declaration of 1917, maintains that the attachment of the British to the Bible as well as the British drive for empire culminate in their policy to rehabilitate the Jews in their ancient homeland after an absence of two millennia (1956:ix, x). Adroitly, she develops through British history the early fascination with the Bible, and hence, the "Holy Land," their involvement in the Crusades, their fascination with the fulfillment of prophecy concerning the Jews, the historic role they saw themselves playing in bringing that about. She also, demonstrating a great feeling for the British instinct for empire, shows how this converged with the religious-cultural preoccupation with the question of the Holy Land from their Christian perspective, and led to the amazing movement to provide the Jews with a homeland again.

In the end, when the British lost interest with the waning of their empire, it was the Americans, like the British, fascinated with biblical history and prophecy, who took up the cause of a homeland for the Jews. The birth of Israel in 1948 could not have happened without the United States. Jewish-Americans responded as volunteers and spilled Muslim blood in vouchsafing the land to the Jews.

The explosion of outrage in the Muslim world was instantaneous. The Muslims have never forgotten. Every ruler of Saudi Arabia from the late King Faisal to the present has proclaimed *jihad* (holy war) against Israel. That it is not being prosecuted militarily at the present in no way means it has been forgotten. The Muslims, in spite of various peace efforts, are waiting for the most propitious time to commence *jihad* militarily.

In addition to the pro-Israel foreign policy posture of the United States government, a segment of the American church, based on its own understanding of biblical prophecy, has given unqualified monetary support to Israel. Because of this, Christians are perceived as being religiously, politically, and militarily anti-Muslim. In plain words, we are perceived as the ultimate enemy.

Undoubtedly, Islam presents a formidable challenge to Christian missions. All cross-cultural missions involve replacing or radically altering a people's worldview with one based on the Bible. The clash between that of Islam and a biblical worldview, on the surface so similar, is so sharp that every effort must be made to avoid any other complicating clashes on lesser issues such as nationality, patriotism, political opinions or military adventurism. That is unless of course, Muslims commit aggressions that force the rest of the world to become involved.

All of these comments, based on recent events, tend to reinforce the impression in Muslim eyes that America is either an extremely suspect friend or a potentially dangerous enemy, or both. The fact that the majority of Protestant missionaries abroad are from the United States (so far) sends mixed signals to our Muslim friends. Their question is, "Are you in league with the political leadership of your country?" Muslims who have never had a personal missionary friend think our answer would be "Yes." They assume Christians are like them. They have seen very few, if any, models of Christians whose supreme loyalty is to a supranational and even a supernatural kingdom of God.

In the several pages we have just been through, we see what happens when Christians disregard our Lord's teaching about the abuse of power. If His kingdom is not to be characterized by soldiers, political boundaries, military adventurism, conquest and forcible subjugation of others, what is it about?

The kingdom of God is about love. It is about serving. It is about humility. It is about truly caring for others. It is about striving to restrain others from their headlong plunge into destruction and instead bringing them into the everlasting kingdom of God's dear Son. The central person of this kingdom is, of course, Jesus Christ. The King who emptied Himself and took upon Himself the form of a servant, and who, in the end, died for us. His teaching is about the renunciation of power, the denying of one's self, giving one's self in service to others.

Muslims, who in my opinion have erred massively in confusing spiritual power with worldly power—power of the sword, fear, and intimidating tactics—are hypersensitive in detecting the same in others. Perhaps no other religion heightens the stark difference between the world's way and the way of God as does Islam. Therefore, the burden is on the Christian to separate himself from the ways of the world, as seen in the history of military states, crusades, colonialism and modern power politics, and to enter the harvest fields equipped only with spiritual weapons and power. The Christian worker who intends to work with Muslims must have come to a deep understanding of the nature of Christ's kingdom, lest he or she become confused and begin to fall back on the use of worldly power, pride, and prejudice.

And the work will not be easy. Jesus, who came as a lamb, sends us as sheep among wolves.

CHAPTER 19

THE KINGDOM OF GOD AND CULTURE

> Jesus declared, "Believe me ... a time is coming when
> you will worship the Father neither on this mountain
> nor in Jerusalem ... the true worshipers will worship the
> Father in spirit and truth ..." (John 4:21, 23).

I n the preceding chapter, we dealt with the stigma of the West's military
history (perceived as Christianity) against Islam. We acknowledged that
our nationality may be a liability as we seek to communicate the Gospel
to people of other nations, especially if our nation has been guilty of hurting
theirs.

In this chapter, we will attempt to deal with a problem far more
nettlesome, pervasive, and possibly, even more difficult to overcome: "How
does the Gospel of the kingdom relate to culture?" Another way to state
the question is, "Did Jesus give an absolute cultural expression to the
kingdom of God?" This has enormous consequences when the Gospel is
believed and received and raises the question of whose culture will triumph
when conversion occurs. Should the new believer adopt the culture of the
one who led him or her to Christ? Or if the cultural background of the
members of the local church is different from that of the new convert,
should he or she adopt the cultural patterns of the local Christians? Or
may the convert respond to the Gospel within his or her own cultural
context? If so, what principles should shape the form of the church?

If we were to trace this problem back through the preceding
generations, we would discover that the Church no longer looks like the
Church of the first century, or the second, or the third, or the fifteenth.
What happened? Who gave it permission to change? When did it change?
How? Why? Was not there supposed to be a once-for-all-time expression

of Christian culture? Is not Christ's rule to be universal? Did not Jesus set the pattern for us all by His own example?

I remember a nightmare I once had while teaching on Christianity and culture to students in a missions course in Pakistan. In the dream, the leaders of a village of five thousand Muslims came to me and said: "Sir, you have been teaching a few of us about Christ for these past two years. Now we all believe. And we have persuaded everyone in our village to believe the Good News of Jesus Christ. Now we want you to come and baptize us and teach us the Christian culture." At that point I woke up in a cold sweat asking myself, "What is the Christian culture? Is it American Presbyterianism? British Anglicanism? Swedish Pentecostalism? The culture of the Southern Baptists? Plymouth Brethren? The Salvation Army?" Gradually, it dawned on me that there is no such thing as the Christian culture; there is only Christ transforming culture wherever the Gospel takes root.

But perhaps we made a mistake in Christianity by not absolutizing first century Jewish cultural expressions of the Gospel. After all, Jesus did say to His early followers, "follow me." Should we have imitated Jesus in everything? Evidently not, or else the New Testament would be a much thicker book. As pointed out earlier, the apostle John explicitly chose not to include a vast body of material about Jesus in the writing of his Gospel simply because it was not necessary to God's purpose.

Before we look at what Jesus and the apostles taught on the kingdom of God and culture, there are certain things we must keep in mind. That is, we are not questioning the moral or ethical teaching of our Lord. He Himself said He came not to destroy but to fulfill the Law (Matt. 5:17). He came in purity, holiness, righteousness, love, mercy, the very embodiment of truth—the truth about God and about man—and then provided us the way back to God through Himself. These things are devoutly embraced and beyond discussion by this author.

But Jesus' enemies accused Him of changing the traditions of their fathers (Mark 7:5). Similarly, false charges were brought against His disciples: "For we have heard him [Stephen] say that this Jesus of Nazareth will destroy this place and change the customs Moses handed down to us" (Acts 6:14). What was it that was changing? Why were the Jews so upset?

Why are the Muslims so upset about the introduction of the Bible and Christian teaching? What will change? What should change?

Jesus in Samaria

In attempting to answer these questions, let us first turn to Jesus' remarkable experience with the woman at the well in Samaria (John 4:1-42). In many ways, the Samaritans of Jesus' day could be compared with the Muslims of our day. They were rivals to the Jews. They were related but not of the same pure bloodlines; they had part of the Holy Books (The Pentateuch); they had set up a rival center of worship in Samaria (Mt. Gerezim), going up to Jerusalem was no longer compulsory for them; and they had their own priests.

Perhaps by looking at what Jesus taught during His encounter with the Samaritan woman we can derive working principles on how to look at the problem of the Gospel and culture. In this passage, we see that Jesus indicates Jewish ceremonial law will be dispensed within the Messianic Age. Other passages, in the next chapter, will help us to further identify principles to use in communicating the Gospel across cultural boundaries to the Muslims. Before proceeding, the reader is urged to read John 4:1-42.

The Samaritan woman, having had her past laid bare by the Lord, counters with a very provocative and penetrating statement that pierces right to the heart of the question between these two rival religions. She said, "Our fathers worshiped on this mountain, but you Jews claim that the place where we must worship is in Jerusalem" (John 4:20). Basically, she is asking which is the right place and which are the right customs whereby we should worship God. This question continues to be a focal point in cross-cultural missions today.

Jesus' answer is startling, unnerving for a traditionalist, and beautifully liberating for non-Jewish people:

> Believe me, woman, a time is coming when you will worship the Father neither on this mountain nor in Jerusalem. You Samaritans worship what you do not know; we worship what we do know, for salvation is from the Jews. Yet a time is coming and has now come when

the true worshipers will worship the Father in spirit and truth, for they are the kind of worshipers the Father seeks. God is spirit, and his worshipers must worship in spirit and in truth (John 4:21-24).

His reply is so bold, shattering and revealing. The Gospel, the Good News of the kingdom, was going to be set free from its Jewish cultural bondage. With His daring words "nor in Jerusalem," Jesus cut the cultural cords of tradition that bound the kingdom of God to the Jewish ceremonial laws given by Moses. From other passages we know that the Jewish temple was to be destroyed (Matt. 24:2; Mark 13:2). Jesus also prophesied the destruction of Jerusalem (Luke 13:35). If Jesus had not had a larger vision of something much more beautiful to come, it would have been a picture of unrelieved gloom. But He could see far beyond to the glory of end times, and the astonishing things that would happen along the way to make the vision come true.

Jesus went on to say some electrifying things to this Samaritan woman. The force of His positive statements was overwhelming: "You will worship the Father." A new idea in both intent and content. She would personally have the genuine experience of worship, and the object of her worship would be the one living, true God revealed to her as Father. That would grab anyone's attention, especially if you had never thought about God as your Father before. Parenthetically, there is not a word in all of Islam about God being our Father. The shock of using this word, "Father," would be greater for a Muslim than it was for this Samaritan.

In the next breath, Jesus swept away any possibility of legitimacy for the Samaritan religion. He could have as well been speaking to the millions of Muslims today who claim God is high and utterly transcendent, unknowable, completely unlike us. Jesus said unequivocally to the woman: "You Samaritans worship what you do not know; we worship what we do know, for salvation is from the Jews" (John 4:22). Jesus displayed God's singular redemptive plan which came through the line of Abraham, Isaac, Jacob, Judah, David, and ultimately Jesus, the Son of God.

But Jesus wanted this woman to be born-again into the kingdom of God, and to have her spirit cleansed of all that hindered her from worshiping God in spirit and in truth. Ultimately, He wanted her to be filled with God's Spirit and Truth. In the early part of His dialogue with her He had promised her "living water" if she would drink from what He offered. Later in the Gospel of John, Jesus explained that the "living water" was the Holy Spirit who had not yet been given (John 7:38, 39). What wondrous love—He wanted to give her the Holy Spirit! And yet another revelation: God is a "Seeking Father." He has been looking for that Samaritan woman. He sent Jesus to find her!

Hardly had the realization of that sunk in when the next words came with searching fire: "God is spirit, and His worshipers must worship in spirit and in truth" (John 4:24). Worship is not tied to a mountain. Worship is not tied to a people. Worship is a direct experience between God and a person willing to encounter the spirit, power and energy of God's Holy Spirit. Worship is the single-minded and passionate thirst for truth, the honest facing of the truth about one's self, and the powerful, transforming encounter with Him who is the Way, the Truth and the Life, Jesus the Messiah, the Savior of the World.

The ramifications of this discourse have shaken the foundations of institutionalized religion ever since. There will be neither empty, hypocritical ceremonialism nor syncretism in God's worship. God refrained from absolutizing the Jewish cultural expression of worship and, with the same stroke, slammed the door shut on the people of any other culture who would try to do the same, "neither on this mountain nor in Jerusalem" (John 4:21). That temple was to be destroyed. No Jews, Samaritans, or anyone else, would be able to hold the truth in old wineskins any more. "God is spirit, and his worshipers must worship in spirit and in truth" (John 4:24). What does this mean about the cultural forms through which we do the worshipping? We will attempt to answer that shortly.

This is not to say that salvation did not come through the Jews, nor that the concept of the temple and Jerusalem were ever to be forgotten. God confirmed that salvation was rooted in time and space. God's great act of redemption, the crucifixion of Jesus Christ, the Messiah, happened at a certain time in the earthly life of Jesus, and at a certain place—outside the walls of old Jerusalem. Jesus was not going to cut loose the idea of salvation from history. Nor would the ideals espoused in these institutions be forgotten; rather, they would be universalized.

Universalizing the Temple

In His economy, God preserved, amplified, and, yes, universalized the meaning of both the Temple and Jerusalem. It was the apostle Paul, to some extent Peter, and last of all, John, who received special insights into the true meaning of the Temple and the city of Jerusalem in the book of Revelation. In his letter to the Ephesians, Paul, talking of our citizenship, described the Temple as made up of people, not stones:

> You are no longer foreigners and aliens, but fellow citizens with God's people and members of God's household, built on the foundation of the apostles and prophets, with Christ Jesus himself as the chief cornerstone. In him the whole building is joined together and rises to become a holy temple in the Lord. And in him you too are being built together to become a dwelling in which God lives by his Spirit (Eph. 2:19-22).

Peter adds to the imagery in this way: "As you come to him, the Living Stone [Jesus]—rejected by men but chosen by God and precious to him—you also, like living stones, are being built into a spiritual house ..." (1 Peter 2:4, 5).

These two passages together present a beautifully transcendent picture of a spiritualized temple—no longer a cold, inanimate building; now a living temple made up of living, human stones. The image is breathtaking in its size and sweep. It will include believers from every age and from every part of the world—the home for God's living Spirit. God Himself will be in our midst. No wonder Jesus could talk about the old temple being done away with; He knew of a greater Temple—the consummation of God's redemptive masterpiece—an eternal living home in the midst of His recovered children from every time and place. A living temple with God in the midst.

Universalizing Jerusalem

Paul, in writing of the two Jerusalems, the earthly and the heavenly ones, wrote to the Galatians—a people still trying to keep the law symbolized by Jerusalem as it then was: "the present city of Jerusalem ...

is in slavery with her children. But the Jerusalem that is above is free, and she is our mother" (Gal. 4:25, 26).

Paul was not willing to get locked into an earthbound Jerusalem with a fixed set of cultural customs. He saw that the spiritual pattern transcended the earthly one, which God was about to abandon. He also realized that the kingdom of God had to transcend the cultural boundaries of any people for it to be truly universal. It would not be necessary to come to the physical Jerusalem anymore. One could go directly to the seat of the kingdom, the throne of God in heaven, the heavenly Jerusalem, through the merits of Jesus Christ the Intercessor-King.

Universalizing Circumcision

When we look at other crucial issues for the Jewish people, issues they had decided were non-negotiable, we find the same principles operating. Circumcision was spiritualized. To the Church at Philippi, Paul wrote: "For it is we who are the circumcision, we who worship by the Spirit of God, who glory in Christ Jesus, and who put no confidence in the flesh ..." (Phil. 3:3). To the church at Colosse, he wrote:

> In him [Christ] you were also circumcised, in the putting off of the sinful nature, not with a circumcision done by the hands of men but with the circumcision done by Christ, having been buried with him in baptism and raised with him through your faith in the power of God, who raised him from the dead (Col. 2:11, 12).

Circumcision has been lifted out of the physical realm and made universal, therefore applicable to both male and female, but in purely spiritual terms, of course. Its meaning is now contained in and swallowed up by all that is symbolized by baptism.

Universalizing the Concept of Israel

Even the word "Israel" has now been universalized. Paul wrote the following to the church at Ephesus: "Remember that at that time you were separate from Christ, excluded from citizenship in Israel and foreigners to the covenants of the promise ..." (Eph. 2:12), and, "Consequently [because of Christ's work], you are no longer foreigners and aliens, but fellow citizens with God's people and members of God's household" (Eph. 2:19). In his closing benediction to the churches in Galatia, Paul wrote these words: "Peace and mercy to all who follow this rule, even to the Israel of God" (Gal. 6:16).

In a spiritual sense, we are now all "Israelis," in the true (non-political, non-cultural, non-racial) sense of the word. If you remember the time when Jacob wrestled all night with God and would not let go until God blessed him, you will recall that God gave the name "Israel" to Jacob because he had prevailed with God, and was now "a prince with God" (the original meaning of the word "Israel"). To be a true Israelite, then, implies no racial overtones, but rather means that one has joined the household of God through faith in our Lord Jesus Christ.

Universalizing the Kingdom of God

We have already noted that Jesus came to introduce the kingdom of God ("Repent, for the kingdom of heaven is near" (Matt. 4:17).) We learned that Jesus had no intention of making this a political, earthly kingdom, with all the trappings of power, territory, police and a military arm. He spiritualized the concept of the kingdom: "My kingdom is not of this world" (John 18:36). Men and women would no longer have to worship God in Jerusalem; they could worship Him in spirit and truth anywhere. Christianity was to be spiritualized and universalized. People would worship Him everywhere in "spirit and in truth."

Therefore, in the flow of fulfilled prophecy, customs that were initially Jewish, such as circumcision, the understanding of citizenship in the Commonwealth of Israel (now called the kingdom of God), and even the concept of Jerusalem as the seat of power for God's reign, have now been made spiritual and open to all. Jewish exclusivism gave way to an incredible universality. Citizenship in the kingdom of God would be for all who recognized Jesus as the rightful King. His sovereignty was to be over human hearts, lovingly surrendered, rather than a kingdom built upon force or fear.

Jesus used several similes to describe what the kingdom of heaven was like. He said it was like salt (Matt. 5:13), like light (Matt. 5:14), and like yeast (Matt. 13:33). These images conjure up pictures of the salt that both purifies and preserves; light that dispels the darkness and shows the safe pathway through an otherwise hostile world; and yeast that permeates and transforms the whole mass of what it is leavening. Each of them work quietly, without force or fanfare, yet unerringly performing their intended function.

Just to make sure there were no misunderstandings, Jesus strictly forbade the use of force in making any judgments before the Last Day. In the parable of the good seed and the weeds (Matt. 13:24-30, 37-43), the good seed stands for "the sons of the kingdom" and the weeds stand for "the sons of the evil one." Jesus warned His disciples not to try to uproot the weeds. This would imply some use of force. At the end of the age, the angels will do that.

The Kingdom and Culture

The implications of all of this for Christian missions are profound indeed. By spiritualizing the Temple, Jerusalem, citizenship in Israel, circumcision, and yes, even the kingdom of God itself, Jesus truly unlocked each of these realities from its Jewish cultural boundness. By saying that the Father is seeking those who will worship Him in spirit and in truth, with no absolute form of worship, Jesus was saying that the Gospel—the Good News of the kingdom of God with Himself as the key to the kingdom—is free to go everywhere. It can be responded to everywhere by men and women from every tongue, tribe, people and nation (Rev. 5:9) in their own cultural way and as long as that worshipful response is in spirit and in truth.

Christ gave no absolute expression to a universal Christian culture. The Christian is there to communicate the essence of the Good News of Christ's kingdom and to let the new believers respond to that teaching in ways that fit their own cultural context. Therefore, Christians must understand that they are there to bring about a spiritual transformation only—to establish the rule of Christ as King in the new believer's heart. The outworking of that should reflect all of the principles and values that Jesus taught, but it does not mandate how the new believer is to worship, dress, eat, or do the thousand-and-one other things particular to that person's culture.

It is with a great deal of pain that we who have studied the Christian movement and the ways in which the Church has been planted in various lands, in so many different cultural settings, have observed how many, many missionaries could not distinguish between their own culture and the essence of the Gospel. As goodhearted as they were, they unwittingly fell into a kind of syncretism, by wedding their cultural forms absolutely to the Gospel message. In order to be saved, not only did the new converts have to believe the Good News of Jesus Christ, which was necessary, of course, but they had to do everything the way the missionary did or taught. In other words, the missionaries imposed their own cultural practices on the new believers, thus communicating the mistaken idea that this was the only Christian way to do it.

Islam as Cultural Imperialism

This is precisely the error that Muhammad and his followers fell into when they tried to derive a universal law from the material in the Quran and from the behavior of Muhammad himself as recorded in the *Hadith*. Orthodox Muslims, then and now, have tried to absolutize that slice of seventh century Arab culture as exemplified in Muhammad.

Orthodox Islam, in contrast to the freedom of the Gospel, has taken a fixed position on the issue of Islam and culture. Muhammad felt that his words were binding on all mankind. He even modeled the cultural expression of how to carry out one's total life response to the words of the Quran. Not only his utterances in the Quran, but all of his sayings and doings became normative for all Muslims. This was first enshrined in the *Hadith* and later formalized in the *Shariah*. Muhammad's representative cultural lifestyle, that is, his seventh century Arabic cultural model, became binding (in Muslim minds) on all humankind.

What is of vital interest to the Christian worker today is what Muslims have done with the idea of the kingdom of God. The kingdom of God is mentioned a few times in the Quran. Maulana Muhammad Ali, in commenting on the opening chapter of the Quran, said:

> The latter [the Christian] is instructed to pray for the coming of the kingdom of God, whereas the Muslim is instructed to seek for his right place in that kingdom,

which had already come, the hint no doubt being that
the coming of the Prophet [Muhammad] was really the
advent of the kingdom of God about whose approach
Jesus preached to his followers [Mark 1:15]
(Ali:1973:1,2).

This is simply Maulana Muhammad Ali's own idea and is not found
explicitly stated in the Quran. He missed the point that Jesus actually
introduced the kingdom in His own day, that the kingdom is a reality in
the lives of Christian believers right now, and at the return of Jesus Christ
will be fully consummated and visibly manifested.

Even though most Muslims believe the kingdom of God is Islam, it is
also true that the Quran hints at a future realization of the kingdom. In
Surah 22:56 we read: "The kingdom on that day is Allah's. He will judge
between them. So those who believe and do good will be in Gardens of
Bliss." Here the kingdom of God seems to mean the rewards of paradise,
as perceived by Muhammad. A chapter in the Quran is actually called
"the kingdom" (Surah 67). Again M. M. Ali's comment on this chapter is
revealing:

The statement here that the kingdom is in Allah's hand
and that he has power over all things is like a prophetical
statement as to the establishment of the kingdom of
Islam, which was really the kingdom of God. This is made
clear by what Jesus Christ said: "The kingdom of God
shall be taken from you, and given to a nation bringing
forth the fruits thereof" [Matthew 21:43]
(Ali:1973:1080).

Ali completely missed the point that Jesus was talking to the Jews and
was saying to them that the kingdom would be taken from them and
given to the Gentiles, that is, those Gentiles who would become followers
of Christ.

Some Muslim leaders have expressed their ideas on what the kingdom
of God means in the Quran. For example, when the late Maulana Abul
Ala Maududi was asked for his definition, he said: "The kingdom of God

is Islam on earth as it is in heaven." In June of 1985, when this writer asked the Director of the Islamic Institute at the University of the Philippines what he thought the kingdom of God was, he replied: "No one has ever asked me that question before. I suppose it means the imposition of Islamic Law on the whole world."

The Kingdom and the Christian Worker

For Muslims who have accepted one of the above Islamic definitions of the kingdom of God, it will be necessary for the Christian worker to patiently show how the kingdom was introduced by our Lord Jesus and explain its spiritual nature—working as yeast in the midst of all human cultures and how it will be fully consummated at Jesus' final return.

In reality, most Muslims do not have an idea of what the kingdom of God is all about. For them, the teaching of a spiritual kingdom pervading and transforming cultures wherever it goes will be seen either as a breath of fresh air or a dangerous threat.

Therefore, it is important for the Christian worker to not only understand what is meant by the "kingdom of God," and the "Good News of the kingdom," but that he or she be able to teach it clearly, without locking it into any given culture. The hallmark of the kingdom of God is not that it be recognized by any particular cultural forms, but that the citizens of the kingdom be those who worship the Father in spirit and in truth.

In living among Muslims, Christians need to be aware of four factors. First, God gave us the capacity to manage the world—invent the systems to be good stewards of creation as we live with one another. This inevitably led to what we call the development of culture. We need to understand that all cultures have been developed by humans in response to the cultural mandate of Genesis 1:26-28.

Second, from the moment of the fall of man and woman in the Garden of Eden, culture will necessarily reflect that fallen state.

Third, from the time of God's judgment on humankind at the Tower of Babel (Gen. 11:1-10) when God caused the birth of new languages and cultures, cross-cultural communication problems were going to be inevitable.

And fourth, God, who has commissioned us to disciple all ethnolinguistic groups in this world, obviously has designed the message of salvation in such a way that it can be considered "supracultural" truth, that is, it is capable of being transmitted to hearers in every human culture.

So far, we have not delved into any detailed discussions of how the "Good News of the kingdom" relates to anyone's particular culture. Let us turn now to some of these issues.

CHAPTER 20

A SERVANT TO MUSLIMS

*Though I am free and belong to no man, I make myself
a slave to everyone... (1 Cor. 9:19).*

In the previous chapter, we noted how the Gospel was set free from its Jewish cultural bondage. The major themes of the kingdom of God, the temple, Jerusalem, circumcision, citizenship in the commonwealth of Israel, all were spiritualized. The work of God was to be primarily characterized by "Spirit and Truth," rather than a specific set of cultural ways of observing "laws." It was our Lord Jesus, of course, who laid the groundwork for this radical innovation. He set the Gospel free to go out among peoples of all cultural backgrounds without forcing Jewish cultural forms on them.

Jesus Empties Himself

I am sure that Jesus was the model for the apostle Paul in all he was able to think through and act upon in his own amazing career. Let's look at one of Paul's key passages on Jesus. On the surface, it looks like Paul was writing to a couple of quarrelsome ladies in the church at Philippi. In doing so, he was exhorting them to humility, and to illustrate his point, he cited the so-called "kenosis" or "emptying" passage:

> Your attitude should be the same as that of Christ Jesus:
> Who, being in very nature God, did not consider equality
> with God something to be grasped, but made himself
> nothing [emptied himself], taking the very nature of a
> servant, being made in human likeness. And being found
> in appearance as a man, he humbled himself and became
> obedient to death—even death on a cross! (Phil 2:5-8).

Yes, this is about humility. The implications of this kind of humility are quite searching. Jesus let go of all of His Godly prerogatives and emptied Himself—"made Himself nothing." Jesus could have held onto His heavenly culture, whatever it was, but He didn't. He emptied Himself and took upon Himself the cultural forms of a Palestinian, Aramaic-speaking, Galilean Jew. He entered completely into the culture of the people to whom He was sent. He did not hold onto any of His heavenly privileges. He entered into His people's world with true humility.

Jesus' quality of humility is rare among us today. Usually, we are deeply patriotic, can be stirred up to fight for our country, and in general consider ourselves better than people of other ethnolinguistic backgrounds. There is a word for this expression of pride—ethnocentrism. It is pride of race and culture. Everyone has it. It is one of the greatest hindrances to the progress of the Gospel. In the Christian worker it becomes a barrier in trying to communicate the Gospel to a people of another culture. This is especially true if there is any sense of antagonism or rivalry between the two cultures.

Jesus was so different. Over and over again, He reached out to people of other cultures: the Roman centurion, the Samaritan leper, the Syro-Phoenician woman, the Gaderene demoniac and the Greek inquirers. When He cleansed the temple of the mercenary money-changers, it was the "Court of the Gentiles" that He cleared and re-opened for all Gentiles.

It wasn't that He ignored His own people, for He showed compassion on Jewish lepers, Jewish demon-possessed people, Jewish sick, and Jewish prostitutes. His love was universal. And therefore, it included what ethnocentric people might call "the religio-cultural lepers and sinners of the world"—the non-Jewish peoples.

Not only did Jesus free Himself from the well-developed prejudices of His own people, but He even refused to let His family ties warp His sense of mission and the true understanding of what it meant to be a son or daughter of God. The crowd urged Him to interrupt what He was doing and go meet His mother and brothers trying to get through the crowd to Him. He turned and asked: "'Who is my mother, and who are my brothers?' Pointing to His disciples, he said, 'Here are my mother and my brothers. For whoever does the will of my Father in heaven is my brother and sister and mother'" (Matt. 12:48-50). The only mark of belonging to the family of God was doing the will of the Father in heaven.

Paul's Understanding of Universal Love

Paul thoroughly understood the heart of the Lord to reach out to all people. He wrote: "God our Savior ... wants all men to be saved and to come to a knowledge of the truth" (1 Tim. 2:3, 4).

We must remember that Jesus emptied Himself to make this a reality. He demonstrated self-denial all the way to the cross. More than simply refraining from creature-comforts, that self-denial was also a positive expression of love—entering into the world, the culture (without becoming its prisoner) of the people to whom He was giving Himself. But wherever Jesus found that the traditions of men were nullifying the intent of God's word, He challenged it: "Thus you nullify the word of God for the sake of your tradition" (Matt. 15:6). So, we must find the balance.

It was left to Paul, that great pioneer of missions, to work out these principles. In due time, and almost accidentally, he gave us his "guidelines of missionary methodology" in the middle of his first letter to the Corinthians. This following paragraph is a powerful summation of these principles:

> Though I am free and belong to no man, I make myself a slave to everyone, to win as many as possible. To the Jews I became like a Jew, to win the Jews. To those under the law I became like one under the law (though I myself am not under the law), so as to win those under the law. To those not having the law I became like one not having the law (though I am not free from God's law but am under Christ's law), so as to win those not having the law. To the weak I became weak, to win the weak. I have become all things to all men so that by all possible means I might save some. I do all this for the sake of the gospel, that I may share in its blessings (1 Cor. 9:19-23).

Let's take time to glean from this passage as many insights as possible. First of all, a look at the key idea in this text: "Though I am free and belong to no man, I make myself a slave to everyone." This is a very interesting parallel to the Philippians passage quoted earlier about Jesus "taking the very nature of a servant." Voluntarily, both Christ and Paul gave up many privileges in order to communicate the Gospel to others. Christ gave up His regal position at the right hand of the Father in Heaven; Paul gave up his status as an up-and-coming leader among the Pharisees. Jesus Himself said, "For even the Son of Man did not come to be served, but to serve, and to give his life as a ransom for many" (Mark 10:45). Paul, in turn, felt there was no alternative but to make himself a servant to the very people he was trying to win. As we enter into Muslim work, like our Lord and like Paul, our first missionary model, we must learn to empty ourselves and become servants to the Muslims we are trying to win.

Paul also wrote of winning "as many as possible." What does this do to a person when it becomes a stated goal? First of all, it generates an undying zeal for getting the task done. It also forces you to experiment, to find out what works to win "as many as possible." You will become an innovator. Instead of holding on to your old cultural ways of doing everything, you will want to enter into the world of your new friends, and discover how to relate the Good News of Jesus Christ and His kingdom to them more effectively.

Paul wrote: "To the Jews I became like a Jew, to win the Jews. To those under the law I became like one under the law (though I myself am not under the law), so as to win those under the law" (1 Cor. 9:20). In Paul's life there are two outstanding examples of this. Whenever he entered a new area, he went to the Jews first. He started at the synagogues. He fit in with the traditions of worship, waiting for his turn to speak. He chose the most appropriate way to express himself in that setting. For example, although his disciple Timothy had a Jewish mother and grandmother, he had never been circumcised. Paul had him circumcised to satisfy those Jews who were making an issue of it (Acts 16:3). The second incident happened toward the end of Paul's life. Anticipating trouble on his last trip to Jerusalem, and to convince the Asian Jews that he was observing the Law, he undertook the vow of a Nazarite: had his head shaved, and gave the money for the burnt offering (Acts 21:24-26). And this was approximately thirty years after Jesus had died on the cross once and for all for the sins of the whole world!

"To those not having the law," Paul wrote, "I became like one not having the law (though I am not free from God's law but am under Christ's law), so as to win those not having the law" (1 Cor. 9:21). Paul was able to radically alter his lifestyle with Gentiles who had no intention of coming under Jewish ceremonial law. And he defended this position when he saw others trying to impose Jewish ceremonial laws on Gentile believers.

Again, there are two illustrations of this. When the apostle Peter visited the Gentile church in Antioch, he adjusted to their cultural lifestyle, that is, until a delegation arrived from Jerusalem. Before the law keeping Messianic Jews arrived, Peter had learned to eat freely with the Gentiles and did not insist on any Jewish customs, particularly, circumcision. When men from James' party arrived, they insisted that all believers be circumcised. Peter wavered, then joined them—insisting that Gentile believers had to keep the law, especially circumcision. Paul nailed this as hypocrisy and confronted Peter with the question, "You live like a Gentile and not like a Jew. How is it, then, that you force Gentiles to follow Jewish customs?" (Gal. 2:11-14).

This controversy ultimately led to the Jerusalem Council as described in Acts 15:1-29. After a thorough airing of all positions and listening to the testimonies of what God had been doing, a remarkable resolution of the problem occurred. James was the one who summarized the decision: "It is my judgment, therefore, that we should not make it difficult for the Gentiles who are turning to God" (Acts. 15:19). Later in the formal letter to the Gentile believers, the official decision was expressed this way:

> It seemed good to the Holy Spirit and to us not to burden you with anything beyond the following requirements: Your are to abstain from food sacrificed to idols, from blood, from the meat of strangled animals and from sexual immorality (Acts 15:28, 29).

That's it. No ceremonial laws were to be applied to the Gentiles. The only two major concerns were the purity of their moral life and the purity of their allegiance to God. No immorality. No compromise with idolatrous sacrifices.

And as if to put a seal on the whole business, Paul adamantly refused to allow Titus, who was a Gentile, to be circumcised when he took him to

Jerusalem (Gal. 2:3). In fact, in referring to the people who came to spy out their freedom while in Galatia, Paul took a very firm stance: "We did not give in to them for a moment, so that the truth of the gospel might remain with you" (Gal. 2:5).

Paul wrote: "To the weak I became weak, to win the weak ..." (1 Cor. 9:22). In this passage, "weak" meant those whose conscience bothered them about eating meat that had been first offered to idols. In his letter to the Christians in Rome, Paul put it this way: "Let us therefore make every effort to do what leads to peace ... It is better not to eat meat or drink wine or to do anything else that will cause your brother to fall" (Rom. 14:19, 21). To the Corinthians, he proclaimed: "Therefore, if what I eat causes my brother to fall into sin, I will never eat meat again, so that I will not cause him to fall" (1 Cor. 8:13). In working with Muslims, this is a very important lesson. Muslims have well known taboos against eating pork and drinking alcoholic beverages. Even though we know we have freedom in these areas, it is a freedom we should not exercise. Our goal is not to flaunt our freedom but to win as many as possible.

Finally, we come to the logical conclusion of this missionary spirit: "I have become all things to all men so that by all possible means I might save some. I do all this for the sake of the gospel, that I might share in its blessings" (1 Cor. 9:22, 23). At first reading this may seem utterly outlandish—a totally compromised position—but after careful thinking, it clearly becomes the only possible attitude for the Christian worker. If there are no absolute cultural forms to the practice of Christianity, then "all possible means" are to be tried in an effort to win others to Christ. This calls for extraordinary flexibility tempered with deep discernment over what would be syncretistic and what would best fit the cultural context.

Applying Paul's Principles to Muslim Work

What does all of this mean with regard to Muslim work? This is what we are going to explore as we look at the many varieties of Islam. Because many of us come from backgrounds that are so different from that of our Muslim friends, and because of the longstanding Muslim animosity to Christian missionary activity, this is not going to be easy. Remember Jesus' challenge to His original disciples: "If anyone would come after me, he must deny himself and take up his cross daily and follow me. For whoever wants to save his life will lose it, but whoever loses his life for Me will save it" (Luke 9:23, 24).

As long as one stays within his or her cultural context, the nature of this self-denial is confined to the area of one's carnal nature and those ideas and practices that are evil. But when one desires to communicate the Gospel across cultural barriers to Muslim peoples, a new factor enters the picture. The way we communicate the Gospel to one another in our own culture may actually hinder effective communication of the Gospel to Muslims of another culture.

This was brought home to me in a very painful way while trying to work with Muslims in Pakistan. The church there was made up largely, but not altogether, of the children and grandchildren of Hindu Untouchables whose forebears had come to Christ in huge numbers (about 500,000) between the years 1890 and 1930. Under British rule the problem did not seem so acute. After the departure of the British and the partition of India in 1947, however, millions of Muslims migrated into the east and west wings of Pakistan, and almost an equal number of Sikhs and Hindus migrated into a Hindu-dominated India. The Christians, not knowing what to do, stayed. The result was that a tiny minority Christian community (1.4%) was enveloped by a 97% Muslim population in what is Pakistan today.

And to these newly arrived Muslims, who had survived the holocaust of the partition of British India, these Christians had many traces of both Western ties to churches abroad and unmistakable roots in the lowest caste of Hinduism. In spite of all the great things missionaries had done in developing these people through education, they were still nicknamed "sweepers," and they had easily recognizable traits of Hindu culture about them—language, music, dress styles, eating habits, a different concept of male and female roles, and a host of minor telltale indications of where they had come from. For all of the above reasons, Christians were not made to feel welcome or wanted under the new Muslim regime.

Tragically, many Christians reciprocated those feelings. They displayed a hostile attitude toward their Muslim rulers. This turn of events had a profound effect on how the Pakistani churches treated anyone who came from a Muslim background and prompted Reverend Aslam Khan (a convert from Islam himself) and I to undertake a survey of converts from

Islam. We counted a total of about 700 in our area. Of them, 350 could no longer be located. Of the 350 we could find, 315 no longer went to church because they did not feel welcome. Of the 35 who still went to church, not one of them was willing, at the time of our interviews, to say that he or she had felt emotionally accepted by the existing church—including two men who had risen to be college presidents. That was devastating.

We found that the church, originally of a Hindu background, had simply made no effort to accommodate people who came from a Muslim background. In fact, more often than not, a Muslim inquirer who appeared at church was held suspect. The Christians assumed he (almost always a male) was out to get one of their women or was looking for employment, or worse, was a spy for the government. In one case, I watched a young man try for two years to be baptized and received into the membership of our local church. It was to no avail. Finally, after witnessing a shoot-out between a heretical group of Muslims and fundamentalist Muslims, he came to me and said:

> Uncle, today I watched Ahmadi Muslims [heretical Muslims] die for their faith. It made me ask myself if I am willing to die for faith in Christ. I am but I have never been baptized. Jesus has commanded baptism; I am willing, but the local church leaders will not receive me. Would you arrange for me to be baptized? Then I will be able to say to the Lord that I have done what He asked me to do.

> With a heavy heart, I arranged for him to be baptized by a Muslim convert evangelist in another city. Even after that he was not received into the fellowship of the church. What could be done in a situation like that?

A burst of insight came to me while sitting in church one Sunday. The pastor was late. The all-male choir began to sing spontaneously while we waited. I joined in. Slowly, it dawned on me that we were singing songs filled with Hindu vocabulary. I froze. In fact, I could not sing anymore. I began to seethe with anger. Under my breath, I remember saying to myself, "You stupid grandsons of Hindu converts. What would a Muslim think if he came in here right now and heard you singing in the language of the enemy?" (Hindu India and Muslim Pakistan have fought three major wars in the last forty years.) And then the Lord rebuked me. He asked: "Don, what do you do when you feel spiritually dry?" I thought of how I sought out fellow missionaries, poured out my heart, sang together from a common stock of hymns and choruses, and prayed in my mother tongue. He said: "That's what these young men are doing. This is their cultural heritage. Join them, but I am going to do a new work among the Muslims."

"A new work among the Muslims!" What does that mean? What will it look like? How will it relate to existing work? Is this divisive? Will this split the church? Is this really from God?

These are very important considerations. Paul wrote: "Make every effort to keep the unity of the Spirit through the bond of peace. There is one body and one Spirit ..." (Eph. 4:3, 4). Can you have unity of Spirit without a worldwide uniformity of style? Or the other way around: Would insisting on uniformity hinder the spread of the Gospel?

What happens when you want to win as many Muslims to the Lord as possible? Will you be willing to try new things? If Paul was able to say: "To the Jews I became a Jew to win the Jews," should we be able to say, "To the Punjabi Muslims I became as a Punjabi Muslim (culturally, but not theologically) that I might win them?" There are some ways in which I think the answer to that question is a qualified "Yes." But it will require tremendous care to avoid syncretism (that is, tolerating Muslim forms that retain Islamic meanings) on the one hand, and a strenuous effort to keep the unity of the Spirit with the existing Christians of non-Muslim background, on the other. This will be no small task. Until recently, few have been willing to try. In the last section of this book, I will discuss the experiments that are underway and suggest what we might do.

CHAPTER 21

THE USE OF SPIRITUAL POWER

> The weapons we fight with are not the weapons of the
> world. On the contrary, they have divine power to
> demolish strongholds. We demolish arguments and every
> pretension that sets itself up against the knowledge of
> God, and we take captive every thought to make it
> obedient to Christ (2 Cor. 10:4, 5).

Having discussed cultural principles involved in communicating the Gospel to Muslims, it is now time to explore the spiritual dimensions of this missionary challenge. In one sense, our problem is not Muslims. They are the candidates for God's love. They are the prisoners of systems and the powers behind them. Jesus came "to proclaim freedom for the captives and release ... for the prisoners ... " (Isa. 61:1). We are in a spiritual war for the souls of Muslim men and women everywhere. Islam itself is our challenge. It is a cluster of ideologies and worldviews that have bound Muslims in a dark, spiritual bondage and denied them the glorious liberty they could have through new birth in Jesus Christ and life in the Spirit.

The Anti-Christian Spirit of Islam

At the outset of this chapter I need to state that I believe there is a deep spiritual aspect to our Christian encounter with Islam. Although only a small percentage of Muslims may be Orthodox, the anti-Christian ideas in Islam have become so pervasive that they predispose Muslims everywhere to resist the preaching of the Gospel. Furthermore, I believe that there is a spiritual intelligence and power behind this resistance. Satan's great desire is to thwart God in reaching and recovering lost human beings through the Gospel of Jesus Christ. In earlier pages we discussed how

Muhammad taught that God could not have a Son, how God could not become a man, that no one could die for anyone else, that Jesus was not crucified, and that if one's good deeds (one's obedience to Islamic laws) outweighed one's bad deeds, that person would go to a sensuous "paradise," otherwise to a frightening hell. We saw how Muhammad, his companions and their successors built a system called Islam which is guarded by rules and which uses the lure of sensuous rewards and threats of a gruesome hell to bind Muslims to itself. No one may leave that system without the threat of death (Q. 4:91). The worldwide notoriety given to author Salman Rushdie, who had the death sentence pronounced against him by the late Ayatollah Khomeini of Iran, is a case in point (*Los Angeles Times*, February 14, 1989).

I also believe that in non-Orthodox forms of Islam, spiritual "powers" are at work, whether they be in Sufism, Folk Islam, or any other sect. For behind each one of the varieties of Islam is the spirit attempting to prevent Muslims from ever learning who Christ really is or why they need Him.

Islam is virulently anti-Christian at its core. It is a stronghold of error which uses arguments directly contradicting everything God has achieved through Christ for the salvation of all humankind, including Muslims. This is not to deny that there is reflected truth in the Quran, for Muhammad, in using the sources he did, received secondhand some of the biblical concepts about God, though not all. But it is to say that Muhammad built a system wholly opposed to God as Father, Son and Spirit; that Islam is opposed to the spread of the Good News of salvation through the preaching of Jesus Christ as the Son of God, crucified, dead, and risen. In its attack on the great work of Christ, the Son of God, Islam is a "pretension that sets itself up against the very knowledge of God" (2 Cor. 10:5), and as such, Christ, with His spiritual power working through the truth we proclaim, will ultimately demolish it. Since Islam is not built on the foundation of Jesus Christ, it will be burned up in the testing fires of God (1 Cor. 3:11-14).

Because of its unusual hostility to the Gospel of Jesus Christ, we have to conclude that behind the system of Islam is a supernatural anti-Christian power. In Scripture we read: "For our struggle is not against flesh and blood, but against the rulers, against the authorities, against the powers of this dark world and against the spiritual forces of evil in the heavenly realms" (Eph. 6:12). We believe that these powers are behind the system of doctrine that so powerfully works against the Gospel. Note the following points of attack on the Christian faith and movement:

- The Quran denies the crucifixion, the central event of Christ's life (Q. 4:157).

- Muhammad, failing to win Christians, cursed them (Q. 9:30).

- Muhammad reduced Jesus to being merely a prophet and then proclaimed himself the "Seal of the Prophets" (Q. 33:40).

- Islam, in the century after Muhammad, vehemently attacked the Word of God and falsely charged that it had been altered at every point where it disagreed with the Quran (Abdiyah Akbar Abdul-Haqq 1980:38).

- Islam is committed to world conquest by every means, including force (*jihad*) (Q. 8:38-39).

- All Christians, according to Islam, are destined to be ruled by Muslims and to pay the humiliating poll tax (*jizya*) (Q. 9:29).

- Any Muslim who becomes a Christian is to be killed (Q. 4:89).

- Saudi Arabia, the heartland of Islam, will neither allow churches to be built, nor congregations to freely meet.

- Church buildings cannot be repaired in Egypt without government permission, which is seldom, if ever, given.

- In Muslim countries where *Shariah* Law has been imposed, Christians are not allowed to preach the Gospel to Muslims.

The Shift to a Biblical Worldview

The phenomena of Folk Islam in the lives of millions of Punjabis among whom I lived for eighteen years in Pakistan caused me to search for biblical explanations. Day after day, we witnessed hundreds, sometimes thousands, going to shrines, holy men, for healing, guidance, protection from evil, power against enemies, deliverance from demonic oppression, knowledge about the future, fertility, blessings on flocks and fields, prayers for rain, in short, help for facing all of the problems of everyday living. The element of the supernatural pervaded their whole way of dealing with their problems. This led to a re-evaluation of secularly-influenced assumptions, namely, that propositional statements of truth are all that matter—that the supernatural phenomena we observed in Folk Islam were just harmless, superstitious ideas.

For a person not accustomed to this kind of thinking, especially those who have embraced a secular worldview from any part of the world, it is a shock to learn that there really are spirit beings who can do what the Punjabis and many others in that part of the world believe. Lest my Western or secularized reader think that I have "flipped out" over these phenomena, let's remember that our secular, Westernized worldview is not a biblical one; Western or secular man has developed a worldview other than the biblical worldview. I take the position that the Western/secular worldview is in error and that the biblical explanation concerning Satan, the Devil, demons, evil spirits, evil spiritual powers and authorities is a true representation of reality. To argue with this is to take issue with the entire picture of redemptive history from start to finish. For the skeptical reader, consider the following review of Scriptures.

Satan is mentioned in the Bible, starting with the fall of man in the Garden of Eden (Gen. 3) to his final disposal at the end of the age (Rev. 20). His presence is implicit throughout the entire span of human history. He waged war in heaven. Many angels joined him in the great rebellion. The forces of God, headed up by Michael, a superior spiritual being, prevailed, and Satan and his angels were cast down to the earth (Rev. 12). He was already in the Garden of Eden at the time of Adam and Eve (Gen. 3).

Job, who predates both Abraham and Moses (Kelso 1968:147), was chosen by God to go against Satan in one of the greatest spiritual duels of all time (Job 1,2). By the time that God gave the Law to Moses (1440-1400 B.C.), people were already sacrificing their own children to demons (Deut. 32:17). Godless people were still doing this in the days of the psalmist (Ps. 106:37). Satan was on the scene in David's day (around 1000 B.C.) and seduced Israel by inciting David to take a census, thereby tempting him to rely on the strength of his army rather than God (1 Chron. 21:1).

Isaiah (740-700 B.C.), after pronouncing judgment on the king of Babylon, taunts the "power" behind the throne (Lucifer, Son of the Dawn) (Isa. 14:15). Ezekiel (593-571 B.C.), after pronouncing judgment on the king of Tyre, then turns, in much the same way as Isaiah did, to make a prophecy against the "power" behind the king of Tyre. Ezekiel details Satan's degeneration from being the "model of perfection" to being reduced to ashes and someone whose very looks are appalling, who will "come to a horrible end and will be no more" (Ezek. 28:12-19). In the book of Zechariah (around 520 B.C.), Satan is pictured as standing at the right hand of Joshua, the High Priest, to accuse him (Zech. 3:1).

Satan's activity and power are described in general terms in the two following passages: "The whole world is under the control of the evil one" (1 John 5:19), and, "The great dragon was hurled down—that ancient serpent called the devil, or Satan, who leads the whole world astray" (Rev. 12:9). When Jesus officially began His earthly ministry, immediately following His baptism, He was driven by the Spirit into the wilderness to be tempted by Satan (Matt. 4:1-11). Jesus' enemies, in trying to explain His extraordinary power over demons, accused Him of being in league with the Devil. Jesus' reply to this charge is significant:

> But if I drive out demons by the Spirit of God, then the kingdom of God has come upon you. Or again, how can anyone enter a strong man's house and carry off his possessions unless he first ties up the strong man? Then he can rob his house (Matt. 12:28, 29).

Implied in this answer is that Jesus had bound Satan and was looting his house, that is, liberating the prisoners, those oppressed by demons, and was setting them free. What is so noteworthy here is that Jesus demonstrated the presence of His kingdom by His deliverance ministry. His worldview is that everyone is either a citizen of the kingdom of darkness (of Satan) or the kingdom of God. This is unlike secular thought which maintains that all things have a rational, scientific explanation, and that no supernatural or evil person exists. Unfortunately, this idea has come into churches all over the world, with the result that many Christians don't even know who or what their enemy is.

Before leaving this subject, we should take a closer look at just what power the enemy has and what he can do. The Devil can sow tares among the wheat (heresy in the midst of truth) (Matt. 13:39). He can snatch the Word of God from hearts that are not receptive (Luke 8:12). He put the idea of betraying Jesus in Judas' heart; he ultimately entered into Judas (John 13:27). Remember that in David's day, he rose up against Israel and incited a believing king to trust in the flesh instead of God by taking a census. He raised up raiding parties to steal Job's flocks and kill his servants. He caused a mighty wind to blow and destroy the house where Job's children were feasting, killing all of them. He even had the power, by God's permission, to afflict Job with boils.

In the New Testament period, we learn that demons could cause muteness (Matt. 9:33), seizures (Matt. 17:15), give people superhuman strength, cause a man to cut himself (Mark 5:2-5), and give a young girl the ability to foretell the future (fortune-telling) (Acts 16:16). Demons could also deceive through false teaching (1 Tim. 4:1). They could haunt places (Rev. 18:2). They could be the key power and presence in pagan religious sacrifices and feasts (1 Cor. 10:20, 21). Demons have the ability to cause miraculous signs to deceive people (Rev. 16:14).

The reason for reviewing so much Scripture on this point is to counterbalance the secular worldview of the West, which denies the very existence of Satan and hierarchies of demons. Most Westerners, due to this powerful molding influence on their respective cultures, know practically nothing about spiritual warfare against these kinds of powers. Secularized Christians have to be brought back to a biblical viewpoint. One of the great ironies of the Western missionary movement is that it has been blinded by its compromise with secularism as to the reality of demonic, even Satanic powers working through the religious systems of the people they go to win. As often as not, the local people know more about the reality of such evil influence than the missionaries.

Charles Kraft's testimony as to what changed in his life and ministry is most informative. (Please note: As I quote from men like Kraft and others, it does not mean I fully endorse the directions their ministries have taken. Nor in the case of healing, do I advocate that all will be healed. But I do believe we have much to learn in moving from secular skepticism to a healthy belief in the Word of God, and that is why I quote from their testimonies.) This is Kraft's confession of how he was ineffective while in the throes of his secularized Christianity.

> As Evangelicals, however, we were totally unprepared to deal with the one area the Nigerians considered most important—their relationships with the spirit world. Time after time Nigerians would turn our discussions to the disruption in their lives they claimed were caused by evil spirits. Such things as disease, accidents, death, the infertility of humans, animals, and fields, drought, and the disruption of relationships were all seen as the work of these evil entities (1989:3, 4).

Kraft pointed out the futility of attempting to meet Nigerian needs with the fruit of Western science:

> Though we talked a great deal about spiritual things, the Nigerians understood most aspects of spirituality much better than we did. I'm afraid we were doing what Paul accuses the Galatians of doing: starting in the spirit but then turning to human power [Galatians 3:3]. In the name of Christ, as if this was the best he could offer, we had simply produced western secularized approaches to illness, accident, education, fertility, agriculture, and every other problem of life. We acted as though western scientific methods were more effective than prayer (1989:4, 5).

Later, as Kraft became a part of the awakening among evangelicals to the spiritual realities of our world and discovered that they match the situation described in Jesus' day, he wrote of the amazing paradigm shift in his worldview:

> What I was experiencing was a classic "paradigm shift," a major change in perspective. I had opened myself up to the possibility of change by exposing myself to new experiences. I was turning *from skepticism to belief* ... All of a sudden I was choosing to believe and behave quite differently... I began to teach on healing in my own Sunday School class ... as time went on, I developed the boldness to ask God to provide opportunities to demonstrate what I was talking about right in front of the class. On a couple of occasions, the results were dramatic (1989:53, 62).

Kraft found that this paradigm shift turned his devotional life upside down:

> I find myself reading the Bible (especially the Gospels) with new eyes—knowing that miracles and deliverances and revelations from God and angels and demons and all those things I used to read about only as inspired history are for us today! I find a new desire to pray, to talk to God and to listen to him ... There is a new power and authority in ministry ... (1987:133, 134).

This was the end result of his newfound worldview: "It wasn't long before I was ... experiencing Christianity with power for the first time in my life" (1989:8).

What was the nature of that paradigm shift? What do we need to learn from it? Basically, it was the discovery of how to use the power and authority that Christ has given His disciples from the beginning. In commissioning His disciples to go on their first evangelistic tours, Scripture says: "He called his twelve disciples to him and gave them authority to drive out evil spirits and to heal every disease and sickness" (Matt. 10:1). And, "he gave them power and authority to drive out all demons and to cure diseases, and he sent them out to preach the kingdom of God and to heal the sick" (Luke 9:1, 2).

I have felt it was necessary to go into this background material because so many of the potential readers of this book are probably like me. That is, they came to Christ through evangelical churches that taught power encounters like these don't happen anymore, that those experiences were only for the apostolic period. I myself have had to undergo a radical shift from anti-supernatural secularistic ideas which had negated large portions of biblical teaching and rendered me ineffective in dealing with the deep spiritual dimensions of the warfare we are engaged in across the world of Islam. I had to learn to believe God for the power to discern the presence of evil spirits, to heal the sick when it was God-led, and to pray for those oppressed by demons to be delivered.

The truth is that God works the same way today as He did millennia ago. Jesus and the Spirit are the same yesterday, today and forever. The gifts and power of God's Spirit are as available today as they were in Jesus' day and were not confined to the apostolic period—they are available for all who believe and appropriate them. This issue becomes especially pointed when we struggle with Folk Islamic practices right where the people live. No demonstration of God's power on our part over the power of the enemy means no lasting fruit. Maybe there will be surface "conversions," but in the absence of knowing how to deal with the demonic power that may have affected the would-be believer (even having been taught by the missionary that they don't exist), the potential convert may never learn how to escape the grip of the evil powers that held him. The missionary, then, is completely mystified as to why his "converts" cannot stand.

In discussing spiritual warfare let us remember that the underlying struggle for the loyalty of the human race is ultimately between Christ and Satan, between the kingdom of God's dear Son and the kingdom of darkness. The Muslims are not our enemy; the mastermind who inspired the system that enslaved them is. Therefore, we go forth in Jesus' name, proclaiming the truth of the Gospel, healing and delivering from demonic oppression. These acts of love manifest the presence and power of the King over the power of the enemy in this world as well as in eternity.

Perhaps no one has spelled out the implications of this truth more eloquently and comprehensively than Don Williams:

The shattering, life-changing news of the Bible is that the King who rules this kingdom both sustains our world from heaven and decisively and irrevocably invades it in the incarnation of His Son who bears His dynamic Spirit. What this means for us is that our lives can and must be changed now. While we may routinely pray, "Thy kingdom come, Thy will be done on earth as it is in heaven," God is actually answering this prayer throughout our world as He manifests His kingdom reign. Thus, He is releasing His Holy Spirit in power, opening hearts to His lively presence, healing wounds past and present, breaking compulsive, addictive behavior, and elevating the poor into His presence by expelling our present darkness and recreating our fallen humanity. We have the unique opportunity to experience this kingdom by faith and to see it personally intersect our lives before we are catapulted into eternity where both faith and unbelief will become sight, either to our joy or to our horror (1989:2).

Williams, whose eyes were opened to the reality of God's miraculous work in the present, later went into great detail pointing out the powerful impact secular, anti-supernatural philosophical views had on molding his quasi-Christian worldview.

Is the Collapse of Islam Possible?: ## An Analogy from the Fall of Communism

Atheistic Communism set out to obliterate the Christian faith and failed. Jesus, in speaking of Himself, said: "Then what is the meaning of that which is written: 'The stone the builders rejected has become the capstone'? Everyone who falls on that stone will be broken to pieces, but he on whom it falls will be crushed" (Luke 20:17-18). One interpretation of this means that whoever falls in worship before Jesus will have his sinful pride broken, but whoever refuses Jesus will be crushed beyond recovery. Today, we are seeing this happen in the former Soviet Union. A nation that vowed it would exalt atheism and crush the Church is now being crushed itself. Many feel that it was the Church in the Soviet Bloc (even Eastern Europe) which brought Communism down.

Before we continue, let me state that I believe in the genuineness and reliability of the Bible, as it is today. I believe the following pillars of Christian faith: that the very heart of God's great redemptive act in offering salvation to mankind is wrapped up in His becoming a man (John 1:14), that Jesus is the express representation of God on earth (Heb. 1:3), that Christ died on the cross for us and we are justified by His blood and saved from the wrath to come through Him (Rom. 5:8, 9), that He was buried and rose again the third day according to the Scriptures (1 Cor. 15:4), that there is salvation in no other name (Acts 4:12), that to reject Him is to reject God Himself (1 John 2:23), and finally that whoever denies the Son, as the Scripture states so clearly, is an antichrist (1 John 2:22).

For any Muslim who may read this, please note that I am quoting Scripture, and that as a believer, this is not a question of my private opinion; it is being faithful to the revealed Word of God. If you have an objection to these cardinal redemptive acts of God in Christ, your basic quarrel is with God Himself, not with me. I am simply His faithful witness.

I have felt it necessary to restate the Scriptural position for the benefit of Muslim readers so they will understand why we perceive their religion the way we do. Again, let me repeat, so there is no misunderstanding: God loves Muslims. So do we. Christ died for Muslims. We give our lives in attempting to bring salvation to Muslims. Muslims are precious in God's sight and in ours. The problem is the religious system that binds them, even blinds them, and, in general, works to keep Muslims from finding salvation in Christ.

Muslims should not only take warning from the illustration of Communism's fall, but even more from the Scriptures themselves. The system to which they belong has set itself against God's Anointed One. On the surface, Islam appears to honor Jesus, but in reality, it is utterly opposed to the heart of the Gospel and is therefore doomed. Listen to David's prophecy against all who would take their stand against the Son of God:

> The One enthroned in heaven laughs; the Lord scoffs at
> them. Then he rebukes them in his anger and terrifies

them in his wrath, saying, "I have installed my King on Zion, my holy hill." [This was ultimately fulfilled in Jesus.]

I will proclaim the decree of the Lord: He said to me, "You are my Son; today I have become your Father. Ask of me, and I will make the nations your inheritance, the ends of the earth your possession. You will rule them with an iron scepter; you will dash them to pieces like pottery."

Therefore, you kings, be wise; be warned, you rulers of the earth. Serve the Lord with fear and rejoice with trembling. Kiss the Son, lest he be angry and you be destroyed in your way, for his wrath can flare up in a moment. Blessed are all who take refuge in him (Ps. 2:4-12).

We know the outcome of this war, for Islam does see itself at war with all other systems until they are "properly subdued." Daniel prophesied long ago what would happen to all kingdoms that oppose the kingdom of God with Christ as the rightful King:

In the time of those kings [Caesar and Herod, who ruled when Jesus was born], the God of heaven will set up a kingdom that will never be destroyed, nor will it be left to another people. It will crush all those kingdoms and bring them to an end, but it will itself endure forever (Dan. 2:44).

The apostle Paul, in his inspired writing, wrote about the endtimes in which Jesus Christ, as the Son of God, will subdue all of God's enemies:

Then the end will come, when he hands over the kingdom to God the Father after he has destroyed all dominion, authority and power. For he must reign until he has put all his enemies under his feet ... When he has done this, then the Son himself will be made subject to him who put everything under him, so that God may be all in all (1 Cor. 15:24, 25, 28).

The Bible closes with a magnificent series of pictures of the warfare and the victory of Christ over all enemies: "the kingdom of the world has become the kingdom of our Lord and of his Christ, and he will reign for ever and ever" (Rev. 11:15). It is comforting to the Christian worker to know that the final outcome is sure. Jesus is the legitimate King. All rivals are to be vanquished. Truth will win over error. Righteousness will be the hallmark of His kingdom. Men of the earth will oppress and terrorize no more, and Satan himself will receive his final judgment and be cast away to deceive no more.

We know that Christ won each of His decisive battles with Satan, beginning with His initial confrontation in the wilderness (Matt. 4:1-11), again in the Garden of Gethsemane as He approached His final test (Matt. 26:36-46), and finally, when He died voluntarily on the cross in our place (Col. 2:13-15), by which He conquered sin and Satan. When He arose from the grave, He also conquered death. We need to avail ourselves of the comfort and strength that comes from the great victory. But even though Jesus has won, the war is not over. There are many battles still to be fought: there will still be many casualties and many martyrs before we finish the work He left for us to do.

He has asked us to disciple the nations—all the thousands of ethnolinguistic groups in the world. We are to go in His name, preach the Gospel, set the prisoners free, heal the sick, cast out demons, expand the borders of His church and trample Satan underfoot (Rom. 16:20). In this titanic struggle, we are to prevail over the enemy, we are to demolish his strongholds and arguments, and "every pretension that sets itself up against the knowledge of God" (2 Cor. 10:3-5). I believe that ultimately this will mean that Muslims will be set free from their system and brought back to God their Father through the Gospel of His Son, our Lord Jesus Christ.

The Place of Prayer

Returning to our discussion of the collapse of Communism, let us examine the place of prayer in that event. Christians in the Soviet Union suffered enormously under dictators like Stalin, Khruschev, Breznev, Chernenko and Andropov. The same could be said of all the Eastern European countries, Vietnam, North Korea, Cuba, and others. Throughout the rule of these oppressive regimes, Christians inside and outside these countries prayed. The big question is, "Did God move as He did in response to those prayers?" My answer is "Yes." The answer took more than fifty years, but what we are seeing today is the result of the faithful prayers of God's people.

When Jesus taught His disciples to pray, among the requests were the following: "Your kingdom come, your will be done on earth as it is in heaven…" and, "deliver us from the evil one" (Matt. 6:10, 13). By asking the Father to bring in His kingdom and that His will be done on earth, we, in a sense, release God to do what He is longing to do. When we ask to be delivered from the evil one, we are acknowledging that "the whole world is under the control of the evil one" (1 John 5:19), and that God, who is in us, is greater than the one who is in the world (1 John 4:4), and can deliver us.

Furthermore, we see how God gave Peter the insight to appropriate a theme from the Mosaic Law and apply it to all believers today: "But you are a chosen people, a royal priesthood …" (1 Peter 2:9). As royal priests, we are to bear before God petitions for the nations. Look at the way Paul also wrote on the same theme:

> I urge, then, first of all, that requests, prayers, intercession and thanksgiving be made for everyone—for kings and all those in authority, that we may live peaceful and quiet lives in all godliness and holiness. This is good, and pleases God our Savior, who wants all men to be saved and to come to a knowledge of the truth (1 Tim. 2:1-4).

God's desire is to see all men saved. He has given us the privilege of intercessory prayer for all men and for their rulers.

We see this so vividly illustrated in the life of Moses. Because of their sin, God was about to destroy the Israelites. Moses staked his life on his intercession for his people, saying, "Please forgive their sin—but if not, then blot me out of the book you have written" (Ex. 32:32). Moses would rather forfeit his life than see his people lost. We need this kind of groaning—this quality of deep intercession that springs out of the groaning of God's Spirit (Rom. 8:26). Who knows? God may bring Muslims out of their bondage to Islam.

Prayer warriors in the spirit of Abraham, Moses, David, Nehemiah, Peter and Paul are needed. Prayer warriors who take the teaching and example of our Lord Jesus to heart. People who will ask God for the Muslim nations of the world, country by country, and ethnolinguistic group by ethnolinguistic group. Prayer is perhaps the mightiest weapon we have in this spiritual war for the salvation of the Muslim peoples of the world.

But there are other aspects and dimensions to this war of liberation to set Muslims free from the restraints of Islam.

<u>Signs and Wonders in the Kingdom</u>

Jesus came to invite people to leave the kingdom of darkness and to enter the kingdom of God. He came in love and compassion. In His tour of Galilee, for example, He preached the Good News of the kingdom and healed every disease and sickness (Matt. 9:35). His was to be a kingdom of love—for He is love (1 John 4:8). Scripture says that when He saw the crowds, He was moved with compassion. How do you show compassion? How do you manifest your love? The most immediate and vexing problem a human being can have is personal illness, a debilitating disease, or even worse, being afflicted with demons. Jesus' response to these very visible needs was always one of compassion. Wherever He went He healed people from their sicknesses and delivered those oppressed by evil spirits. Not only did Jesus demonstrate the power of God in this way, but He also empowered His disciples to do the same by giving "them power and authority to drive out all demons and to cure diseases, and he sent them out to preach the kingdom of God and to heal the sick" (Luke 9:1, 2).

In the above quote, Jesus linked healing and deliverance with the preaching of the kingdom of God. Healing seemed to be the evidence of the presence of the kingdom. Later, Jesus gave the same authority to thirty-six teams which He had appointed to go before Him and prepare the places He was about to visit. What is so very interesting in this last reference is that Jesus linked this to the harvest:

The harvest is plentiful, but the workers are few. Ask the Lord of the harvest, therefore, to send out workers into his harvest field ... When you enter a town and are welcomed, eat what is set before you. Heal the sick who are there and tell them, "The kingdom of God is near you" (Luke 10:2, 8, 9).

Jesus' response to the elation and joy of the returning teams was most revealing. Instead of rejoicing at this evidence of the relief of human suffering, He saw far beyond to the ultimate undoing of the enemy who caused it all: "I saw Satan fall like lightning from heaven. I have given you authority to trample on snakes and scorpions and to overcome all the power of the enemy ..." (Luke 10:18, 19). Jesus was the one who opened His disciples' eyes as to who the real enemy was. Therefore, John was able to write: "We know ... that the whole world is under the control of the evil one" (1 John 5:19). And it was John who articulated so succinctly the purpose of Jesus' coming: "The reason the Son of God appeared was to destroy the devil's work" (1 John 3:8).

Power Encounter in Muslim Work

In our work with Muslims, it is inevitable that we will encounter power, for Islam itself is about power. Although there are many references to mercy and compassion in the Quran, the overriding impression of God in that book is one of irresistible power. Some Muslims see themselves as the instruments of that power—for example, Muslim *mujahidin* (holy warriors) commissioned to impose the Quranic "will of God" upon the whole world—by force, if necessary. In Islam there is no place for incarnation, suffering love and redemption. These are contrary to Muhammad's concept of divine sovereignty and the use of force (Cragg 1984:137). Islam's power is the power of force, of fear, of persecution, of economic discrimination, of the control of media, of the denial of visas, of the effort to drive Christian presence out from its borders and to frustrate the birth of any new movement among its populace.

For the Christian, forgiveness and healing are inextricably linked to Jesus' death on the cross (Isa. 53:4-6; 1 Peter 2:24). His conquest of Satan was possible because of His conquest of sin (John 14:30). His conquest of death was by the Spirit of Holiness whereby He was declared to be the

Son of God (Rom. 1:4). His pouring out of the Holy Spirit upon us was to manifest the Good News of God's great redemptive work in Christ (Acts 1:8). This Good News of God's kingdom is to be testified to by God Himself through "signs, wonders and various miracles, and gifts of the Holy Spirit distributed according to his will" (Heb. 2:4). As the true kingdom of God invades the world of Islam, its hallmarks should be the love of God and the power of God expressed in forgiveness of sins, healings, deliverances from demonic oppression, and other signs and wonders. This is a different kind of power—the power to minister to human needs. It stands forth in great contrast to Islam, which has none of this kind of power or certification from God.

The Bible tells us that Satan knows his time is short: "But woe to the earth and the sea, because the devil has gone down to you! He is filled with fury, because he knows that his time is short" (Rev. 12:12). Even though Satan knows that he is a defeated enemy, he is going to vent his fury on Christ and those who identify with Him, that is, the Christians. He will use whatever weapons, people, ideology, or religion he can control and direct toward his hated enemy, Christ. Because of its anti-Christian nature, we can expect vigorous opposition from Islam in all of its varieties, especially as the Gospel successfully encroaches on Satan's domain.

Truly, Christ sends us forth as sheep among wolves (Matt. 10:16). We may not use earthly weapons. Humanly speaking, we are defenseless against such an enemy. But spiritually, we have the privilege of prayer. Angels come to our assistance in response to those prayers (Dan. 10:4-11; Heb. 1:14). We also have the Word of God in our hands, that word which is called "the Sword of the Spirit" (Eph. 6:17). And, of course, in that Word is the blessed Gospel of our Lord Jesus Christ, which is described as "the power of God for the salvation of everyone who believes ..." (Rom. 1:16). This Word is also called "truth" (John 17:17), and Jesus explained that it is the "truth" that would set people free. And finally, we have our sovereign God Himself who lives in us and fights for us, delivering us from all the power of the enemy (Luke 10:19).

In seeking to win Muslims to Christ, then, we need to use the mighty weapons and the power that Christ makes available to us. He Himself is our strength, He responds to our prayers, He empowers us to heal and deliver the prisoners from Satan's power. We are exhorted to demolish

CHAPTER 22

THE PRACTICAL SIDE

Greater love has no one than this, that he lay down his life for his friends (John 15:13).

There are certain universal qualities of attitude that should characterize us no matter who we are working with, especially when we are attempting to reach people of another culture.

Overcoming Negative Attitudes

Because of the long history of animosity between Muslims and Christians, Christians may be tempted to allow an unforgiving and resentful spirit to poison their attitudes. This was brought home to me by two unforgettable experiences: one in Egypt, the other in India.

I happened to have been in Egypt in the early 1990s at the time of the Iranian-led uprising in Mecca during the annual pilgrimage. My Egyptian companion, a Christian, was relaying the news to me. These are his words: "There has just been a riot in Mecca. Several hundred Iranians and others have been killed by the Saudi army. Praise the Lord! We wished that they had killed thousands. We hate Muslims!"

The second event took place during a conference in the city of Calcutta in eastern India. I was in the middle of a lecture on developing a positive attitude toward our Muslim neighbors when a young man collapsed and fell out of his seat weeping uncontrollably. When I went up to him and asked what was the matter, he repeated over and over again, "Can God ever forgive me?" I asked, "Brother, what have you done?" This is the story as he told it:

> I just moved into a new apartment here in the city. As we were moving in, a man from another apartment down the hall came up to me and said: "I have heard that you

are a Christian family moving in here. We are so happy. We are Muslims and we have always wanted to have Christian friends. Can we be friends?" I replied: "No! We never make friends with Muslims." And I closed the door in his face.

And then, still sobbing, he asked again: "Can God ever forgive me?" After assuring him that God could, we prayed. Then I said to him: "You can't stay in the meeting. You must go back to your apartment and find that man and apologize and begin your friendship with him. Then you can come back to these meetings." The next day, he was in the meeting and his face was radiant. He had received my counsel and was absolutely liberated from his old hatred and prejudice. He had made friends with his Muslim neighbor.

Love is the proof that we are Jesus' disciples. He called it a "new commandment" (John 13:34, 35). We are to love our neighbors as ourselves—no exceptions (Matt. 22:39). We are to love Muslims. God does (John 3:16). Even in the event that they make themselves our enemies, there is no exemption. Jesus' teaching is radical indeed: "But I tell you who hear Me: Love your enemies, do good to those who hate you, bless those who curse you, pray for those who mistreat you" (Luke 6:27, 28).

Several years ago, in interviewing several Malay men and women, all former Muslims who had come to Christ, I discovered to my amazement that every single one came because of a Christian friend or neighbor whose loving attitude attracted them to Jesus.

The apostle Paul has summed up in his own unique way the epitome of having a loving attitude toward every individual:

> I have become its [the church's] servant by the commission God gave me to present to you the word of God in its fullness—the mystery that has been kept hidden for ages and generations, but is now disclosed to the saints. To them God has chosen to make known among the Gentiles the glorious riches of this mystery, which is Christ in you, the hope of glory. We proclaim him, admonishing and teaching everyone with all

wisdom, so that we may present everyone perfect in Christ (Col. 1:25-28).

Applied to Muslims, what a goal—to see every Muslim become complete, perfect in Christ Jesus. I believe this is the only legitimate attitude a believer can have toward any other human being—and in the case of this study, toward every Muslim in the world—to long for every Muslim to become perfect in Christ. All other attitudes lead to a non-caring, non-engaging, non-harvesting attitude toward Muslims.

A thankful spirit goes a long way in any kind of work; it is essential in working with Muslims, otherwise the difficulty of the work could lead to discouragement. Muslims, too, in spite of their treatment of Christians, were made in the image of God. The apostle Paul understood this when he wrote:

> I urge, then, first of all, that requests, prayers, intercession
> and thanksgiving be made for everyone—for kings and
> all those in authority, that we may live peaceful and quiet
> lives in all godliness and holiness. This is good, and pleases
> God our Savior, who wants all men to be saved and to
> come to a knowledge of the truth (1 Tim. 2:1-4).

So, just on biblical principles, we are bound to give thanks for all Muslims. But for those who have lived among them, there are countless times when we have been their guests, have lived as part of their systems, and have been helped by them.

Twice in my own experience, Muslims have intervened to save my life. The first time was during the second Indo-Pak War over Kashmir. A rumor had spread among the villages outside the Pakistani mountain town where we were living that we had signaled the Indian airplanes flying overhead. Enraged Muslim villagers came to torch our houses and kill us. They were stopped at the bottom of the hill by the local Muslim shopkeepers who said: "Those people would never do what you think they did. You may not do this terrible thing. You will have to kill us first." And they barred the way and turned the villagers back.

The second time was during the Yom Kippur War between Israel, Egypt, and Syria. Palestinians and Pakistanis had taken to the streets of

Lahore in protest against Israel and America. They were stopping all cars, looking for Americans. They stopped mine. When they learned that I was an American, they began screaming "*Amreeki, Amreeki,*" and rocking the car to turn it over and burn it. A tall Jordanian came up to my window, saw the desperate situation I was in and turned to the crowd and shouted, "This man is not American; he is French. Viva la France! Viva la France!" And he drove the crowd away.

Of all the many other kindnesses done to me by Muslims, the most memorable happened on the edge of a West African Malinka village. We had been driving all day and pulled into a clearing at the edge of a village at sunset. As we unpacked a picnic basket to have our evening meal before driving on through the night, an African woman passed with a bundle on her head. She turned to look at us, walked on about ten paces, then stopped and took the bundle down, untied it, fished something out and stuck it in the sleeve of her copious garment. She came over to the leader of our three-man group and went through an extended exchange of greetings in the Malinka language. After about ten of these exchanges she brought a giant tuber of manioc out of her sleeve and presented it to our leader. Then there were many more polite exchanges. After that she returned to her bundle, tied it up, and went on in to her village.

When it was all over, I turned to my friend and asked, "Brother, what was that all about? That woman knew you from somewhere before, didn't she?" He said, "No, I have never stopped here before." Then I said, "Well, she must have been a Christian and figured out that we were Christians, too, and that's why she was being so kind to us." He said, "No, that lady was a Muslim." And I asked, "Well, what was that all about?" He replied, "Brother, in this culture, when a stranger arrives at the edge of your village at nightfall, you are obligated to take him in, cook his evening meal, and offer him a place to sleep for the night. That lady did just that. She offered to cook our meal and to give us her house for the night." I asked, "Did you catch her name?" He said, "Her name is Saadi Kamara." I said, "I am going to tell the story of Saadi Kamara to Christians everywhere because Jesus would. She is the 'good Samaritan' of our day. Jesus would tell the story of this 'Good Muslim,' if He were here today; therefore, so will I."

Another incident happened in Bel Air, California. After teaching a Sunday School class on "Loving Your Muslim Neighbor," an agitated lady came up to me and said, "I think I live next door to Muslims." I asked, "How do you know?" She replied, "They have olive colored skin, speak a foreign language and the woman is covered with a black veil from head to foot." I said, "Yes, you live next door to Muslims. How long have they lived there?" "Six months," she replied. Then I asked, "Well, what have you done about it?" "Nothing," she replied, "I'm scared to death of them." Then I asked, "Would you do whatever I suggest?" "What are you going to suggest?" she asked. I said, "This afternoon, when you get home from church, I want you to bake or buy a cake, take it next door to your Muslim neighbors, and say, 'I am your neighbor, forgive me for not coming sooner to welcome you to our neighborhood. Here is a small present for you. I would like to become friends with you.'"

The next Sunday, the woman was waiting for me when I arrived to teach the Sunday School class. "It worked," she said joyfully. "They invited me in. A nice young man spoke English and introduced me to his mother and the rest of the family. The woman was not wearing a veil indoors and she is very nice, too. We have become good friends." The woman simply needed someone to make a suggestion on how to start a friendship with a next door neighbor.

Most of us have probably not given Muslims a chance to show their spirit of hospitality, or generosity, or kindness. The image of God is still there inside of them, damaged by sin, like it is in the rest of us. Nevertheless, they reflect the image of their estranged Heavenly Father whom they do not know. Ours is the responsibility to love our Muslim neighbors, to befriend them, and to allow them the privilege of ministering to us, too. Jesus was very good at this. Remember how He started the conversation with the woman at the well in Samaria? "Would you give me a drink of water?" We need to get close to them if we are going to be recipients of their kindness.

So, our spirit of thanksgiving for Muslims can have two roots. The first is because the Bible teaches us to be thankful for them. The second is for deeds of kindness they do for us.

Cultural Sensitivity

Love and thankfulness will carry you into the other person's culture, too. Our prime example is Jesus. Scripture teaches us that He lived in glory in the presence of God the Father before the creation of the world (John 17:24). Yet He emptied Himself and became one of us—a human being in a specific time and place (Phil. 2:6, 7). In particular, He came as a Palestinian Jew, thus identifying with the primary group of people He gave His life to win. In the life of Paul, we learned that he was willing to become all things to all people so that by any means he might win some (1 Cor. 9:22). And we suggested that in order to win Muslims, we might well have to become culturally, but not theologically, like the Muslim we are trying to win. Bashir Abdol Massih, writing in *The Gospel and Islam*, combines these models of Jesus and Paul under the theme of "Incarnational Witness." His description is appropriate:

> The incarnational witness is one in whom love has worked so deeply that he seeks in every way possible to become like the hearer so that he can manifest the gospel in thought, communication, and religio-cultural forms that relate meaningfully to the hearer (Massih 1979:87).

All too often, the Christian worker is blind to the whole issue of cultural sensitivity. Living with the misunderstanding that the only thing necessary is communication of the Good News in the other's language, the Christian unconsciously teaches his or her culture as part of the Gospel. This is often a hindrance to the spread of the Gospel, especially if there is a vigorous clash between the culture of the Muslim to be won and the Christian attempting to do the winning. The message is often rejected not because it was understood and deemed unacceptable, but because of the way it was presented, that is, in its cultural trappings, which were so offensive to the hearer that he could not receive the message.

Earlier, the question was raised, "Has God decreed that there would only be one cultural form of Christianity?" The answer is "No." Otherwise, Jesus would have taught it to us. But He said true worship would not be "on this mountain, nor in Jerusalem," but rather "in spirit and in truth." The Gospel would not be bound in Jewish cultural forms—the temple and its trappings. It would be accessible and received in every cultural milieu.

Therefore, the burden is on the Christian witness to decide what that "supracultural" truth is, the essence of the Good News from God to man.

Each worker will have to discern just how he or she should develop his or her approach in ways appropriate to a particular target culture. This should lead one, then, to gain a thorough knowledge of the target culture and what parts of it could and could not be appropriated for Christian worship. Such discernment necessarily involves determining which forms are flawed beyond recovery by evil meanings and which forms would lend themselves easily to God's holy purposes in worship and service.

As Kraft pointed out, cultures can be used by God, Satan or man (1979:113). Because sin is so pervasive, cultural forms will be affected by it. God seems to be in the business of transforming human beings who in turn modify their respective cultures as they learn to discern the difference between following the Spirit of God and the "spirits" that are in the world.

Islam, because of its inherent anti-Christian teaching, has misappropriated innumerable forms for its own ends. As Christian workers make inroads among these Muslim peoples, we will have to continually test and evaluate to see what can be retained or modified from the cultural background of these new believers for Christian purposes.

Since language is the "womb" of a culture, it is imperative that along with learning the culture, the Christian worker should set about to learn the language of the people he or she is seeking to win. Reyburn's brilliant research on Bible translations in Muslim languages shows that, even though Christians have lived among Muslims from A.D. 622 to the present, it has only been since 1800 that the Christian missionary movement has begun to take seriously the translation of the Bible into Muslim languages (Reyburn 1979:363).

There must be a deep commitment to language learning and translation of the Scriptures if we are to see a healthy discipling of the yet unreached hundreds of Muslim peoples.

Responding to Human Need
Earlier I wrote of healing, deliverance from demon oppression and the possibility of other "signs and wonders" in the spiritual warfare over the souls of Muslim people. But, there is another side to the expression of our love for them. Again, Jesus is our Teacher:

> Then the King will say to those on his right, "Come, you who are blessed by my Father; take your inheritance,

175

the kingdom prepared for you since the creation of the world. For I was hungry and you gave me something to eat, I was thirsty and you gave me something to drink, I was a stranger and you invited me in, I needed clothes and you clothed me, I was sick and you looked after me, I was in prison and you came to visit me ... whatever you did for one of the least of these brothers of mine, you did for me" (Matt. 25:34-40).

A refugee, hungry, thirsty, naked, sick, in prison—these are the characteristics of millions of Muslims today in Afghanistan, Iraq, Jordan, Kashmir, Pakistan, Bangladesh, Somalia, Sudan, Chad, Palestine, and Kosovo Province in Yugoslavia, to name a few. Millions live in spiritual darkness and economic deprivation. There seems to be no end to human suffering when we look at the Muslim world. The disasters which catch our attention on such massive scales should not deter us from noticing the individual cases of human need right where we live, whether as a guest in their countries or having them as guests in ours.

In spite of the fact that our motives are misunderstood (for Muslims think we "buy" converts by responding to their human needs), Christ has asked us to minister to them as though we were ministering to Him. What better way to demonstrate His love and their worth in His eyes. We must not allow the twisted thinking of that old devil working through beguiled Muslims to dissuade us from ministering to human need wherever we find it.

The question of how to inherit eternal life—a question posed by an expert in law—was answered not by a belief system, but by the story of a Samaritan responding to human need. Who was the true neighbor to the one who fell into the hands of robbers? The lawyer could no more escape Jesus' lesson than we could: "The one who had mercy on him" (Luke 10:25-37). "For Christ's love compels, because we are convinced that one died for all, and therefore all died" (2 Cor. 5:14). Christ's love compels us to love those for whom He died.

Henry Martyn's Life: A Model

Henry Martyn (1781-1812) has been considered the first Protestant missionary to Muslims. He was eminently qualified in languages, having been trained in Urdu, Persian, Arabic and Sanskrit at Cambridge University. He was an extremely dedicated young man whose desire, after reaching India, was "to burn out for God." This literally happened. He died at the age of 32 in Turkey on his way back to England.

The period of his active ministry covered only a short period of time (1806-1812). Yet his accomplishments in debates with Muslims, translation of Scriptures (the New Testament in Urdu, Persian and Arabic), brilliant tracts explaining Christianity to Muslims, and most of all, his personal life and witness, left a profound impression on all of his contemporaries, both Muslim and Christian.

Martyn was a quick learner and soon realized that formal public debates with Muslim scholars were not effective. Accordingly, he changed his approach and eventually developed seven principles of working with Muslims that foreshadowed many of the things we have advocated in this book. They are as relevant and as appropriate today as when they were first worked out by Martyn around 1810. This material, by the way, is taken from Lyle Vander Werff's invaluable book, *Christian Mission to Muslims: The Record*, 1977:31-36.

Following are Martyn's seven principles of working with Muslims:

1. Share your own personal experience—your testimony of how you experienced the forgiveness of sins and peace with God through Jesus Christ.

2. Appreciate the best in your Muslim friend and ascribe such qualities to God working in his life. The same could go for those elements in Muslim culture that are genuinely approved by God.

3. Keep your message Christ-centered, as you talk about the grace of God and how it is mediated through Christ and carried forward by the sanctifying work of God's Spirit.

4. Draw your Muslim friend into the study of the Scriptures so that he can discover these new truths for himself.

5. Play the role of a supporting friend as your Muslim friend goes through this time of critical investigation and decision-making.

6. Create a favorable atmosphere in society by ministering to human needs.

7. Trust the Holy Spirit to work in your Muslim friend as he seeks his place as a believer in his Muslim context.

PART FIVE

APPROACHES TO SPECIFIC
KINDS OF MUSLIMS

INTRODUCTION

We have covered a lot of ground regarding attitude. I have written about Jesus' way of using spiritual power in contrast to the world's way of physical force. We have explored the subject of how the kingdom of God relates to human cultures. From Paul, we drew principles of how to relate to Muslim cultures. I wrote of the nature of spiritual warfare. And finally, we dealt with practical issues of relating to your Muslim friends and neighbors, ending with the model of Henry Martyn's life.

All these things must be kept in mind as we now take up the issue of how to relate to different kinds of Muslims. All of the above principles should come into play as they are needed.

But, what kind of Muslims are you seeking to win? Do they hold beliefs which make them different from other kinds of Muslims? Should these distinctive beliefs elicit approaches modified by your knowledge of their background, their belief system, and their particular set of assumptions in their worldview? I think so. In some cases, the Christian worker will be able to capitalize on what Muslims already believe or practice, filling it with new Christian meaning. But in other cases, the worker may have to differ with Muslim assumptions and show him or her an entirely new way.

So, in this section we are going to suggest how to respond to these different kinds of Muslims. We will attempt to project how Jesus might handle these issues if He were facing them today.

How would Jesus respond to Sunnis, Shias, Secularists, Militants, Sufis, Folk Muslims, Ahmadis or African-American Muslims? As we continue, please remember that these are suggestions that need to be tested in the fire of personal experiences. They are not meant to imply this is the only way the Lord could work in a given situation with these specific kinds of Muslims.

Remember also that, as often as not, Muslims are drawn initially to Christ by the attractive lives of their Christian friends, not by arguments. Nevertheless, some Muslims are won because the Christian worker was sensitive to the issues and knew how to use them skillfully in showing that Christ was the answer to his or her unmet needs.

CHAPTER 23

JESUS AND THE SUNNIS

Woe to you, teachers of the law ... You shut the kingdom of heaven in men's faces. You yourselves do not enter, nor will you let those enter who are trying to (Matt. 23:13, 14).

Sunnis, you will recall, are those Muslims who follow the exemplary model of Muhammad (*Sunnah*) and consider the Quran and the *Hadith* as authoritative. An Orthodox Sunni would want to live under *Shariah* Law. This type of Muslim, in all probability, would be very similar to the Orthodox Jews of Jesus' day. We propose that Jesus would, therefore, relate to a Sunni much the same way He related to those Jews who tried to keep the Mosaic Law and the traditions of the elders.

Jesus' Attitude toward Mosaic Law

Even from the age of twelve, Jesus was intensely interested in religion as it was perceived and practiced by the scholars of the Scriptures, the Old Testament (Luke 2:46, 47). He was interested also in motives and attitudes of the heart on the part of the practitioners (Luke 16:15). When He began His ministry, Jesus attested to the validity of the Law. In fact, He saw all of His future ministry as a fulfillment of that Law. Concerning this, He said:

Do not think that I have come to abolish the Law or the Prophets; I have not come to abolish them but to fulfill them. I tell you the truth, until heaven and earth disappear, not the smallest letter, not the least stroke of a pen, will by any means disappear from the Law until everything is accomplished (Matt. 5:17, 18).

Jesus also knew the difference between a practical love and application of the principle intent of the Law, in contrast to barren legalism. On one occasion He summarized the Law in these words:

> "'Love the Lord your God with all your heart and with all your soul and with all your mind.' This is the first and greatest commandment. And the second is like it: 'Love your neighbor as yourself.' All the Law and the Prophets hang on these two commandments" (Matt. 22:37-39).

Love for God and love for neighbor were to be the measuring stick for the test of true goodness and godliness. We might point out also, that Jesus, as far as we know, kept all of the Jewish ceremonial Law contained in Scriptures, but did not feel at all bound by manmade traditions.

The Sunni Problem: Shariah Law

Sunni Islam, as it developed under Muhammad's and his followers' guiding hands, represented a highly Arabicized, Semitic adaptation, not so much of Mosaic Law but Jewish traditions to it as found in the *Talmud* and the *Mishnah*, plus a few more ideas inspired by his contacts with Eastern Christians, Zoroastrians and Arabic culture.

Islam emerged as a growing body of law, based on Muhammad's dicta in the Quran and his own pattern of living. Its driving thrust was to bring everything about Islam under a binding set of laws of which he was the sole pattern and originator. Sunni Islam has come to stand for that branch of Islam that is bound to the *Sunnah* of the Prophet as derived from his Quranic and extra-Quranic actions and sayings. It is supremely characterized, then, by law. Sunni Muslims are bound by *Shariah* Law and the *Hadith*, as conceived by Muhammad and his followers.

Jesus Sees the Heart

From studying the Gospels, we see certain patterns emerging as to how Jesus related to various types of people. For example, Scripture tells us Jesus loved the rich young man who came to Him asking how to receive eternal life. The young man had kept all of the Law from his youth.

However, he loved his riches more than the Lord. For him, the question was not keeping the Law—he did that. Rather, it was lifestyle—being willing to give it all away to the poor when the Lord asked him to do so.

To the Scribes and the Pharisees who laid heavy legal and financial burdens on others that they would not carry themselves, Jesus was merciless—because they were merciless. He read their hard hearts and severely rebuked them (Matt. 23:4). Jesus had no mercy on those who pretended to be religious, but inwardly were ferocious wolves (Matt. 7:15).

On the other hand, to the brokenhearted, Jesus granted instantaneous forgiveness. The unnamed sinful woman who loved Jesus, wept over His feet, dried them with her hair and anointed them with costly perfume was forgiven all her sins because her faith had saved her. Jesus sent her away in peace (Luke 7:36-50).

How would Jesus relate to a Sunni? It would depend on what He saw in his or her heart. In the above stories, Jesus saw the love of money in the rich young ruler, hypocrisy in the lawyers, and heartache in the fallen woman. And He responded appropriately in each situation.

Although we can in no way come up to Jesus' level of accuracy in reading people's hearts, we do know that He has given us the gift of the discerning of spirits (1 Cor. 12:10). By His Spirit, He gives us insights into the true condition of people's hearts and He expects us to minister accordingly.

Reaching the Sunnis

To those Sunnis who are genuinely toiling in the idea that keeping *Shariah* Law can save them, our way of dealing with them may take great prayer and patience. They have been deceived into believing that Muhammad's word was the last word in Scriptural tradition and that salvation is obtained by keeping the Law. There is a veil over the minds of these people that can be removed by intercessory prayer and by patiently showing them the hopelessness of that approach. First, they must be shown the true function of law: it kills (2 Cor. 3:6). This is explained quite pointedly by Paul in his letter to the Romans:

> Now we know that whatever the law says, it says to those
> who are under the law, so that every mouth may be

silenced and the whole world held accountable to God. Therefore no one will be declared righteous in his sight by observing the law; rather, through the law we become conscious of sin (Rom. 3:19, 20).

Islam labors under the idea that salvation is possible by merit; that is, if one's good deeds outweigh one's bad deeds, paradise is the reward. Neither Muhammad nor his followers understood that in God's eyes, "the wages of sin is death" (Rom. 6:23), or that "whoever keeps the whole law and yet stumbles at just one point is guilty of breaking all of it" (James 2:10). It takes patience to show this to a devout Sunni Muslim from our Scriptures.

Undoubtedly, the charges will be raised that our Scriptures have been changed, and you will have to show your friend why this is not so.

Furthermore, the Sunni Muslim is apt to drag in a comparison between Christ and Muhammad. Current trends to proclaim Muhammad infallible, and in some quarters, divine, notwithstanding; the Quran exposes Muhammad's sinfulness in the following passages:

16:61   If God was to punish men for their wrong-doing, He would not leave, on the (earth), a single living creature [including Muhammad].

40:55   Ask forgiveness for thy fault [applied to all].

42:5   Pray for forgiveness for (all) beings on earth [Muhammad is included].

42:30   Whatever misfortune happens to you, is because of the things your hands have wrought, and for many (of them) He grants forgiveness [Muhammad had his share of misfortunes].

47:19   Ask forgiveness for thy fault, and for the men and women who believe [Muhammad included].

48:1,2   Verily we have granted thee a manifest victory: that God may forgive thee thy faults of the past and those to follow [Muhammad included].

This may seem tedious to the Christian reader, but it is necessary to disabuse Muslims of any exaggerated image they may have of Muhammad. To quote these verses does not mean that we believe the Quran is inspired, but that Muslims who do are unable to hold an inflated opinion of Muhammad.

Jesus would patiently show Sunnis that there is no rational hope in the system given to them by Muhammad. Jesus knew that God's Law (much less *Shariah*) could not bring salvation, and consequently, all that awaited all men and women was death. He also knew that He, as the sinless Son of God, Lamb of God, Living Sacrifice, would pay the death penalty for all humankind. He knew that He held the key to forgiveness because He was going to go to the cross as a substitute sacrifice for all humankind. Jesus, knowing the futility of "salvation by law," be it the Mosaic Law or the *Shariah*, would present Himself to the Muslim as the Savior of the world by virtue of His having satisfied the demands of God's Real Law on the cross.

We, as ambassadors of Christ, have to learn how to show Muslims the necessity of a divinely provided atonement on behalf of their sins. We could even refer our Muslim friends to the Quran where there is a hint of an idea that God provided a ransom (atonement): "And we ransomed him with a momentous sacrifice" (Q. 37:107). This, of course, refers to God providing a substitute sacrifice in place of Abraham's son, whereby He ransomed him. Using this analogy, we could show that Jesus is that sacrifice of such momentous proportions that His blood alone was sufficient to atone for the sins of all mankind.

Jesus or Muhammad

All of this inevitably brings us to the question of choosing between Jesus and Muhammad, since they are so diametrically opposed in their understanding of law, grace and salvation. Jesus is set forth as the Son of God, crucified, risen, glorified and now ascended to the right hand of the throne of God. Muhammad, on the other hand, died a natural death at about the age of 62 and was buried in Medina. These questions will always arise: "What do you think of Christ?" and "What do you think of Muhammad?"

It is usually pointless to say anything to the Muslim initially about the biblical evaluation of Muhammad. It is best to do everything you can to point your friend to Jesus. If you succeed in bringing your friend into a study of the Scriptures, he or she will soon find out the sharp and divergent contrast between the Son of God and Muhammad. In concluding this chapter, I cannot emphasize enough the place of intercessory prayer for your Muslim friends, the patience required in drawing them to Christ, the love that will not quit, and the utter dependence on the Holy Spirit to help you.

CHAPTER 24

JESUS AND THE SHIAS

> Did not the Christ have to suffer these things and then enter his glory? And beginning with Moses and all the Prophets, He explained to them what was said in all the Scriptures concerning himself (Luke 24:26, 27).

Shia Islam is characterized by three distinctive doctrines that are not found in Sunni Islam.

Shias believe that "Divine Light" indwelt Muhammad, his son-in-law, Ali, and Ali's son, Husayn. They believe this "Divine Light" also dwelt in each successive *imam* and it lives in the present day supreme ayatollah. In some cases, this "Divine Light" is equated with deity itself.

Second, Shias believe Husayn (martyred at Karbala in A.D. 680) died for his people. In other words, there is in Shia Islam an idea of vicarious atonement. The Shias celebrate this martyrdom during the first ten days of the first month of the Muslim calendar (Muharram) with passion plays re-enacting the suffering and martyrdom of Husayn, which reach a climax on the tenth day of Muharram. As pointed out earlier, the tenth of Muharram corresponds to *Ashura*, the Jewish Day of Atonement (*Yom Kippur*).

Allied with these two ideas is a third: Shiism has always functioned as a protest movement within Islam.

> Shias engaged in movements of protest, including socioeconomic protest, which often heralded a messianic mahdi who would bring back justice and equity after the current reign of injustice and oppression (Keddie and Cole, 1986:4).

It is probable that these ideas developed as a result of Muslim exposure to Christians who lived around them. The problem is that these distinctive Shia concepts are now tied to their own sense of identity as Muslims and, in the case of Iran, to ethnicity. In passing, it should be noted that Shiism was originally an Arab phenomenon, but in due time it was adopted by the Persians, and tends to be linked to Persian-speaking people, or others, such as the Kurds, who live in close proximity to them.

For the Christian worker, the "passion theme" of Shia Islam predisposes the Shia Muslim to understand the Christian idea of the atoning death of Christ on the cross for the sins of the whole world in a way that is not true of Sunni Islam. Both Sunni and Shia Islam believe God rescued Christ from the cross and took Him alive to heaven. But for the Sunnis, recognizing as they do, the tenth of Muharram, there is still great significance to the day because it coincides with the Jewish Day of Atonement. On that day, *Ashura*, the door of the *Kaaba* (the House of God) is opened to visitors (Gibb and Kramers 1974:48). It is reminiscent of what happened on that day when Jesus was crucified and the veil of the Temple was rent, thus, opening up the "Holy of Holies" to ordinary believers.

The challenge, of course, is how to bring the true knowledge of Christ to these Muslims who are already predisposed to accept these key ideas of incarnation, atonement and suffering. In order to do so, a Christian presence must exist among the Shias so that there can be exposure to the real Christ. In the case of Iran, the attitude to Christians has not been very hospitable. Christian missionaries are no longer welcome, Bibles are no longer allowed in, some churches have been closed, and several Muslim convert pastors, as well as those from Christian Aremenian backgrounds, have been martyred in the last decade.

Christian Advance in Iran

In spite of the seemingly admirable traits in Shiism which lend themselves to Christian fulfillment, the trend is to deify the *imams*, to claim "Divine Light" exists in them, and allow them to rule. This has led to a nightmare of revenge, oppression, war, and the suicidal sacrifice of their best youth on the fields of battle. The terrors perpetrated on the people of Iran by the Islamic Revolutionary Government of Khomeini and his successor are beyond anything known before. Satan has had a field day working through these Shia leaders and this system, causing massive destruction of land and people.

Yet there have been several wonderful developments throughout this rule of the ayatollahs. First, Christ Himself, in response to Christians' prayers I'm sure, seems to have taken the initiative by causing Shias all over Iran to have visions and dreams about Him (Yaghnazar 1991:1). This has created a great hunger among those affected, and they have searched for Christians to answer their questions.

A second development, independent of the dreams and visions phenomena, has been an insatiable demand for Christian Scriptures. The problem is how to get enough Bibles into Iran to satisfy the demand. For a while, new Bibles were allowed in and printed in Iran. Now it is forbidden.

And third, the story of a prominent government figure being raised from the dead has caused quite a stir in Iran. It happened this way. The government leader needed emergency surgery during a period when all of the doctors were on strike, protesting Khomeini's law that no male doctor could treat a female patient. Revolutionary guards rounded up a team of six surgeons at gunpoint, along with the necessary assistants, to perform the operation. During the course of the operation, the patient died. The doctors knew they would be accused of causing the death and be executed. In desperation, based on two things they knew about Christ from the Quran, namely, that He could raise the dead, and that He was alive in heaven today, they prayed to Him. Their prayer, as they reported in a church afterwards, went something like this:

> O Christ, we know that you can raise the dead and that you are alive in heaven right now. You know this man has died and that we are as good as dead men ourselves. We beseech You to raise this man from the dead and to spare our lives. If you do, we promise to give ourselves to You and to serve You the rest of our lives (an Iranian Christian, (an Iranian Christian, name witheld 1986:1).

Jesus raised that man from the dead right there on the operating table. Today, those six doctors are all baptized believers and have attended a downtown church in Tehran. Needless to say this event has caused a commotion in the city, with a large number of Muslims showing a new interest in Christ. Reportedly, churches in Iran are now full and many Muslims are now coming to the Lord, in spite of persecution (Yaghnezar 1991:1).

The stress of war, loss of loved ones, economic collapse, police brutality on a scale never known before, and all in the name of Shia Islam, have caused a widespread openness to the Gospel. The tiny Christian presence in Iran and the distribution of the Word of God, the use of Christian radio programs, correspondence courses and the showing of the *Jesus* film are all contributing to a growing harvest in Iran today. The peculiar Shia beliefs have also been a predisposing factor in this move toward Christ. Let's think for a few minutes about how the following doctrines would find a resonating point in the Gospel.

Jesus as Divine Light

Shias believe "Divine Light" has indwelt their leaders from Muhammad to Ali to Husayn and through the chain of *imams*. As you will recall from our previous discussion, the last *imam*, having disappeared, lives in a suspended state somewhere between heaven and earth, and supposedly communicates guidance to the reigning ayatollah. He is believed to have passed on this light to the supreme ayatollah today. This person functions as the Chief Steward of the faith until the return of the occulted *imam*, whom Shias believe will also be the *Mahdi*. Along with this, many Shias believe that Christ will return with the *Mahdi* to establish a worldwide rule of Islam!

Jesus, you may remember, said of Himself: "I am the Light of the world. Whoever follows me will never walk in darkness, but will have the light of life" (John 8:12). Since Shias have already accepted the possibility of "Divine Light" living in a human ayatollah (whom some would consider divine), the ground has been prepared for them to believe in the idea that Jesus is the manifestation of "Divine Light." In Jesus' case, we also read, "In him was life, and that life was the light of men" (John 1:4). No ayatollah, of course, could impart life to anyone, as Jesus did.

And that leads us to another point of attraction for the Muslim who is fascinated with this concept of light. Jesus said to His followers, "You are the light of the world." Jesus, by giving us life and empowering us to do righteous deeds, said we also would shine as lights in the world. This life is available for all. In his light, we see light, and he is the fountain of life for us all (Ps. 36:9).

Shia Islam has the concept of divine light. It just awaits a Christian witness to explain to the Shia friend from the Word of God that this teaching predates Islam by six hundred years. Moreover, God intended for all believers to reflect this light, which finds its source in Jesus Christ, the Light of the world. From the acknowledgment of "Divine Light" in Jesus, it is just a short step to show the full glory of the incarnation, of how and why Jesus came as the Son of God, to reveal the Father, to show that all of God's fullness dwelt in Him, and that He is the exact representation of the Father (Col. 2:9; Heb. 1:3).

The Suffering Savior

We had just finished watching the crucifixion scene in the film *Ben Hur.* I turned to speak to the manager of the cinema house who was next to me. Tears were streaming down his face. I asked him: "Suleman, do you believe Jesus died on the cross for your sins?" Still weeping, he said: "I believe it with all my heart." The story could be repeated hundreds of times among Shiite Muslims, wherever they have had a chance to see the suffering of Christ acted out, for example, in the *Jesus* film. There is an incredible receptivity to the Gospel when it is presented in film or video. Shiites have been preconditioned for centuries to believe in the death of a vicarious sufferer for their sins. What the early Shiites borrowed from the Christian passion plays can now be recovered as we have opportunity to show them the original story in film or Scripture. And this is what is happening, wherever there is an open door.

One of my former professors, Dr. M. Daud Rahbar, so succinctly said: "I could never believe in a God who would not identify with human suffering." At the risk of his life and his career, after reading the New Testament, Dr. Rahbar sought baptism and chose to follow our "Suffering Savior." Ours is the task of not only telling Jesus' story, but living it out in front of Shia eyes, that they might believe and have life through Jesus' name.

Kingdom Teaching and Social Protest

Jesus, in His own day, lived out a life of social protest. His ear was finely tuned to the cries of injustice and the despair of the poor. His indignation burned against the heartless rich, the crooked government officials, and the hypocrisy of the religious leaders. He championed the dispossessed.

But His method was different. Instead of advocating violent remedies, He taught the necessity of the new birth. It starts in the human heart. The ethics of the kingdom of God have to be personal before they can become communal. And even the non-violent method of achieving change was radical. He combined righteousness, divine light and suffering all into one powerful message. And He lived it out to the death. Again, ours is to follow His example as we carry His message into the world of Shia Islam. They wait and they respond when they see it and understand it. Shias are ready for the call to take up their crosses daily and follow a suffering Savior, who gives all of His disciples divine light and who prepares them for a new heaven and new earth characterized by righteousness.

CHAPTER 25

JESUS AND THE SUFIS

> I have been crucified with Christ and I no longer live, but Christ lives in me. The life I live in the body, I live by faith in the Son of God, who loved me and gave himself for me(Gal. 2:20).

Before reading this material, please turn back to chapter 12 and review the teaching on Sufism—Islamic Mysticism. Sufism, having taken much of its early inspiration from Christian ideas circulating throughout Muslim lands, is most susceptible to the mystical side of the Gospel. For example, when Ibn al-Arabi (A.D. 1165-1240) was summoned before an Islamic inquisition in Aleppo (Syria) to answer the charges of non-conformity, he asserted that his poems were to be taken metaphorically, "the basic message being God's perfection of man through divine love" (Shah 1971:x).

This hunger for God's love opens the door wide for us to talk about how God actually expressed His love for us in the gift of His Son, Jesus Christ. Galatians 2:20 expresses this so well in Sufi terms: "I am crucified with Christ; it is no longer I who live but Christ who lives in me; and the life I now live in the flesh, I live by faith in the Son of God who loved me and gave Himself for me." Jesus could meet the Sufis on the common ground of love.

Cultural Flexibility

One other characteristic that may render Sufis more receptive to Christian approaches than other Muslims is how flexibly those approaches accommodate the local environment. This often leads to great compromises with the Law and Orthodox Islam. As mentioned earlier, many Sufis became quite syncretistic and fall into what has been called Folk Islamic practices (Parshall 1983:16). These practices do not fascinate us as much as the accommodative tendency, the weakening of allegiance to *Shariah* Law.

Seeking after the inner experience, the "interiorization of the motive" over the slavish devotion to the Law, opens the door wide to a genuine Christian experience of God. It also, I might add, opens the door to the possibility of other kinds of spirits coming to live in or be attached to the Sufi. In addition to seeking union with God, the Sufi effort to achieve the annihilation of self lends itself to that aspect of Christian thought that talks of death to self, of "crucifying the flesh with its affections and desires."

Perhaps most damaging of all, Sufis have been taught that their psychologically induced states of ecstasy were genuine experiences of union with God. Thus, they no longer feel a need to seek any other "god," in this case, God as revealed in Christ.

From the point of view of the Christian worker, one can see that Sufism offers both hope and obstacles to the Gospel. Hope because there is such an apparent hunger for God and such a willingness to undergo strict discipline to achieve it. Obstacles because there is a new kind of bondage, namely, to a human head of the order and also the possibility that in seeking to get in touch with "god" outside of Jesus Christ, the devotee is wide open to getting in touch with something from the demonic spirit world.

Jesus would have an easier time among the Sufis than He would among the secularized Muslims. Sufis have already exhibited a hunger for God. Before tackling suggested approaches to Sufis, lest we think this will be too easy, we need to remember that the devotee's loyalty (total obedience) is already to someone other than Christ, and that the obsession with "inner light" may draw the disciple into the grip of enemy "powers" posing as true light, and that syncretistic practices may open the door in a different way to the world of the demonic spirits opposing Christ.

Therefore, the very first concern in attempting to reach Sufis is to remember that Christ who lives in you is greater than whatever spirits may control or indwell the Sufis (1 John 4:4). It is up to us to exercise the authority and power that Christ has given us over all the power of the enemy (Luke 10:19). Furthermore, because Sufis are concerned with "death to self" and "union with God," we must assume that in the absence of

Christ, they are deceived about their experiences. Satan may have blinded their minds (2 Cor. 4:4). Therefore, we should not take it for granted that it will be easy to win them. Prayer will be a powerful element in seeking to win Sufis. Remember that Christ has the power to bind or expel evil spirits.

Having duly noted that the ultimate nature of our work is a kind of spiritual warfare, let us now turn to some of the Sufi concerns that might open them up to functional equivalents in true Christian experience. As an aside, when we use the word "functional equivalent," our assumption is that religious experiences can either be genuine or false, that the only genuine experiences are those rooted in Jesus Christ, and that all others are spurious. From this, it can be seen that a form or practice could be just as easily used by the Devil as by Christ. Our goal is to capture the form or practice for Christ. Having established this premise for our approaches, we assume that Sufi experiences are imitations of real experiences. They express hunger of the human heart for what really is a possibility in Christ. The Sufi has been denied access to Christ by these substitute forms and practices, with some alien spirit taking the place that rightly belongs to Him. In looking over the ways that Sufis might be open to Christian approaches, the following areas of common interest may provide places to start.

Love for God

The true Sufi's concern is love for God. Along with this comes a consciousness of sin and a genuine concern for repentance and, ultimately, a renunciation of the world. Sufis, according to their limited understanding of religious phenomena, are able, up to a point, but not without distortion, to make distinctions between the ways of the world and the ways of God. Only the Spirit of God working through revealed Scriptures is able to remove that distortion.

The very heart of the Judeo-Christian message is love for God. Moses, writing under the inspiration of God's Spirit, gave us these immortal lines: "Hear, O Israel [people of God]: the Lord our God, the Lord is one. Love the Lord your God with all your heart and with all your soul and with all your strength" (Deut. 6:4, 5).

Jesus, who came 1400 years later to fulfill the law, not abrogate it, reinforced this teaching when He responded to a Jewish legal expert's question as to which was the greatest law with these words: "'Love the Lord your God with all your heart and with all your soul and with all your mind.' This is the first and greatest commandment" (Matt. 22:37, 38). Today, this love is best demonstrated in the life of the Christian worker. Let the Christian worker beware if his or her life does not reflect this all-out love for God. One's own life must reflect this love of God, especially when the other person already thinks he or she is deeply in love with God. There will have to be unmistakable evidences of this love in the Christian's life. After all, Jesus said that it was by love that the world would know we are His disciples (John 13:34, 35).

The Sufi will expect this love to be manifested in the area of personal piety, an intoxication with God, a God-centeredness that is truly other-worldly. But the Christian love for God will necessarily go far beyond this Sufi understanding. We know that true love for God results in love for fellow humankind as well. So on the one hand, there is a way to be a holy people and thus measure up to Sufi expectations. On the other hand, we will have to unashamedly go beyond their limited and hence, distorted understanding of love. The real always exceeds the substitute. Hopefully, by life and word, your Sufi friend will see the superiority of the genuine love of Christ in you when compared with his or her inadequate experience.

True Repentance

When it comes to the issues of repentance, understanding of sin, renunciation of the "world" and death to self, the scriptural understanding goes far beyond that of Sufism. We need to remember that Sufism got some of its ideas from Christian monasticism. Monasticism, unfortunately, instead of staying true to its biblical roots, adopted ideas from Neoplatonism, namely, that the physical world of flesh and matter is evil and that all good exists in the spiritual world (Wilson 1989:90). Sin was thought to consist of paying attention to anything in the physical world. Piety was thinking of God only. Repentance, by this rule, was to renounce the world and focus solely on God. Sufism took over these ideas from Neoplatonism through the monastic influence of aberrant Christians. What was lost was the biblical perspective of seeing that the original creation, including man and woman, was good. Instead of seeing man as morally fallen and recoverable, Sufism saw "flight from the world" as the final solution. This, of course, led to a neglect of serving and seeking to save fellow-humankind.

The Christian worker, in this case, is going to have to be very sure of his or her understanding of the biblical explanation of creation, the Fall, God's redemptive acts reaching their climax in the death of Jesus Christ on the cross, the resurrection of Christ with an incorruptible body, and what it means to look forward to a new heaven and a new earth characterized by pure righteousness. The Bible affirms creation and the celebration of life. It affirms humanity with its sexuality. What is to be repented of is the improper use of these gifts and the perverted and selfish distortion of the stewardship of life. The burden is on the Christian worker to show the inadequacy of the Sufi understanding of Creation, the Fall, and Redemption. Sufis believe that man was created weak, not sinful. The "Fall" in the Quran is described as a literal fall or casting down from a lovely garden (paradise) in the heavens. Orthodox Sufis (Sufism can be compatible with Orthodox) believe that redemption is obtained when good deeds outweigh bad deeds. The introduction of biblical truths is the only way to lay the foundation for a true understanding of regeneration (the new birth), baptism (filling of the Holy Spirit), the exchanged life, righteousness by faith, the walk of faith in the Spirit, and the hope of the new heaven and the new earth when Jesus returns as Lord. This leads us on to our next bridging point with Sufism.

Jesus as the Light of the World

As an expression of the Sufi's love for God and concern for internal, spiritual illumination (Divine Light), the devotee is driven to seek a deep, satisfying inner experience of God. In the pursuit of this experience, Sufis, like all "seekers," fall into two camps: those who seek the ecstatic experience itself with its subtle appeals to human pride, and those who are genuine seekers after God. To the first group, all you can do is caution them about seeking the "gift" instead of the Giver. To the second group, we have everything to offer through faith in Jesus Christ. In His own lifetime, Jesus said: "I am the light of the world" (John 8:12), thus claiming deity for Himself. A thousand years before, David had written: "For with you is the fountain of life; in your light we see light" (Ps. 36:9). And John, under the inspiration of the Holy Spirit, wrote of his Lord: "In him was life, and that life was the light of men. The light shines in the darkness, but the darkness has not understood it" (John 1:4, 5).

Truly, in every sense, Jesus is the Light of the World. Not only does He understand in His infinite wisdom how all things were made and why they were made (for He is the one who made them), but He actively sustains all things to this present moment. The Christian worker must learn to present Jesus as the Light of the World, as the Omniscient Creator, as the totally wise and adequate Sustainer and the very epitome of love. On this latter point, John's first letter is so helpful: "God is love. Whoever lives in love lives in God, and God in him" (1 John 4:16). Jesus is God's ultimate expression of that love: "The Son is the radiance of God's glory and the exact representation of his being ..." (Heb. 1:3). Jesus is the embodiment of that love which the Sufi is seeking.

A Christian Understanding of Death to Self

In addition to the life of love, our Sufi friends need to know that the other aspect of "putting on Christ" is death to self, death to the old nature, death to sin. We are now alive to God. It is in this sense, death to sin, that we experience what the Sufis call "annihilation." The apostle Paul wrote of his "annihilation" in the following way: "I have been crucified with Christ and I no longer live, but Christ lives in me. The life I live in the body, I live by faith in the Son of God, who loved me and gave himself for me" (Gal. 2:20). And what a life: the Son of God Himself living in us, living out the perfect life of love in us, through us. Total union with God in Christ. It is what Sufi seekers have been looking for all their lives. And so much more the Sufi never dreamed of: "And we, who with unveiled faces all reflect the Lord's glory, are being transformed into his likeness with ever-increasing glory, which comes from the Lord, who is the Spirit" (2 Cor. 3:18). In God's way, through Christ, by the Spirit, we are being transformed into the very image of God, and we live out that love in practical ways, not by withdrawing from the world, but by plunging back into it to help fellow-humankind. Jesus' own prophetic words become a reality for us. By doing so, we walk in that "Light" for which the Sufi seeks. The proof of the indwelling Light are the good deeds that lead men to recognize the presence of the Father and to give Him the praise.

Sufism's Contextualizing Tendency

Sufism's tendency to be accommodative to its local environment could work for or against a Christian approach. Let us use principles of flexibility and adaptability to afford Sufis the chance to respond to the Gospel in their own local context. This would be characterized by newly written Christian hymns applied to local styles of music. It would mean worship in the vernacular of the people. It would mean we teach Sufis how to be filled with God's Spirit both individually and corporately, God Himself living in them. But it would have to guard against the Sufi tendency to accommodate to the other spirit world.

Sufi Circles to House Churches

And finally, especially in situations where the majority population may be Muslim and even hostile to Christianity, the Sufi tendency to meet in small groups, even closed circles, may lend itself beautifully to the birth and formation of similar patterns of grouping in low-key "house church" movements. This may not only be advantageous, but even necessary in those Muslim countries where there is open persecution of the Christian Church.

CHAPTER 26

JESUS AND THE FOLK MUSLIMS

> Now, Lord, consider their threats and enable your
> servants to speak your word with great boldness. Stretch
> out your hand to heal and perform miraculous signs and
> wonders through the name of your holy servant Jesus
> (Acts 4:29, 30).

Before delving into this chapter, you may want to do a careful review of the material in chapter 13 on Folk Islam. You will recall that by the term "Folk Islam" we mean that on the surface, the people perceive themselves as some kind of Muslim, but in reality, they practice a kind of animistic religion. This form of religion takes the spirit world seriously— very seriously. The whole system of thought, no matter how vague or informal, attempts to explain life as the devotees see it. And what they see are spiritual forces at work either hindering or helping them in their daily lives. For them, there is a spiritual reason for everything that happens. Life, then, consists of appeasing these spiritual powers or attempting to harness them for their good or evil, or at the very least neutralizing them so they cannot cause any harm to anyone or anything. Spirits are seen residing in almost anything, depending on the local variety of religion.

Meeting the Needs of Folk Muslims

Folk Muslims need healing, deliverance, forgiveness, guidance, comfort, strength, encouragement, protection from evil in all of its manifestations. Tragically, they have turned for help to the enemy. And that enemy is more than willing to give the illusion of help through his own kind of "signs and wonders," as long as he can keep them in his power. Folk Muslims, unlike Orthodox Muslims who think they have the answers, are looking for answers. They are looking for "power" against "the powers" that beset them at every turn in life. They are ready, at an experiential level, to consider Jesus who has conquered these "powers" and has given the same power and authority to His disciples today against these enemies. Therefore, while God can certainly reach Folk Muslims in any way He chooses, the most practical level for Christian workers to meet the needs of Folk Muslims is in the spiritual realm, with all the resources they have in Christ.

Remember what Jesus said when the seventy-two returned to Him with great joy because God had used them to heal and to cast out demons:

> I have given you authority to trample on snakes and
> scorpions [an obvious reference to demonic forces] and
> to overcome all the power of the enemy; nothing will
> harm you [that is, no evil from them will enter into you]
> (Luke 10:19).

We who belong to Jesus have access to the same power today. In facing the practices and practitioners of Folk Islam, then, we can expect far more open confrontations and power encounters than in a theological or theosophical form of Islam. It is not that we won't encounter the demonic in other forms of Islam, we will; but in Folk Islam the demonic, the traffic with the spirit world, is more open and apparent.

Major Concerns for the Christian Worker

What then are the major concerns that should guide the Christian worker as he or she attempts to minister among Folk Muslims? Following is a list of qualities that for me are indispensable in working with Folk Muslims:

The worker should know we are engaged in a deadly war (Eph. 6:10-18; 2 Cor. 10:3-6). Peter, who boasted he would never deny Christ, fell. After he recovered, thanks to Christ's intercession, he wrote:

> Your enemy the devil prowls around like a roaring lion
> looking for someone to devour. Resist him, standing firm
> in the faith, because you know that your brothers

throughout the world are undergoing the same kind of sufferings (1 Peter 5:8, 9).

We must develop the mentality of one at war. The enemy is ready to pounce on any weakness in loyalty of heart or performance in battle. This calls for constant alertness.

Jesus must be Lord of your life. Again I turn to Peter, who lived through a major failure in his life on this point. "In your hearts, set apart Christ as Lord. Always be prepared to give an answer to everyone who asks you to give the reason for the hope that you have" (1 Peter 3:15). Satan knows too well how to "devour" the one whose loyalty has slipped. Peter feared people more than God, and he fell. A "household divided against itself will not stand" (Matt. 12:25). Jesus is the active commander in this warfare and He would like to direct the action. We must be in the most intimate relationship with Him and utterly sensitive to His voice as He leads us into these encounters.

The Christian worker, to the best of his or her ability, must have renounced all sin. No gateway must be left open for Satan to enter, accuse or render ineffective. Satan's only way of gaining access or even control of us is through our own sin. Paul wrote to his young disciple Timothy:

> If a man cleanses himself from the latter [that which is ignoble or dishonorable], he will be an instrument for noble purposes, made holy, useful to the Master and prepared to do any good work (2 Tim. 2:21).

John wrote to his readers: "Everyone who has this hope [of the appearing of Jesus Christ] in him purifies himself, just as he is pure" (1 John 3:3). The Christian worker must be filled with the Holy Spirit. Jesus cautioned His disciples to wait until they were "clothed with power from on high" (Luke 24:49). He promised them power for witnessing (Acts 1:8). Paul urged his readers to continue being "filled with the Spirit" (Eph. 5:18). When those of the young persecuted church sought the face of the Lord in prayer for power to do "signs and wonders" in Jesus' name, they were filled afresh and became exceedingly bold in the face of opposition as they preached the Word of the Lord (Acts 4:31).

Every major character in the Bible who accomplished great things for God did so after a special anointing of God's Spirit. It is by the power of God's Spirit that we do anything for the Lord (Zech. 4:6). It is the Holy Spirit who both empowers and leads in these spiritual encounters with Folk Muslims. The Spirit often takes the lead through our intuitions or "words of knowledge" as to what people's problems are. These divinely given insights are usually the clue to the healing or deliverance that follows. The Holy Spirit also gives us special gifts for the warfare: the discerning of spirits, healing, faith, words of knowledge, words of wisdom, the ability to work miracles, prophecies, the ability to speak in other languages, and to interpret languages (1 Cor. 12:7-11).

Love must be supreme in the life of the Christian worker. Jesus, when He walked among the people, was moved with compassion. He saw them "as harassed and helpless, like sheep without a shepherd" (Matt. 9:36). The apostle Paul in explaining his ministry, revealed his motivation: "For Christ's love compels us, because we are convinced that one died for all, and therefore all died" (2 Cor. 5:14). He also wrote that Christ is "in you, the hope of glory. We proclaim him, admonishing and teaching everyone with all wisdom, so that we may present everyone perfect in Christ. To this end I labor, struggling with all his energy, which so powerfully works in me" (Col. 1:27-29). The love of Christ led him to seek out the lost and to do all in God's mighty power to present them perfect in Christ. Our goal as we seek to win Folk Muslims (and every other Muslim too) can be nothing less.

Faith is indispensable in this kind of warfare. How Jesus upbraided His disciples for their unbelief. What open-ended promises He gave them:

> I tell you the truth, if you have faith and do not doubt, not only can you do what was done to the fig tree, but also you can say to this mountain, 'Go, throw yourself into the sea,' and it will be done. If you believe, you will receive whatever you ask for in prayer (Matt. 21:21, 22).

Speaking as a child of the West again, I can testify how all my own education in science, including medical school, worked against my having the kind of faith that expected to see God work supernaturally in response to my faith. But thank God, I am returning to a biblical worldview and am not only learning to believe God for these "great and mighty things," but am discovering how Jesus expects us to imitate Him, to do things the way He modeled them for us even as the first disciples did. Charles Kraft's testimony parallels mine: first you start teaching what the Bible really says, and gradually you learn that these supernatural gifts and power are available to you today. Just say "No" to your unbelief. Believe God for victory in these "power encounters" with the other spirits ruling the lives of Folk Muslims.

Prayer and fasting have a place. The faith mentioned above doesn't necessarily come easily. The reason is our own reluctance and unbelief. For many of us, a good deal of time spent in prayer works changes in us. Christ becomes more real; we become more sensitive to the leading of His Spirit. Faith grows stronger through prayer and studying His Word. Fasting also has a place. Being able to say "No" to your body is often a great help in being able to say "Yes" to the Holy Spirit. Vivienne Stacey's testimony on the preparation in prayer and fasting that preceded the exorcising of a haunted house in Muscat (Oman), where all who entered felt the presence of evil and some even felt depressed or suicidal, is a marvelous demonstration of how power to exorcise came through a long period of prayer and fasting (1986:4-7).

It is best to work in teams in this kind of spiritual warfare. Jesus sent His disciples out two by two (Luke 10:1). Kraft talks about "accountability" (1989:175). Stacey highly recommends approaching these "encounters" as a team (1986:7). Bishop Michael Green approaches teams under the theme of "unity" (1981:251). There is, apparently, an incremental increase in power when two or three are gathered in Jesus' name to do this work:

> Again, I tell you that if two of you on earth agree about anything you ask for, it will be done for you by my Father in heaven. For where two or three come together in my name, there am I with them (Matt. 18:19, 20).

The care in counseling and discipling those who have been helped, healed or delivered is so important following their experience of the Lord's touch. It is especially important to see that they acknowledge Christ as

Lord and are filled with His Spirit. Otherwise, what Jesus warned could happen:

> When an evil spirit comes out of a man, it goes through arid places seeking rest and does not find it. Then it says, 'I will return to the house I left.' When it arrives, it finds the house unoccupied, swept clean and put in order. Then it goes and takes with it seven other spirits more wicked than itself, and they go in and live there. And the final condition of that man is worse than the first ... (Matt. 12:43-45).

Further Concerns

The Christian worker is faced with a two-edged challenge in Folk Islam. The first is the "power encounter": Christ versus Satan and his demonic forces. This takes place at every level in Muslims' lives. No matter where you turn, you see these all-pervasive Folk Islamic practices. Each one represents an open door for alien spirit power. When Muslims come to Christ, they will have to renounce all of it, each and every practice. Satan does not easily let go of his subjects. There will be prices to pay after the successful encounters in which ordinary Muslims are healed, delivered from their lifelong fear of spirits and death, set free from demonic powers, and brought into the kingdom of God's dear Son, Jesus Christ.

The second concern is to provide the young believer with a whole new way of life to replace the one he or she has just been delivered from. Paul Hiebert aptly comments:

> We are called to challenge the structures and beliefs of existing religious systems, even as we invite their followers to turn to Christ. There are important truths in other religions that need not be destroyed, but other religions exist in systems in rebellion against God. They, therefore, oppose those from their ranks who turn to Christ (Hiebert 1989: 56).

Folk Muslims will first have to see power operating in the life of the Christian worker. They will have to see that the One who lives in Christians is greater than the one who lives in the world. The Christian worker will have to demonstrate that Christ's power is superior, that we can live a life free from fear, that there is a Holy Spirit who can guide us, empower us, even thwart our enemies. There will be various kinds of miracles of healing, deliverances and possibly raisings from the dead. But after "trampling underfoot all the enemy," and restoring the new believer to wholeness, there remains the even more daunting task of providing a whole new way of looking at life. Jesus must be the new focal point for this new worldview.

It may be appropriate to develop equivalent Christian ceremonies to replace the old for passing through the stages of life, from the "cradle to the grave." New celebrations could be invented to take the place of the old in terms of the religious year: an appropriate celebration of the Incarnation (Christmas), the Atonement (Good Friday) and the Resurrection (Easter). In rural societies, taking cues from the Old Testament, Christian celebrations may need to coincide with the seasons of the year to replace the local ones. The Christian worker dare not fall into the sterile compartmentalization of secularized Christianity, with its do-nothing approach to the seasons of life; he or she must have thought through what a new worldview would look like for the new believers coming out of Folk Islam. And for all the stages of life—birth, naming, puberty, marriage, childbearing, death—which are so richly celebrated in Folk Islamic circles, the Christian worker should provide thoroughly biblical, and in so far as it is appropriate, functional substitutes.

In addition to ceremonies, whole new sets of values need to be taught in personal lifestyle, family relationships and relationships to the larger society, as well as to the physical environment, based on the biblical values of stewardship concerning creation.

Finally, the Christian worker must be prepared for serious backlashes from Folk Islamic practitioners who will be deprived of their businesses, their incomes, their places in society, and/or their livelihoods. Almost every time the apostles demonstrated the mighty power of God over the other powers, it was followed by persecution, beatings, jail and even martyrdom. The Christian worker has to be ready to pay with his or her life for daring to challenge the enemy powers and setting their prisoners free.

CHAPTER 27

JESUS AND THE MILITANT MUSLIMS

One wonderfully unique quality about Jesus was His ability to cope with any situation. His diagnosis was always correct. His response was always appropriate. He would not have been put off by militant Muslims. After all, one of His disciples was Simon the Zealot (Acts 1:13)

What is it that drives a zealot? The most obvious answer is dissatisfaction with the status quo. In Jesus' day, religion had become a sham. The secularized Sadducees were opposed by the supernaturalistic Pharisees. The Essenes had developed a pietism of withdrawal. Politically, the Jewish leaders were compromised. A foreign army occupied the land. The king, part Jew and part Arab, was the son of a man who had bought the Kingdom from Rome. The people, in their shame and frustration, were divided about what to do. Some looked for a deliverer, the Messiah. Others wanted to take matters into their own hands, revolt against Rome and its puppet king, and install a leader from a purified Judaism. Still others thought the Messiah would lead such a revolt.

Is the Muslim world any different today? Not much. It is true that now the Western colonial powers no longer occupy Muslim lands, but the hateful shadow of Western influence lingers. Muslim peoples no longer have a caliph as the worldwide head of their community. *Dar al-Islam* is divided into forty-nine countries, at the present time, which represent seventy-seven percent of all Muslims, and the other twenty-three percent live as minorities in other lands. Furthermore, as we have seen in earlier chapters, Muslims are subdivided into 408 different major ethnic groups. Theologically, they present a wide variety of persuasions from Orthodox to Mystics, and with various levels of compromise ranging from secularism to syncretistic blends of Islam and animistic religions.

Economics, too, is a concern. With the exception of those Muslim countries which have been blessed with oil, the remainder are, as a group, at the bottom of the economic scale of all the world's countries (see appendix E). There is widespread dissatisfaction with the status quo in most of the Muslim world. In Orthodox Muslim thinking, these things should not be. Islam is "the best and final religion." It should be in the ascendancy everywhere on its march to world domination.

The question a militant Muslim asks is, "What went wrong?" The usual Muslim answer to that question is, "It is because we have departed from original pristine Islam. That is why God has not blessed us and why our enemies get the best of us. And it is because of what those enemies have done to us that our people are so poor. If we return to Islam, the way it is supposed to be, then God will begin to bless us again and we will surely dominate the world the way God intended for us to do."

Painfully, scores of leaders and would-be leaders throughout the Muslim world feel that they have the solution to Muslim problems and they intend to impose their solution on their Muslim subjects and neighbors. This has led to interminable squabbling between rulers and would-be rulers, as well as to destructive power struggles between rulers of various Muslim countries.

From my own observations, militant Muslims fall into at least two groups. One group is quite sincere in lamenting the unwholesome condition of their people. The second group is focused on acquiring power—naked power to conquer others. The first group, not knowing the true Gospel, turns back to what they know of God and His ways through the Quran and the teaching of Muhammad. In reality, the Quran mirrors biblical material pointing to high ethical and moral standards on many issues. To these sincere searchers of righteousness, Jesus would have a lot to say in pointing them to His kingdom teaching. He always cared about the plight of the people and He offered them a better way of life. In the Sermon on the Mount, Jesus ensured blessings for those who were poor in spirit, mournful, meek, hungry and thirsty for righteousness, merciful, pure in heart, peacemaking and willing to be persecuted because of righteousness (Matt. 5:3-10).

On another occasion, through a parable, Jesus described the ones who would be blessed by the Father as those who fed the hungry, gave drink to the thirsty, invited strangers in, gave clothes to those who needed them, took care of the sick and visited those in prison (Matt. 25:34-36). On yet another occasion, in response to a woman who had the wrong concept of blessing, Jesus said, "Blessed rather are those who hear the word of God and obey it" (Luke 11:28).

Yes, Jesus cared about bettering the lot of mankind. Like Abraham of old, He sought to bring blessing to all the people of the earth. But Jesus also knew that how we obtained these blessings was just as important as our concern for righteousness. He knew the power of the evil one to deceive. He knew that rulers, claiming to be benefactors, bringers of blessings to their subject people, would resort to the most heinous and ruthless methods to bring these long-sought "blessings." And so He spoke against using the sword as a way to bring the kingdom of God (John 18:36). He opposed the idea that the ends justify the means. The wrong methods could actually bring a curse (Genesis 3:17; Genesis 12:3; Joshua 8:34). Innocent people would be harassed or put to death along with the bad in such a ruler's effort to impose his or her will on the country or party.

For those militant Muslims who have been deceived in thinking they were justified in their violent measures, not realizing that they were perpetrating evil in the name of "good," Jesus would have hard words to say. He would challenge and call attention to their oppressive methods. He would say to them, as He did to His own generation, "For all who draw the sword will die by the sword" (Matt. 26:52). Jesus taught us that we are like salt and yeast and light. All work quietly, yet they change the quality, the texture and the landscape of life. As He said to Peter long ago, so He would reiterate today, "Put your sword back in its place …" (Matt. 26:52). And we who work in His stead will have to find ways to say to the Muslim militants who would advocate violence, "There is a better way."

CHAPTER 28

JESUS AND THE SECULAR MUSLIMS

> Don't you know that friendship with the world is hatred
> toward God? Anyone who chooses to be a friend of the
> world becomes an enemy of God (James 4:4).

Muslims who have compromised themselves with modern secular thought may exhibit a wide range of Islamic religious behavior. The dilemma faced by this type of Muslim is that Islam claims too much for itself.

The Absolutistic Model of Muhammad

Muhammad set his life forth as the norm for all humankind for all time. This might have worked if he had separated the religious side of his life from his political and military involvement, but he did not. The Muslim anxiety goes deeper when we learn that Muhammad made no arrangement for a successor regarding how the *Ummah*, the "Community of Believers," should govern themselves after his demise. But perhaps the most crushing omission of all was Muhammad's failure to anticipate the rise of the technological society.

The rise of the West and the amazing technological achievements of a non-Islamic civilization have left Islam in a predicament. Islam, as a total way of life, was supposed to be the divinely revealed way for humankind for all time. But it neither fits the present century, nor can it explain how leadership has passed to non-Islamic peoples. The result is that we are witnessing a bewildering array of Muslim reactions to this phenomenon of the ascendancy of the West.

Today, on the one hand, many kinds of reactionary Islamic movements want to renounce the West altogether along with its technological achievements and go back to the rudimentary seventh century lifestyle of Muhammad. On the other hand, there have been and continue to be countless ways in which Muslims have sought to accommodate to the ideas and technological achievements of the West.

At the far right of the spectrum, we find such reformers as Muhammad Abduh (1849-1905) of Egypt, who in the journal *al-Manar* tried "to find in Quranic verses anticipation of modern technical discoveries in medicine, biology and geology" (Cragg 1965:40). A whole stream of devout Muslims have followed this line ever since.

Equally devout, even passionate in his defense of Orthodox Islam, Muhammad Haykal advocated that Muslims learn all they can from the West in order to recover their former glory:

> Nevertheless, the Orient [Muslim world] stands today in great need of learning from Western thought, literature and art. The present of the Orient is separated from its past by centuries of lethargy and conservatism which have locked its old healthy mind in ignorance and suspicion of anything new (1976: xlix).

It is interesting to note that a figure like the late Dr. Muhammad Kamil Husain of Cairo ridiculed this idea in his *Miscellany*, in an article entitled, "Scientific Exegesis of the Quran—A Stupid Heresy" (Cragg 1985:132). Husain's reasoning was that the Quran was only intended as a religious book and never meant to be used the way the above mentioned scholars were trying to use it. Other Muslim thinkers have not been so devout as they have sought to loosen the grip of *Shariah* Law on their lives. We once again look at the astonishing case of Salman Rushdie, who attempted to write, in novel form, about his search for identity as he sought unsuccessfully to fit into English society after abandoning Bombay and his Islamic roots. In an interview with *Newsweek*, he said of his book, *The Satanic Verses*, "It is a migrant's eye view of the world", and it "is, in part, a secular man's reckoning with the religious spirit" (*Newsweek*, February 12, 1990:53). The Iranian Shiite government concluded that he had gone too far in embracing secularism.

The Disenchanted

Somewhere between these extremes is a vast array of Muslim men and women who, for whatever reason, do not say their prayers regularly, do not keep the fast, do not give regular alms to the poor or to religious causes, do not intend to go on a pilgrimage, do not even believe Muhammad is relevant today, and certainly are not ready to fight in a holy war for Islam. And yet by reason of birth, ethnicity or nationality, they perceive themselves as Muslims. I have heard the following statements in my travels throughout the Muslim world: "I was born a Muslim; I cannot leave the faith of my family," "To be a Turk is to be a Muslim," and "Everyone in Saudi Arabia is a Muslim; you cannot be anything else." Outwardly, they claim to be Muslims; inwardly, they are something else. It is that "something else" that fascinates us. What kind of "something else?"

Jesus Among the Materialists

Jesus, moving among the irreligious materialists of His day, I'm sure, tailored His approach to whatever He found in the human heart. In the case of people like Muhammad Abduh and his followers who have retained their piety while trying to find prophetic indications of scientific inventions in Quranic verses, He might ask, "Why are you trying to credit Muhammad for what I have shown my children in other parts of the world? Watch out for jealousy. Watch out for misguided zeal that would cause you to attribute to Muhammad what I never gave him. I did not show these things to Muhammad. Be honest. His teaching was only a reflection of seventh century Arabic culture. I will teach you the meaning of life. I will show you how my teaching relates to the world at any point in history." And then Jesus might have added these words: "I am the way, the truth and the life. No one comes to the Father except through me" (John 14:6).

Jesus and the Downtrodden

I think of the Muslim weighed down with the cares of the world and too poor to have leisure time—no time out while trying to put bread on the table. He would like to be more religious than he is, but because of life's grinding needs he finds no time for religion. I can hear Jesus saying again as He did when He walked the earth:

> Come to me, all you who are weary and burdened, and I
> will give you rest. Take my yoke upon you and learn

217

from me, for I am gentle and humble in heart, and you will find rest for your souls. For my yoke is easy and my burden is light (Matt. 11:28-30).

Jesus would continue to exhibit the same compassion today as He did when He saw the oppressed, the sick, the hungry, and those oppressed by demons in His own day. He would heal the sick. He would deliver those oppressed by demons. He would live out the true ethics of His kingdom. He would still fit His description found in Matthew 9:36: "When he saw the crowds, he had compassion on them, because they were harassed and helpless, like sheep without a shepherd." He would tell again the parable of the Good Shepherd who went looking for His lost sheep until He found it. He would live among the poor again. He would share their poverty and their suffering. But He would also bring joy and the strength to endure into the midst of their troubles. The guilt and despair of their "compromised" faith would give way to inexpressible joy in the presence of their Savior. They would discover that His mercies are everlasting and His compassion never fails. This is the kind of Christian worker needed among these people, those in whom the Spirit of Jesus lives.

Jesus and the Disillusioned

For those who have turned away from religion because they saw through its sham, concluded there was something not quite right about Muhammad and his teaching, and therefore became disillusioned, Jesus would invite them to overcome their cynicism. He would invite them to come and see what He is really like for themselves. He would awaken faith in them again, just as He did in the days of Nathaniel. Jesus saw past the cynicism of the crushed idealism in Nathaniel, and He appealed to that when He said: "Here is a true Israelite, in whom there is nothing false" (John 1:47). Nathaniel was drawn immediately to Him.

Jesus and the Rebel

But there are other types of secularized Muslims. There are those who rejected Islamic religion, all or in part, because they really did not want to submit. They wanted to follow their own desires. They wanted to take advantage of the extraordinary freedom developed in secular societies to follow their own selfish natures. Jesus met the same kind of people in His own day. He told them stories so they could draw their own conclusions about themselves. To the man who gave way to materialism and went on building bigger and better barns so he could "Take life easy; eat, drink and be merry" (Luke 12:19), Jesus said, "You fool! This very night your life will be demanded from you. Then who will get what you have prepared for yourself?" (Luke 12:20). In spite of our desire to be sympathetic with Muslims in cultural ways—to appreciate the best in their culture—and to try not to be offensive, there comes a time when those Muslims who are heedless must be shocked back to reality, just like the same kind of foolish pleasure-seeker in any other culture.

Jesus and the Socialist Muslim

There is one more kind of Muslim who deserves attention. He or she is the one who has embraced some form of socialist or communist teaching. Probably, for very good reasons, this kind of person has become fed up with the status quo in his or her own society. He or she sees a wide gap between the rich and the poor. He or she sees the insensitivity and brutality of those in power. He or she is convinced that the situation is hopeless unless radical action is taken. Unlike the Muslim fundamentalist who feels the solution is to return to pure Islamic roots, this person sees religion as the problem, the soporific that lulls people to sleep so that they no longer can see or think. For this person, socialism or communism promises a better world. The only problem is that it commits the believer to endless class warfare, with the senseless destruction of human life, and results in the rise of a new ruling class just as abusive as the ones they eliminated.

Buried deep within this kind of Muslim, at least initially, is a deep sense of indignation, a longing for righteousness. This person burns within when he or she sees the injustices of life. The problem arises when he or she feels matters should be taken into one's own hands. Things should be made right, even if it means resorting to violence. This type of Muslim feels the ends justify the means. Unbeknownst to this activist, he or she has subtlety slipped over the edge from being a subject of God to playing God—taking things into one's own hands. In anger, the "kingdom of man" has been substituted for the kingdom of God. We can rejoice that this person is free from the grip of Orthodox Islam, but we have to find a way to bring him or her back to God.

In dealing with this kind of secularized Muslim (for he or she might still call himself or herself a cultural Muslim, if not a religious one), the Christian worker will need a very strong sense that God controls events in the world and the ultimate triumph of good over evil. Moreover, this Christian worker will have to be well grounded in the principles of how the kingdom of God operates. Jesus came to introduce the kingdom of God (Mark 1:15). He taught a level of ethics and morality higher than anything else the world has ever seen (Matt. 5-7). But He also taught patience and suffering, the inevitability of persecution from those who had not yet, and maybe never would, convert to God's ways. He taught the inexorable spread of the "yeast" of the Good News, of the spread of "light" into a dark world, of the believer being like "salt" in the midst of what otherwise would decay and be thrown away.

The Christian worker, in dealing with a Muslim socialist, really needs to have thought through the biblical teaching on the kingdom of God and be able to explain it convincingly to this shattered idealist who may otherwise commit himself to a path of senseless violence—and to no avail. In the end, this type of Muslim has to be gently led back to a belief in God, to the fact that God is in control, and that all things are leading to the great day when God shall step back on the stage of human history in visible form to make all things right. And, of course, Christian workers must first be convinced of these things themselves before they can persuade others.

CHAPTER 29

JESUS AND THE AHMADIS

Watch out that no one deceives you. For many will come
in my name claiming, 'I am the Christ,' and will deceive
many (Matt. 24:4, 5).

The doctrine of the *Mahdi* is common to the Sunnis and the Shias.
There is a minority opinion that the *Mahdi* is Christ; but the majority
believe that he is separate from Christ and will return before Christ to
restore the pristine purity of Islam. After this, the Antichrist will come to
lead away his followers, and then Christ will appear to destroy the
Antichrist. Unfortunately for Christians, Mirza Ghulam Ahmad perverted
the above doctrine by saying that one of the signs of the *Mahdi* was the
ability to discern the *Dajjal* or Antichrist, and that as the *Mahdi*, he
discerned this spirit in present-day Christianity.

The strange doctrines which he introduced concerning Christ were
that Christ insulted His mother at the wedding at Cana, showed cowardice
on the cross in crying out to God, "My God, my God, why have you
forsaken me?", and only appeared to die on the cross, whereas, He merely
swooned, revived, itinerated to Kashmir, preached until He was 120 years
old, and then died there. Ahmadis will show you His tomb in Srinagar
today. Cragg feels that Mirza Ghulam Ahmad has had a pernicious effect
on Muslims, causing them to feel even more animus towards Christians
than they already do (1956:251).

Ahmad's attraction for his followers is that he nullified the orthodox
doctrines of killing apostates and "holy war" as military conflict. He also
taught that Islam was totally compatible with modern scientific inventions.
Even though the Ahmadi Movement was declared non-Muslim by the
Pakistan High Court in 1974, it continues to flourish throughout large
parts of the Muslim world with the exception of the Middle East. This

sect is included here because it is so widespread and so visible. It demands our attention.

Ahmadi Effect on Christians

Relationships between Muslims and Christians have been much damaged by this energetic sect. In addition to claiming the spirit of antichrist worked in present-day Christianity, Mirza Ghulam Ahmad concluded that Christianity had strayed from its origins and could no longer be considered a religion of the *Ahl-i-Kitab*, "The People of the Book" (Glasse 1989:28). Mirza Ghulam Ahmad's zeal for Islam, as re-interpreted by him, was to rid Islam of any "Christian dimensions implanted in it by orthodox Muslim tradition" (Cragg 1965:161), meaning that the idea of Christ returning as a Muslim to lead the whole world to Islam should be eliminated. Ahmad's followers have also vilified Christ by suggesting that his relationship to Mary Magdalene was unsavory. Cragg has neatly summarized this negative effect:

> This contemptuous attitude to Jesus is checked, and in many cases excluded, by the Orthodox Muslims' recognition of Him as "one of the prophets." Nonetheless, in so far as the Ahmadiyya Movements have changed Muslim attitudes toward Christianity, they have done so in the direction of greater alienation and a more rigid Muslim self-sufficiency (Cragg 1956:251).

Vulnerability of Ahmadis to Truth

On two counts, then, the Ahmadi Movement attracts our attention as Christians. The first is the need to "stand firm in one spirit, contending as one man for the faith of the gospel without being frightened in any way by those who oppose you" (Phil. 1:27, 28). We must "always be prepared to give an answer to everyone who asks you to give the reason for the hope that you have" (1 Peter 3:15).

Second, Ahmadis are in an untenable position vis-a-vis the Orthodox Muslim community. They have been officially declared non-Muslims in Pakistan, the land of their adopted citizenship, and are perceived as such throughout much of the Muslim world. They cannot justify their position from the Quran or the *Hadith* to their Muslim audiences.

Similarly, they are unable to justify their vilification of Christ from scriptural grounds; either theirs or ours. They are susceptible to well-reasoned Gospel presentations, as evidenced by the conversion and life of the well-known ex-Ahmadi Christian evangelist, the late Chowdhry Inayatullah Mujahhid of Pakistan. Even these misled and spiteful "sons of Ishmael" are winnable. We should make every effort to win them for the sake of the Gospel.

Reaching the Ahmadis

Working with these kinds of Muslims requires a great deal of love, patience, and tenacity of scholarship. Ahmadis tend to know the Bible very well, but for the wrong reasons. They look for the problem texts, the apparent contradictions between passages, and all kinds of what they consider to be logical fallacies. Ever since 1974, because they have been officially declared non-Muslims, Ahmadis have been somewhat more open to dialogue with Christians, at least, according to this writer's personal experience.

In attempting to develop a sympathetic attitude towards the Ahmadis, I think there are two areas in which we can show that sympathy. The first is in their revulsion towards the extreme harshness of Orthodox *Shariah* Law, as mentioned above in connection with apostasy and *jihad.* And second, in trying to show the compatibility of religion with modern technological and scientific achievements of twentieth century man.

But in two other areas, the Christian worker is going to have to be very skillful in showing the impossibility of Ahmad's position both from the Quran and from the Bible. The Christian worker must have a sufficient grasp of both in order to show that Ahmad is a false prophet in the eyes of both Muslims and Christians. In the case of Orthodox Islam, Ahmad's teaching does not agree with the approved text of the Quran. The Christian worker will have to show enough familiarity with the Quran to support the following points.

According to Orthodox Islam, there can be no prophet after Muhammad. Muhammad to them is the "Seal of the Prophets," meaning the last and greatest Prophet: "Muhammad is not the father of any of your men, but (he is) the Apostle of God, and the Seal of the Prophets: and God has full knowledge of all things" (Q. 33:40). Yusuf Ali's comment on this verse is typical of all Muslim commentators: "The holy Prophet Muhammad closed the long line of apostles. God's teaching is and will always be continuous, but there has been and will be no Prophet after Muhammad" (1977:1119, footnote 3731).

Holy War is incumbent upon every true Muslim: "Fighting is prescribed for you, and ye dislike it. But it is possible that ye dislike a thing which is good for you, and ye love a thing which is bad for you. But God knoweth, and ye know not" (Q. 2:216).

The penalty for apostasy in Orthodox Islam really is death: "But if they turn renegades, seize them and slay them wherever ye find them" (Q. 4:89). The famous Muslim commentator, Baidhawi, who is representative of all, wrote on the above passage: "Whosoever turns back from his belief, openly or secretly, take him and kill him wheresoever ye find him, like any other infidel" (Zwemer 1924:33).

The question to ask the Ahmadi is always, "By what authority do you teach your doctrine?" It is certainly not by authority of the only official sourcebook Orthodox Islam ever had, the Quran.

The Christian worker will have to show extreme patience in dealing with Ahmadi attacks on Christian doctrine and the claim that Mirza Ghulam Ahmad is the returned Christ. The Christian will have to show the Ahmadi that neither the Bible nor subsequent Christian history can support the outlandish claims of Mirza Ghulam Ahmad. This will necessarily plunge the Christian into a laborious and detailed defense of the genuineness, authenticity and divine inspiration of the Bible in the originals and the reliability of the present day translations of it. For a detailed rebuttal to Muslim attacks, the reader should turn ahead to chapter 31.

Having established the credibility of the Bible, the Christian worker may then proceed to use it to overturn these false claims of Mirza Ghulam Ahmad. On the basis of the Bible and history, the Christian worker should have no trouble presenting the irrefutable material for the actual death of Jesus on the cross, His burial and resurrection from the dead, and His appearance to hundreds before His ascension to heaven (1 Cor. 15:4-8), to say nothing of His pouring out the Holy Spirit on His believers from the day of Pentecost, the same Holy Spirit who is with us today. The healings, deliverances and miracles are present testimonies to the reality of His kingdom and His rule.

But it is on Ahmad's claim to be the returned Messiah that the Christian, using the biblical prophecies about Christ's return, should have the easiest time. For example, just consider the following selection of verses concerning Christ's return:

> At that time the sign of the Son of Man will appear in the sky, and all the nations of the earth will mourn. They will see the Son of Man coming on the clouds of the sky, with power and great glory. And he will send his angels with a loud trumpet call, and they will gather his elect from the four winds, from one end of the heavens to the other (Matt. 24:30, 31).

> For the Lord himself will come down from heaven, with a loud command, with the voice of the archangel and with the trumpet call of God, and the dead in Christ will rise first. After that, we who are still alive and are left will be caught up together with them in the clouds to meet the Lord in the air. And so we will be with the Lord forever (1 Thess. 4:16, 17).

> But the day of the Lord will come like a thief. The heavens will disappear with a roar; the elements will be destroyed by fire, and the earth and everything in it will be laid bare [or burned up] (2 Peter 3:10).

The signs and wonders, the awe, the power, the majesty attending the return of Christ are so stupendous, so unmistakably evident, worldwide, to the people of all nations, that the claims of this false pretender seem ridiculous in comparison. Because Ahmadis tend to be contentious, and very good debaters, the Christian worker will need to be skillful in his or her use of Scripture.

Ahmadis Are Winnable

There are three reasons why the Ahmadis are winnable. First, their position is untenable with regard to the Quran. They have no basis of authority other than the writings of their founder, as the Quran has already been rejected as their final authority. Second, they have been officially declared non-Muslims and are perceived as such throughout the Muslim world. In other words, they have no real base in Islam. They are an isolated group and are even heavily persecuted by Orthodox Muslims. This sense of isolation has made many of them open to Christian friends. Third, they already have an unusual familiarity with the Bible. Since they use it to build their case, it only remains for the Christian worker to show that all of the Bible is trustworthy in order to persuade them of the full biblical truth.

We might add to the above that because of the spiritual nature of the kingdom of God as taught in the Bible, there is no incompatibility between the Bible and modern scientific inventions, one of their own points of concern. And of course, all the other principles of ministry we have discussed earlier in this book apply. We are to love them, meet them at their points of human need, and witness in the power of the Holy Spirit, while praying that God would deliver them from the deceptions that have bound them through their false prophet's teaching.

CHAPTER 30

JESUS AND THE AFRICAN-AMERICAN MUSLIMS

> Is not this the kind of fasting I have chosen: to loose the
> chains of injustice and untie the cords of the yoke, to set
> the oppressed free and break every yoke (Isa. 58:6)?

The above quote was spoken by the Lord to His people, reflecting His concern for the oppressed in the land. Today, these words have become a universal cry for the oppressed of the whole earth. They could be applied anywhere, including all of the Muslim countries of the world. But in this work, because I live in the United States, the words are applied to the still unsolved racial problems in my country. God cares about oppression anywhere, because we were all made in His image. And His nature is to show that He cares. The Lord truly is, as our Muslim friends say every day of their lives, "The All Merciful One, the All Compassionate." They got it right. This is how He has revealed Himself in word and deed from the time of Adam and Eve to this present moment. "When he [Jesus] saw the crowds, he had compassion on them, because they were harassed and helpless, like sheep without a shepherd" (Matt. 9:36).

Healing the Racial Wounds

At one point in time, I wanted to team up with leading African-American pastors from the inner city of Los Angeles to reach those African-Americans who were disposed to move toward Islam or had already become Muslims. Representatives of five of the leading downtown African-American churches came to my office for a consultation on this subject. We never got around to the subject for which the meeting was called! Instead of joining forces with them to reach African-American Muslims, I listened for two hours to non-stop complaints against white evangelicals who fled the inner city with their congregations! These pastors felt utterly abandoned by their white Christian brothers. They informed me that African-American Muslims could not be reached until these Muslims could see unity between white and African-American Christians. The healing will have to start where the African-American pastors feel wounded.

This was reinforced in a conversation I had with both African-American and white evangelical leaders concerning why there had to be an African-American National Association of Evangelicals, when there already was a National Association of Evangelicals ostensibly for all. The answer I received was that the white leaders were not willing to share their power with emerging African-American leaders. African-American Christians could only lead by forming a separate organization based on race and color.

What would Jesus do if He were here today? There is not a doubt in my mind that He would lead us right into the heart of the African-American areas of our population, love them, heal them and bring salvation to them— and shame anyone on either side who was prejudiced. In His own day, Jesus led His disciples into the territory of the hated Samaritans. Here in the United States, our African-American brothers and sisters are our "Samaritan" neighbors.

It will take a deep sense of repentance on the part of the white majority Christian population of this country to convince alienated African-Americans that we love them, that God loves them, and that God's love lives in us. This repentance can take many forms.

Moses, Daniel and Nehemiah took their forefathers' sins to heart and confessed them to God. They interceded for their people. And God was pleased to respond to their prayers. Read how Moses prayed:

> The next day Moses said to the people, "You have committed a great sin. But now I will go up to the Lord; perhaps I can make atonement for your sin." So Moses went back to the Lord and said, "Oh, what a great sin these people have committed! ... But now, please forgive their sin—but if not, then blot me out of the book you have written" (Ex. 32:30-32).

Moses knew that God was going to destroy the people for their great sin. He went before God and confessed the sins of the people, even though he personally had not been part of their sin, and God heard him.

Daniel, living in exile and recalling the reason why his people were in exile, prayed to the Lord his God and confessed:

> O Lord, the great and awesome God, who keeps his covenant of love with all who love him and obey his commands, we have sinned and done wrong. We have been wicked and have rebelled; we have turned away from your commands and laws ... Lord, you are righteous, but this day we are covered with shame ... because of our unfaithfulness to you ... O Lord, in keeping with all your righteous acts, turn away your anger and your wrath ... We do not make requests of you because we are righteous, but because of your great mercy. O Lord, listen! O Lord, forgive! O Lord, hear and act! O my God, do not delay, because ... your people bear your Name (Dan. 9:4-19).

And the Lord heard his prayer. This prayer led to the return of the Israelites to their homeland. God sent an angel to explain the unfolding of the future to Daniel. He obviously moved on the heart of Cyrus, the ruler, too. The restoration took place because Daniel prayed for it and for forgiveness for his people.

Nehemiah, also living as an exile, inquired about how things were back in Jerusalem. When his brother told him what it was really like, he took it to heart and prayed for his people:

> O Lord, God of heaven, the great and awesome God, who keeps his covenant of love with those who love him and obey his commands, let your ear be attentive and your eyes open to hear the prayer your servant is praying before you day and night for your servants ... I confess the sins we ... including myself and my father's house, have committed against you. We have acted very wickedly

> toward you ... Remember the instruction you gave your
> servant ... saying, 'If you are unfaithful, I will scatter
> you among the nations, but if you return to me and obey
> my commands, then even if your exiled people are at the
> farthest horizon, I will gather them from there and bring
> them to the place I have chosen as a dwelling for my
> Name' ... Give your servant success today by granting
> him favor in the presence of this man (Neh. 1:5-11).

God heard the prayer of Nehemiah, too. He granted Nehemiah favor
in the eyes of a foreign king and used him to rebuild the broken walls of
Jerusalem, to restore the Law, and ultimately, to restore the proper worship
of God in the Temple.

In my opinion, despite the unique history of the United States, with
its early experience of slavery followed by the Civil War and emancipation
of the slaves, discrimination against African-American families still occurs.
The continuing discrimination and inequalities between the races must
be dealt with by the majority community if a sense of dignity and equality
is ever to be restored to our African-American brothers and sisters.

Reaching African-American Muslims

Assuming that the major problem in reaching African-American
Muslims in the United States is a racial issue, I suggest that it is the
obligation of white Americans to address this racial problem. This can be
done in two ways. The first way is to show a genuine repentance for what
our white forefathers did to cause suffering among African-Americans in
the United States. We also need to be concerned about alleviating that
suffering, publicly and privately, by doing whatever needs to be done to
make amends and insure equal opportunity for all. The second way is to
pray for God's forgiveness for what we and our forefathers may have been
guilty of. Below is a suggested type of prayer.

> O Father God, You who have made us all in Your image,
> You who have created us all from one common mother
> and father, we come to You with broken hearts because
> of the hatreds that we have created between the various
> races in Your family.

We confess our sins and the sins of our forefathers who enslaved millions of the African-Americans, beat and abused them, allowed many to die, raped and shamed their women, and separated their rightful husbands from their wives.

We confess that to this present time, in spite of the progress in equality and race relations, we still have not conquered our prejudices and discrimination. We confess that this is hurting the healing of African-Americans families, is contributing to their pain in terms of loss of economic opportunity, damaged self-image, and general malaise in their approach to life.

We remember Your teaching about respecting the minorities in our midst, admitting that at one time we ourselves were strangers in this land and confess that we have failed to live up to the teaching of Your Word.

Forgive us, Heavenly Father, for all the ways in which we have not loved our African-American neighbors as ourselves. Forgive us for the ways in which we have accepted the power structures that have deprived our African-American neighbors of equal educational, economic and social advancement opportunities.

O Father, teach us Your ways of loving and relating to our African-American neighbors. Teach us Your way of aiding in the restoration of the dignity of the African-American father and the rebuilding of the family. Forgive us for the ways in which we have made our brothers feel inferior, inadequate, even unwanted.

Lord, teach us how to put the same value on their lives as we believe You have put on ours.

Forgive us for aggravating their pain to the point that they feel more drawn to the teachings of Islam than to the teaching of Your dear Son, Jesus Christ.

Show us the way to recover them for Your blessed kingdom, to bring them to the true light, and to show them by our love and concern the way of salvation.

O Father, forgive these racial sins, past and present, and restore our fellowship with one another in the bond of love through Jesus Christ our Lord. Amen.

This prayer should be followed by practical concern as we each do our part to redress this grievous wrong in our society. My own conviction is that African-American Islam will lose its racist attraction when love is exhibited between members of the white and African-American Christian communities.

Once we have done everything we can to redress the wrongs that we and our ancestors have committed, we will be free to tackle the absurdity of the religious heresy of the racist Islamic movement among the African-Americans, as well as the orthodox African-American Muslims, the same way we would any other orthodox Muslims.

Those readers who may not have come from the stock of those responsible for the race problem in the United States should feel free to minister to African-American Muslims the same way they would any other kind of Muslim. That is, minister to their human, material or physical needs, help them escape the theological deceptions of all varieties of Islam, and bring them into the kingdom of God's dear Son.

As an aside, thank God that millions of African-Americans have found their new identity in the Suffering Savior, and that today proportionately more African-Americans are evangelical Christians than whites.

There are deep and abiding wounds in the psyche of the African-American citizens of the United States. By and large they still are a wounded people, wounded by the continuing, sometimes open, sometimes subtle, discrimination that exists. It will take time and changes of attitude on the part of the white majority to bring complete healing to these wounds.

PART SIX

THEOLOGICAL ISSUES BETWEEN ISLAM AND CHRISTIANITY

INTRODUCTION

Islam teaches an attractive form of monotheism and salvation by works. Whether it arrives by war, businessmen who stay and marry, or the "singing" Sufis doesn't matter. It boasts that it is the religion of the natural man. Polygamy, concubinage, and slavery are taught. It appeals to the male ego and the male sex drive. It teaches vengeance more than forgiveness. In the beginning it is accommodative (Quran 2:256 "No compulsion in religion"). In Sudan, it tolerated ancestor worship. Almost everywhere, it tolerates animistic, spiritualistic practices. Later, as it tightens its grip on the new adherents, it goes back to *Shariah* Law, the *Hadith*, and the Quran. It establishes the model behavior of the founder, Muhammad—who was a seventh century Arab man.

I doubt if anyone would embrace Islam if they knew from the beginning what was going to happen later as orthodox Islam—*Shariah* Law—imposed itself on its subjects. This issue is the root of unrest and war in numerous parts of the world, including the following:

1. Afghanistan (Taliban)
2. Sudan (Civil war)
3. Algeria (Civil war)
4. Nigeria (near Civil war)
5. Indonesia (genocide of Christians)
6. Iran (student uprisings)
7. Pakistan (random bombings by militants)
8. Egypt (assassination attempts on President Mubarak)
9. Turkey (secular government trying to crush fundamentalists)
10. Philippines (agitating for a separate Muslim country)

Nevertheless, Muslims from the beginning have contested the cardinal doctrines of the Christian faith. Later, they challenged the authenticity of the Bible. Their present-day contentions and attitudes over these matters may well provoke you to anger, and in general, tempt you to lose your composure in your effort to convince them of the truth of the Gospel. For the Christian worker, keep in mind several guidelines before you enter into discussions with Muslims who question your Book and your basic beliefs. Remember that Muslims are more often won by your demeanor than your words. The presence and power of Christ in your life are the real attraction for Muslims. Nevertheless, we are called upon to give answers. Muslims expect it of us, in fact, they admire boldness of conviction in the matters of God. Following are passages from Scripture that will prove helpful in preparing you spiritually for these kinds of encounters:

> But in your hearts set apart Christ as Lord. Always be prepared to give an answer to everyone who asks you to give the reason for the hope that you have. But do this with gentleness and respect, keeping a clear conscience, so that those who speak maliciously against your good behavior in Christ may be ashamed of their slander (1 Peter 3:15-16).

What is crucial is keeping Christ central to your thinking and behavior. He is Lord. No matter where Muslims are coming from in their thinking, they are ultimately attacking the Lordship of Christ. It is honoring the Lord and focusing on Him which gives you that inner stability to answer with gentleness and respect.

The next passage illustrates further qualities that are to be evident in the Christian response to Muslim opposition:

> The Lord's servant must not quarrel; instead, he must be kind to everyone, able to teach, not resentful. Those who oppose him he must gently instruct, in the hope that God will grant them repentance leading them to a knowledge of the truth, and that they will come to their senses and escape from the trap of the devil, who has taken them captive to do his will (2 Tim. 2:24-26).

To gentleness should be added the ability to teach the Muslim who has been led astray. And it should be done with the special desire to see him recovered from the error of his way and brought to true repentance and the knowledge of the truth. Satan is the real enemy, not the Muslim. By whatever device, the Muslim has been taken captive to do his will. Remember Jesus' early words in Luke's Gospel: "He has sent me to proclaim freedom for the prisoners" (4:18). A word of caution: Notice that Paul in writing to Timothy does not guarantee success, but rests the issue with God, "in the hope that God will grant them repentance leading them to a knowledge of the truth" (2 Tim. 2:25). We must be persuasive, but only God who can change a heart.

A third passage that has proven helpful is Colossians 4:6: "Let your conversation be always full of grace, seasoned with salt, so that you may know how to answer everyone." Grace can only come from the indwelling presence of God. Salt, in this sense, means being able to answer in such a way that it engages the minds of Muslims—satisfies their hunger with a tasty answer. This presupposes a knowledge of the Scriptures, the leading of the Holy Spirit, and the ability to explain clearly what you believe.

Furthermore, you would be wise to have a supportive prayer group behind you. The apostle Paul put it this way, "Pray also for me, that whenever I open my mouth, words may be given me so that I will fearlessly [this does not mean rudely or stridently] make known the mystery of the Gospel" (Eph. 6:19). Our human nature being what it is, we may either lack courage or communication skills unless God strengthens us and gives us gracious words to use in response to Muslim disputations. And the prayers of fellow Christians play a role in this.

Remember that we who acknowledge Christ as Lord have the power of the Holy Spirit dwelling in us. We do not have to fight in our own strength. Again, turning to Paul's explanation:

> The weapons we fight with are not the weapons of the world. On the contrary, they have divine power to demolish strongholds. We demolish arguments and every pretension that sets itself up against the knowledge of God, and we take captive every thought to make it obedient to Christ (2 Cor. 10:4, 5).

Although the above passage may lead you to believe that you will win over your Muslim friend, it doesn't always work that way. A person may actually harden his heart against the Gospel of Jesus Christ. Failure to persuade a Muslim of the truth of the Gospel may not necessarily be due to any inadequacy on your part, provided you have prepared yourself spiritually and intellectually. There is another power at work: "The god of this age has blinded the minds of unbelievers, so that they cannot see the light of the gospel of the glory of Christ, who is the image of God" (2 Cor. 4:4).

Now let us take a look at the typical charges Muslims bring to bear on our Christian beliefs and our Scriptures. We also will take note of Muslim claims for Muhammad and the Quran. And, of course, we shall try to give the Christian reader, as well as the Muslim, material to uphold the claims for the Bible and Christian doctrine. These topics do not always appear in the same order. My arrangement follows the level of frequency these subjects have come up in my own encounters with Muslims.

Outline of Major Issues

A. Muslim Questioning of Christian Doctrine.
    1. The Questioning of the Word of God.
    2. The Denial of the Deity of Christ.
    3. The Opposition to the Concept of Incarnation.
    4. The Denial of the Idea of Atonement.
    5. The Denial of the Crucifixion.
    6. The Denial of the Trinity.

B. Muhammad's Claim to Prophethood.
    1. Muhammad Puts Himself in the Class of Biblical Prophets.
    2. Muhammad's Claim That Jesus Prophesied His Coming.
    3. Muhammad's Claim That He Was the Seal of the Prophets.
    4. Muhammad's Insistence on Obedience to His Words.
    5. Muslims Claim Many Biblical Prophecies for Muhammad.
    6. Muslims Use the Gospel of Barnabas to Support Muhammad.

C. Muhammad's Claims for the Quran.
    1. The Quran Confirms All Previous Scripture.
    2. The Quran Is Equal to All Previous Scripture.
    3. The Quran Supersedes All Previous Scripture.
    4. Muhammad Claims the Words of the Quran Are God's, Not His.

CHAPTER 31

MUSLIM QUESTIONING OF CHRISTIAN DOCTRINE

1. Questioning the Word of God

Almost anywhere you go in the Muslim World you are likely to meet Muslims who will try to counter your witness by the list of issues you read on the preceding page.

Their first effort is to discredit the Bible. They warn their fellow Muslims not to buy or read it, as it would lead them astray. When we ask them why, their answer is that what we have in our hands are no longer the "books" that God gave to the Prophets Moses, David and Jesus. They claim our forefathers corrupted or changed the originals. Nowhere in the Quran, by the way, is there any understanding of what the Bible really is, how it was put together, or what the central theme is.

No Quranic Attack on the Scriptures

It is interesting to note that nowhere in the Quran does it actually say the Bible has been changed, although there are passages where Muhammad charges opponents with distorting the words, and Jews in particular of mispronouncing and juggling Scriptures. But never does he say the originals have been changed. Dr. Abdiyah Akbar Abdul-Haqq points out that in the early years of Islam, when the Bible was not available in Arabic, Muslims made no charge that the Bible was corrupted. But after copies of the Bible fell into Muslim hands and they began to compare the Bible with the Quran, they found wide discrepancies between biblical and Quranic accounts of the same stories. It was at this point in time, somewhere between ninety and one hundred and fifty years after the death of Muhammad, that Muslims who assumed their Quran was authentic fabricated the charge that Jews and Christians had changed the Scriptures (1980:38).

But this charge will not stand up to Muhammad's testimony to the Scriptures in the Quran. Let us examine some of these statements. Parenthetically, please note that my use of the Quran does not mean that I count it as authoritative for myself. My rationale is that since Muslims consider it as authoritative, they should at least acknowledge its testimony to the authenticity of the Bible.

Quranic Affirmation of Previous Scriptures

The words of God can never be changed: "There is none that can alter the Words (and Decrees) of God ..." (Q. 6:34), and "No change can there be in the Words of God. This is indeed the supreme Felicity" (Q. 10:64).

The words Muhammad puts forth as divine revelation actually were given to confirm and guard the previous Scripture: "To thee We sent the Scripture in truth, confirming the scripture that came before it, and guarding it in safety... ." (Q. 5:51), and the "Quran ... is a confirmation of (revelations) that went before it... ." (Q. 10:37), and "before this, was the Book of Moses as a guide and mercy: and this Book [The Quran] confirms (it) in the Arabic tongue ..." (Q. 46:12).

Muslims were also enjoined to consult with Jews and Christians. "If thou wert in doubt as to what We have revealed unto thee, then ask those who have been reading The Book [The Bible] from before thee ..." (Q. 10:94).

Jesus and Christians were even enjoined to take their stand on their own Scriptures: "Say: 'O People of the Book! Ye have no ground to stand upon unless ye stand fast by the Law, the Gospel, and all the revelation that has come to you from your Lord'" (Q. 5:71).

Finally, Muhammad is commanded to believe in the "books" given to Moses, Jesus and the Prophets.

> Say: "We believe in God, and in what has been revealed to us and what was revealed to Abraham, Ismail, Isaac, Jacob, and the Tribes, and in (the Books) given to Moses, Jesus, and the Prophets, from their Lord: we make no distinction between one and another among them, and to God do we bow our will (in Islam)" (Q. 3:84).

Even though there are passages in the Quran that charge "The People of the Book" with "concealing the truth" (Q. 2:77; 2:216), and with writing "The Book with their own hands" (2:79), these do not undermine Muhammad's repeated affirmation of the unchangeable canonized Scripture. Every religion has its deviants. The actions of these Jewish and Christian deviants do not nullify the truth from which they have departed.

Therefore, this above-mentioned collection of Quranic injunctions adds up to a powerful affirmation of previous Scriptures. According to Muhammad, he believed in them and was sent to confirm them. But along with these verses we find others in which Muhammad puts his words on the same level and of the same value as these inspired texts of the Bible. This will be discussed in more detail later.

Muslim Charges Against the Scriptures Are Unfounded

In spite of these abundant references in the Quran as to the validity and authenticity of the Scriptures as they existed in Muhammad's day, the Christian worker will find that Muslims tend to dodge the issue by claiming Christians somewhere down the line have altered the text. This charge is their way of explaining the numerous contradictions between the Quran and the Bible. Understandably, Muslims are reluctant to face the possibility that Muhammad was wrong, and therefore, not a true prophet of God. To do so would cause the collapse of their whole religious system.

Out of fairness to Muhammad, it should be pointed out that he had no access to the canonical books of Scripture. He gained most of his knowledge by hearsay, and that was "based especially on extracanonical and apocryphal sources and on heretical forms of Christianity and Judaism" (O'Shaughnessy 1953:68).

Much patience is therefore required on the part of the Christian worker in explaining to the Muslim that our Scriptures are divinely inspired, trustworthy and authentic translations of a vast collection of early texts, all of which predate Muhammad, and copies of which are preserved in museums throughout the world today.

Refutations of False Muslim Charges

Several volumes have done an excellent job of presenting the case for the authenticity of our present Scriptures with special regard to Muslim charges against them. The Christian worker should become well acquainted with them. They are:

Share Your Faith with a Muslim by Abdiyah Akbar Abdul-Haqq.
The Islam Debate by Josh McDowell and John Gilchrist.
Christian Reply to Muslim Objections by W. S. Clair-Tisdall.

Following is a brief summary of their defense of the Scriptures:

1. There are thousands of documents that predate Muhammad from which the text of the present Bible has been established.

2. The text of the Dead Sea Scrolls of the Old Testament, many of which go back to the first century before Christ, is essentially the same as that of the Hebrew text as we have it today.

3. There is no evidence from any period of Christian history, after the canon was established, that indicates the text of the Bible was any different from what we have today or what existed in Muhammad's day.

4. Many of these pre-Islamic texts of the Bible, in the original languages, are on display in various museums around the world and they are in basic agreement with the text of the Bible as we have it today.

5. Discrepancies existing between the various texts can be attributed to errors in copying, and have not altered any doctrines of the Christian faith.

6. The differences in the many versions of the existing Bible simply reflect the principles of translation by which various translators went about their work. In no case have their preferences for different word choices affected a single doctrine of the Scriptures.

7. If Muslims persist in their allegation that Christians and Jews have corrupted the text of the Bible, both the Old and New

Testaments, then the burden is on them to:

a. Bring forth an uncorrupted authentic original.
b. Through reputable scholarship, show who corrupted the original texts.
c. Demonstrate historically when the tampering occurred.
d. Show exactly what the corruptions were as distinguished from the original.

It might be well to remember that Satan's original attack on Adam and Eve was to entice them to doubt the Word of God. Jesus, in His encounter with Satan, answered each temptation by quoting the Word of God. We must not be beguiled into not using the Scriptures, but rather follow Jesus' example. Remember how Jesus answered Satan's attacks. Each time He said, "It is written …" and then quoted from the appropriate passage.

2. The Denial of the Deity of Christ

The treatment of Jesus in the Quran is a fascinating subject. Muhammad mentions Him ninety-three times. In fact, an objective reader would find Jesus the most attractive personality in the Quran. Following are some of the relevant materials:

- Jesus is named "Messiah," but with no understanding of what the name means.
- He is called the "Servant of God," but without insights like those found in the prophecy of Isaiah.
- He is called a "Prophet," but Muhammad supersedes Him in importance.
- He is called an "Apostle," in the sense of a Messenger sent to warn.
- He is called "a Word from God," but not in the full Gospel sense of God's total expression of Himself to humankind.
- Muhammad described Him as "a Spirit from God," and there is great obscurity in the Quran on what is meant by "Spirit."

- Jesus is further described as "a Sign," "a Parable," "a Witness," "a Mercy," "Eminent," "One Brought Near," "One of the Upright," and "Blessed."

Parrinder discusses each of these in great detail in *Jesus in the Quran*, (1977:30-54).

For a scholarly discussion of what the Quranic phrases "a Word from God," and "a Spirit from God" mean, O'Shaughnessy's two works will prove most helpful (*The Koranic Concept of the Word of God (1948), and The Development of the Meaning of Spirit in the Koran* (1953)).

With all due gratitude to Muhammad for the favorable treatment of Jesus as mentioned above, we now face the unhappy task of looking at Quranic material that questions the heart of the Gospel message.

No other Christian doctrine seems to draw as much vehement denial from Muslims as the teaching on the deity of Jesus Christ. In their zeal to defend the oneness of God against all competitors, they insist that Allah could have no "partners." Muhammad went so far as to claim that the one unforgivable sin was to associate anything or anyone with God (*shirk*). Hence, Jesus is reduced to one of the prophets. To be sure, He stands out as superior to all of the others mentioned in the Quran, and ultimately to Muhammad himself, but nevertheless, Muhammad insisted that Jesus was only a prophet. Let's look at some of the Quranic passages that deny the deity of Christ: "In blasphemy indeed are those that say that God is Christ the son of Mary. Say: 'Who then hath the least power against God, if His Will were to destroy Christ the son of Mary?'" (Q. 5:19).

In the above quote, Muhammad not only disclaims the deity of our Lord, but goes on to say that God could have destroyed Christ if He had wanted to. It was beyond his comprehension that Jesus was eternally and intrinsically part of the Godhead.

Muhammad's categorical denial of the deity of Christ is reinforced by several more references asserting that God could not have a son. Muhammad, and almost all Muslims ever since, think the expression "Son of God" implies that God had a wife (Mary) and that Jesus was conceived from sexual union, thus literally being "The Son of God." Note the following passages: "They say: God hath begotten a son: Glory be to Him— Nay, to Him belongs all that is in the heavens and on earth: everything renders worship to Him" (Q. 2:116). And, "the Christians call Christ the Son of God. That is a saying from their mouth; (in this) they but imitate what the Unbelievers of old used to say. God's curse be on them: how they are deluded away from the Truth" (Q. 9:30). "It is not befitting to (the majesty of) God that He should beget a son. Glory be to Him! When He determines a matter, He only says to it, 'Be,' and it is" (Q. 19:35). Finally, "Say: He is God, the One and Only; God, the Eternal, Absolute; He begetteth not, nor is He begotten; and there is none like unto Him" (Q. 112:1-4).

These above quotes are only a sampling on this theme. They are enough to show that Muhammad zealously guarded the doctrine of oneness of God, to the exclusion of any idea of plurality within the Godhead. To say that God had a son was blasphemous. To say that God procreated diminished His glory. God only had to speak and it was done. No begetting. No begotten.

Yet, curiously enough, Muhammad incorporated several Christian concepts of Jesus into his accounts that certainly make Him more than a prophet, even suggesting several attributes of deity. For example, Jesus' virgin birth is stoutly proclaimed by Muhammad and all Muslims today. In addition, several more startling claims are made for Jesus:

> Behold! the angel said: "O Mary! God hath chosen thee and purified thee—chosen thee above the women of all nations" … Behold! the angels said: "O Mary! God giveth thee Glad tidings of a Word from Him: his name will be Christ Jesus, the Son of Mary, held in honour in this world and the Hereafter and of (the company of) those nearest to God" (Q. 3:42, 45).

In addition to the idea of the Virgin Birth, Jesus is described as a "Word from God," and among those nearest to God in eternity. Other attributes bordering on deity are also recorded in the Quran. For example, Jesus is reported as saying:

> I have come to you with a sign from your Lord, in that I make for you out of clay, as it were, the figure of a bird, and breathe into it, and it becomes a bird, by God's leave:

> And I heal those born blind, and the lepers, and I quicken
> the dead, by God's leave; and I declare to you what ye
> eat, and what ye store in your houses (Q. 3:49).

Here Jesus is portrayed as having creative power, the power to heal and raise the dead, and even to visualize what people are doing far away. In the following passage, we read that God took Jesus alive to heaven: "Nay, God raised Him [Jesus] up unto Himself; and God is Exalted in Power, Wise" (Q. 4:158). In the following passage, in addition to things already mentioned, we read that Jesus is a "Spirit" proceeding from God:

> O People of the Book! Commit no excesses in your
> religion: nor say of God aught but the truth. Christ Jesus
> the son of Mary was (no more than) an apostle of God,
> and His Word, which He bestowed on Mary, and a Spirit
> proceeding from Him (Q. 4:171).

It should be pointed out that Muhammad did not have a biblical concept of the Holy Spirit as He is presented in Scripture, but in his effort to win Christians to his cause, he used this idea with which heretical Christians were familiar (O'Shaughnessy 1953:59). In the following two passages, the additional thoughts are that Jesus is a "Holy Son" and He is to be a sign for all peoples, and that sign is to be interpreted as a "mercy" from God. The angel says to Mary: "I am only a messenger from thy Lord, (to announce) to thee the gift of a holy son " (Q. 19:19). And, "(We wish) to appoint him as a Sign unto men and a Mercy from Us" (Q.19: 21). And, "(remember) her who guarded her chastity: We breathed into her of Our Spirit, and We made her a son and her Son a Sign for all peoples" (Q. 21:91).

From these references, we see that Jesus is set forth as the Messiah (Christ) with creative and healing power, even the power to raise the dead. He is also described as God's Word, a Spirit from God, a Holy Son, a Sign for all peoples. He is to be highly honored in this life and among those nearest to God in the next. O'Shaughnessy points out that even though Muhammad used these words with which Christians whom he sought to win might be familiar, he had no understanding of Christ as "Word," "as expressing a divine activity hypostatized" [that is, as an intrinsic person of the Trinity] (1948:55). And similarly, Muhammad's use of "Spirit" in no way conveyed what we understand as a person of the Trinity (O'Shaughnessy 1953:60).

Yet, these passages pose great difficulties for Muslims. For we see that, while Muhammad perceived Christ only as an apostle, he attributes to Him qualities, virtues and powers that could only belong to God. Therefore, one approach to Muslims who believe in the Quran (for many know nothing about it), is to show them these passages and ask them to tell us what they mean. Some will give weird interpretations; others will be puzzled and will start to wonder who Jesus really is. Dr. Abdiyah Akbar Abdul-Haqq's opinion is that the Quran contains material on both the humanity and the deity of Christ (1980:114).

But in addition to working from the Quran, we must remember we are working toward the Bible. Since the Quran itself enjoins the Muslim to do so, you should help him discover what the Scriptures really say about Christ. And this is where you will need to be familiar with passages that point to His deity. No two workers will ever have the same list, so I will only suggest some as a starter. These have been especially chosen because of relevance they may have for a Muslim:

> A star will come out of Jacob [not Ishmael or his sons]; a scepter will rise out of Israel (Num. 24:17). [This "scepter" is applied to deity in Heb. 1:8]

> I have installed my King on Zion, my holy hill ... Ask of me, and I will make the nations your inheritance, the ends of the earth your possession. You will rule them ... (Ps. 2:6, 8, 9). [Muslims emphasize that only God can rule the world; man is merely a vice-regent or steward for God.]

> Your throne, O God [a prophecy about Christ], will last for ever and ever; a scepter of justice will be the scepter of your kingdom (Ps. 45:6). [Quoted in Heb. 1:8; applied to the Son of God.]

The Lord says to my Lord: "Sit at my right hand until I make your enemies a footstool for your feet … You are a priest forever in the order of Melchizedek … He will judge the nations …" (Ps. 110:1, 4, 6). [All Muslims admit Christ is coming back to judge the world. In this prophecy He is also called "Lord."]

Therefore the Lord himself will give you a sign: The virgin will be with child and will give birth to a son, and will call him Immanuel [God with us] (Isa. 7:14). [The Quran teaches the Virgin Birth. Here the Son is called "God with us."]

For to us a child is born, to us a son is given, and the government will be on his shoulders. And he will be called Wonderful Counselor, Mighty God, Everlasting Father, Prince of Peace. Of the increase of his government and peace there will be no end (Isa. 9:6). [Here "child" (Son), "Mighty God" and "Everlasting Father" are one and the same.]

In those days and at that time I will make a righteous Branch sprout from David's line … This is the name by which it will be called: The Lord Our Righteousness (Jer. 33:15, 16). [In this passage, Jesus, descended from David, is called "The Lord."]

For this is what the Sovereign Lord says: I myself will search for My sheep and look after them. As a Shepherd looks after his scattered flock when he is with them, so will I look after My sheep (Ezek. 34:11, 12). [Here the Sovereign Lord is equated with the Good Shepherd—a name Jesus took for Himself in John 10:11, thus equating Himself with the "Sovereign Lord."]

All of the above prophecies are taken from the Old Testament to show that the promised Messiah would be truly divine. All in all, at least three hundred prophecies about Christ in the Old Testament could be cited. The above are just those that can readily be used in reference to His deity. Others deal with different aspects of His person and ministry.

In the New Testament also, an abundance of passages show the deity of Christ. Just a few will be singled out here from the Gospels; many others are found in the Epistles.

> All this took place to fulfill what the Lord had said through the prophet: "The virgin will be with child and will give birth to a son, and they will call him Immanuel"—which means, "God with us"(Matt. 1:22, 23). (Again, linking the Virgin's son, Jesus, with God.)

> At that time the sign of the Son of Man [Jesus] will appear in the sky, and all the nations of the earth will mourn. They will see the Son of Man coming on the clouds of the sky, with power and great glory. And he will send his angels with a loud trumpet call, and they will gather his elect from the four winds, from one end of the heavens to the other (Matt. 24:30, 31).

Jesus Christ will come in glory with innumerable angels under His command. And He will summon all people for the final judgment. This is something only God can do.

> Then Jesus came to them and said, "All authority in heaven and on earth has been given to me. Therefore go and make disciples of all nations, baptizing them in the name of the Father and of the Son and of the Holy Spirit, and teaching them to obey everything I have commanded you. And surely I am with you always, to the very end of the age" (Matt. 28:18-20). [Only God could have such authority; only God could be omnipresent with all His disciples.]

> In the beginning was the Word, and the Word was with God, and the Word was God ... The Word became flesh and made his dwelling among us. We have seen his glory, the glory of the One and Only, who came from the Father, full of grace and truth (John 1:1, 14). [Most Muslims agree that the Word of God is eternal; therefore Jesus as the Incarnate Word is divine.]

> I and the Father are one (John 10:30). [Jesus declared Himself one with God.]

3. The Opposition to the Concept of Incarnation

In trying to understand where Muslims are coming from, we must remember that the cardinal doctrine in Islamic theology is the oneness of God. The absolute aloneness of the unity of God. Nowhere is this stated more clearly than in Surah 112 of the Quran: "Say: He is God, the One and Only; God, the Eternal, Absolute; He begetteth not, nor is He begotten; and there is none like unto Him." George Sale points out that in his day this chapter was held in special veneration by the Muslims and they considered it equal to one third of the value of the Quran (1850:504).

Even though Muslims are apt to argue that God is all-powerful and can do anything, they seem to stop short of really meaning it by asserting that His absolute transcendence makes it impossible for him to suffer such a detraction from His glory as to become incarnate in a man. In their minds, this would be to confuse the Creator with something created.

Therefore, when Muhammad attempted to refute the doctrine of the Sonship of Christ, he missed the point, as we shall see in the following quote: "(Far exalted is He) above having a son [added to him] ..." (Q. 4:171). The Arabic verb used in this passage bears the meaning of a son being added to God, as though God needed something else to be added to Him to make Him complete. Technically, we can agree with this Quranic statement, because when we talk about the incarnation and the Son of God, this is not what we mean. We believe in the all-sufficiency of God within Himself: Father, Son and Holy Spirit. It is not a question of adding a son to God.

The next quote puts a new angle on Muhammad's disavowal of Christ's Sonship: "It is not befitting to (the majesty of) God that He should beget a Son. Glory be to Him! When He determines a matter, He only says to it, 'Be,' and it is" (Q. 19:35).

In the above passage, the Arabic signifies that God is so powerful that He does not need to resort to the human method of sexual relation to acquire a son. He only needs to speak to bring something into existence. Again, we are in agreement. But this, too, is based on the misunderstanding that the Son is not eternal and co-existent with the Father and the Spirit in the Godhead. In other words, this and the preceding quote do not preclude the possibility of a pre-incarnate Son who in the fullness of time becomes fully man through the power of God working in the body of the Virgin Mary.

Thus, Muslims vigorously deny that God had sexual relations with Mary. So do we. But there are other ways to talk of Christ's Sonship. For the Muslim, the discussion hinges on the nature of the Word of God. The great majority will agree that the Word of God is eternal and uncreated. (For that small minority who don't, the following argument is irrelevant.)

One way to help Muslims see the need for a pre-incarnate Christ or Word is to show them the impossibility of their own position. If Muslims admit that the Word of God is eternal and uncreated, they are in essence saying that two things exist from all eternity. By their rules, this is committing *shirk,* associating something else with Allah. And, of course, if they shift to the position that the Word of God is created and, therefore, not eternal, it is tantamount to saying there was a time when God did not or could not speak, and that later on He changed His state and could speak. That violates their precept that God is unchangeable. It's at this point that we should try to explain to them the Scriptures, such as the following.

> In the beginning was the Word, and the Word was with God, and the Word was God. He was with God in the beginning. Through him all things were made; without him nothing was made that has been made. In him was life, and that life was the light of men (John 1:1-4).

From this passage we can draw the following inferences:
1. God has expressed or articulated Himself from the beginning. This expression of Himself is inseparable from Him. Without

this expression or definition of Himself He would not be God; He would be a "dumb nothing" in space. His Person and the Expression of Himself are, therefore, one. The Word is, therefore, divine.

2. All of creation came into being through the Living Word. He, the Word, brought life. (Muslims fail to make this link between the Word and Life.) When we proceed with the passage, we read: "The Word became flesh and made his dwelling among us. We have seen his glory, the glory of the One and Only, who came from the Father, full of grace and truth" (John 1:14). We have, then, the fullest possible expression of God to man; He became one of us to fully express Himself to us; He became the Living Word. The author of Hebrews further develops this theme in the following passage:

In these last days he has spoken to us by his Son, whom he appointed heir of all things, and through whom he made the universe. The Son is the radiance of God's glory and the exact representation of his being, sustaining all things by his powerful word (Heb. 1:2, 3).

In other words, God has chosen to reveal Himself to us by the perfect expression of Himself, the Living Word, His Son, Jesus.

4. The Denial of the Idea of Atonement

Islam, as Muhammad perceived it, is based on several premises which preclude the idea of atonement: the possibility of someone becoming a substitute sacrifice to atone for or pay the penalty for another's sins. For Muhammad, Islamic Law became everything. Man was given the *Shariah* Law and man was to submit to it, that is, become a Muslim. In the end, there will be a Day of Judgment. One's good deeds will be weighed on a balance scale against one's bad deeds. If the good deeds outweigh the bad, the person will go to paradise; otherwise to hell. In this system, there is no place for the idea of God providing an atoning sacrifice through Christ. This above explanation is based on scores of passages in the Quran which we will not quote here. We have selected only one as a sample of many that show the fear people have of judgment: "Every soul that hath sinned, if it possessed all that is on earth, would fain give it in ransom" (Q. 10:54). For further reference, see Quran 10:3.

And yet, strangely enough, there is a passage in the Quran that holds the door open for the idea of ransom: "And we ransomed him [Isaac; Muslims say Ishmael] with a momentous sacrifice" (Q. 37:107). Muslim commentator Yusuf Ali says concerning this verse, "Note that the ransom, that is, the commutation of sacrifice, was made not by men, but by God" (1977:1206). After calling the Muslim's attention to the above passage, I suggest you show him or her Hebrews 9:22, which says: "In fact, the law requires that nearly everything be cleansed with blood, and without the shedding of blood there is no forgiveness." Following this, make the link to the atoning death of Jesus Christ by quoting Jesus' words in Matthew 26:28: "This is my blood of the covenant, which is poured out for many for the forgiveness of sins."

I also suggest the use of Paul's passage in Romans 5:9-11:

> Since we have now been justified by his blood, how much more shall we be saved from God's wrath through him! For if, when we were God's enemies, we were reconciled to him through the death of his Son, how much more, having been reconciled, shall we be saved through his life! Not only is this so, but we also rejoice in God through our Lord Jesus Christ, through whom we have now received reconciliation [atonement].

5. The Denial of the Crucifixion

As far as we can tell, Muhammad never read the Bible in any language; moreover, it was not even available in Arabic in his day. He was utterly dependent on what he picked up in the marketplace and from friends. Many kinds of Christians lived throughout Arabia and the Middle East. They were in constant strife over the doctrine of Christ. Egyptian Christians (Monophysites) claimed Christ had only one nature; Syrians (Nestorians) claimed He had two natures. With regard to the crucifixion, the Nestorians maintained that Christ suffered in His human nature only, and that His God-nature was not crucified. Moreover, Muhammad heard the Jews and

Christians quarreling over who was to blame for the crucifixion. The following quote from the Quran reflects his own opinion of the matter.

> That they [the Jews] said (in boast), "We killed Christ Jesus the son of Mary, the Apostle of God";—But they killed him not, nor crucified him, but so it was made to appear to them. And those who differ therein are full of doubts, with no (certain) knowledge, but only conjecture to follow. For of a surety they killed him not:—Nay, God raised him up unto Himself; and God is Exalted in Power, Wise. And there is none of the People of the Book [Jews and Christians] but must believe in him before his death; and on the Day of Judgment he will be a witness against them (Q.4:157-159).

This passage has been the cause of many and varied explanations among Muslim scholars as well as Christian ones. According to the noted Muslim authority, al Baydawi (d. 1291), quoted in George Sale's *The Koran*, (1850:43), some Muslims believed that Jesus did die on the cross and argued as to how many hours He hung there. Others, usually much later commentators, maintain that Jesus did not die but was taken alive to heaven, with someone else being substituted in His place (Yusuf Ali, 1977:230).

Sadly, today Muslims almost universally deny that Jesus died on the cross. How tragic that Muhammad, seizing on the controversy among Christians over Christ's natures, as well as the controversy among the Jews and Christians, assumed a position that was not only contrary to Scripture, but tore the very heart out of the Gospel.

On the other hand, some Christian apologists, working with the same passage (Quran 4:157), argue that the text only means that the Jews did not kill Christ, because under Roman Law it was illegal for them to execute anyone, and that the text does not rule out the idea that the Romans did put Him to death by crucifixion. Technically, the early part of the verse quoted may allow that interpretation, but what comes later in the verse mitigates against this ("For of a surety, they killed him not.")

Two Quranic texts allow the interpretation that Christ would die in His natural lifetime. Muhammad attributes the first quote to God, the second to Jesus. The following verses have several interpretations based on readers' understanding of Arabic tenses, uses and the intended meaning of the verbs that are used:

> Behold! God said: "O Jesus! I will take thee [that is, cause thee to die in your earthly lifetime] and raise thee to Myself [that is, after, your death] and clear thee (of the falsehoods) of those who blaspheme..."(Q. 3:55).

> So peace is on me the day I was born, the day that I die [in this lifetime], and the day that I shall be raised up to life (again) [in this lifetime] (Q. 19:33)!

Unfortunately, for the Christian to be able to use these texts to convince the Muslims that Jesus did die in His earthly lifetime, he or she should have a working grasp of the Arabic language. Again, the burden is on the Christian to move the discussion from Quranic passages to the Bible. The worker should have an easy familiarity with biblical texts from Genesis to Revelation to show that the cross was at the heart of God's redemptive activity from start to finish. Suggested texts are as follows:

> I [God] will put enmity between you [Satan] and the woman, and between your offspring and hers; he [ultimately, this is Christ] will crush your head [fatally defeat you], and you [Satan] will strike his heel [mortally wound Christ] (Gen. 3:15).

> Each man is to take a lamb for his family ... slaughter them ... take some of the blood and put it on the sides and tops of the doorframes ... when I see the blood, I will pass over you (Ex. 12:3, 6, 7, 13).

> He was pierced for our transgressions ... the Lord laid on him the iniquity of us all ... he was led like a Lamb to the slaughter ... he bore the sin of many, and made intercession for the transgressors (Isa. 53:5, 6, 7, 12).

Look, the Lamb of God, who takes away the sin of the world (John 1:29)!

For even the Son of Man did not come to be served, but to serve, and to give his life as a ransom for many (Mark 10:45).

He himself bore our sins in his body on the tree, so that we might die to sins and live for righteousness; by his wounds you have been healed (1 Peter 2:24).

You are worthy to take the scroll and to open its seals, because you were slain, and with your blood you purchased men for God from every tribe and language and people and nation. You have made them to be a kingdom and priests to serve our God, and they will reign on the earth (Rev. 5:9, 10).

6. The Denial of the Trinity

"You Christians worship three gods!" How many times those of us working in the Muslim world have been accused of this! And no wonder. Its source is found in Muhammad's own teaching in the Quran. Listed below are selected references:

O People of the Book! Commit no excesses in your religion: nor say of God aught but the truth. Christ Jesus the son of Mary was (no more than) an apostle of God, and His Word, which He bestowed on Mary, and a Spirit proceeding from Him: so believe in God and His apostles. Say not "Trinity": desist: It will be better for you: For God is One God: Glory be to Him (far exalted is He) above having a son (Q. 4:171).

In blasphemy indeed are those that say that God is Christ the son of Mary. Say: "Who then hath the least power against God, if His Will were to destroy Christ the son

of Mary, his mother, and all—everyone that is on earth?
For to God belongeth the dominion of the heavens and
the earth, and all that is between. He createth what He
pleaseth. For God hath power over all things" (Q. 5:19).

They do blaspheme who say: God is one of three in a
Trinity: for there is no god except One God. If they desist
not from their word (of blasphemy), verily a grievous
penalty will befall the blasphemers among them (Q.
5:76).

From other verses, we learn that Muhammad had the impression that
Christians actually worshiped Mary, Jesus and God as separate deities.
Tisdall, in his study of the apocryphal gospels that existed in Arabia in
Muhammad's day, confirmed that Muhammad saw the worship of Mary,
of Mary and Jesus, and heard those who ill-advisedly said that "God is
Three" (1910:179-182). Again, it is tragic that Muhammad apparently
never met what we would call an evangelical Christian who could give a
clear explanation of the Oneness of God, while talking of the Father, Son
and Holy Spirit.

For the Christian who works among Muslims, it is imperative to come
to a very sound understanding of the oneness of God and be able to
convince the Muslims from the Scriptures that we indeed worship One
True God, without denying Him as Father, Son and Spirit. The following
passages may prove helpful:

Hear, O Israel: The Lord our God, the Lord is one. Love
the Lord your God with all your heart and with all your
soul and with all your strength (Deut. 6:4, 5).

O Lord, God of Israel, there is no God like you in heaven
above or on earth below—you who keep your covenant
of love with your servants who continue wholeheartedly
in your way (1 Kings 8:23).

I am the Lord; that is my name! I will not give my glory
to another or my praise to idols (Isa. 42:8).

> For even if there are so-called gods, whether in heaven or on earth (as indeed there are many "gods" and many "lords"), yet for us there is but one God, the Father, from whom all things came and for whom we live ... (1 Cor. 8:5, 6).

> Then the end will come, when he hands over the kingdom to God the Father after he has destroyed all dominion, authority and power. For he must reign until he has put all his enemies under his feet ... When he has done this, then the Son himself will be made subject to him who put everything under him, so that God may be all in all (1 Cor. 15:24, 25, 28).

This list of references include some of the most difficult in the Bible (but not all) on the subject of the Triune God, as well as simple, straightforward verses that unambiguously address God as One. No doubt there are things almost impossible to understand and explain about our God: Father, Son and Holy Spirit. Before we proceed with any further discussion, it is of interest to note that the word "trinity" does not occur anywhere in the Bible. It is a Greek philosophical term applied to God as revealed in the Bible. Therefore, I feel no compulsion to use the term. If Christ and Paul did not, why should I?

The Bible itself may hold a way to get at this difficult subject. In Genesis 1:26, 27 we read: "Then God said, 'Let us make man in our image, in our likeness' ... So God created men in his own image, in the image of God he created him, male and female he created them." It is possible that by analyzing ourselves we may discover clues pointing to the nature of God in whose image we are made. Even though the Scripture speaks of us as "spirit, soul and body" (1 Thess. 5:23), the analogy breaks down because in the Bible, the Father, Son and Holy Spirit function as distinct personalities while being of one essence, whereas we function as only one personality, with mind, spirit and body. Nevertheless, even though we are each a single person, we can be described in terms of our spirits, souls and bodies; yet we are not three, we are each one.

Similarly, God is One, even though He has revealed Himself to us as Father, Son and Spirit. I would not be me without either my spirit, soul, or body. God would not be able to function as God without being at the same time Father, Son and Spirit. They are one inseparable entity. They are not each one-third of the whole, they are intrinsically One. They function as one—one mind, one will, one spirit, one God.

The Triune God: A Dance of Love

C. S. Lewis, starting with the idea that God is love, tried to explain God in terms of a dance of love. There has to be a lover, a beloved, and the phenomenon of love itself. And yet because this pertains to God, the dance goes on internally, inside of an all-sufficient God, able to exist by Himself in love because there is a Father, Son and Spirit (1943:152). Again, every analogy is inadequate. In this one, the Spirit is not given full due as "the phenomenon of love itself." In other words, He is not presented as a full Person.

The Triune God as the Master Artist

Dorothy Sayres, in her book, *The Mind of the Maker*, describes God as an Artist, totally perfect and sufficient within Himself. She likens the Father to the conceptional mind of the artist. She describes the Son as the eternal and fullest expression of the artist's creative genius. And the Spirit is the creative energy of God in full and perpetual use, as the Master Artist expresses all the fullness of His being in His eternally-being-generated Masterpiece, His Son (1964:40ff.). Again, as in the illustration from C. S. Lewis, the analogy fails to do justice to the Holy Spirit. Since we are finite, it is impossible to take in all the possible dimensions in which God can express Himself. Yet, even with our limited understanding, the concept of the Triune God makes more sense that anything else.

The Muslim Dilemma

Consider the terrible dilemma the Muslims find themselves in. Allah is totally alone. Most Muslims agree that the Word of God is eternal; but He or It is not part of Allah. If Muslims say the Word is uncreated, then two things exist eternally, by Muslim accounts, an intolerable blasphemy. If they say the Word of God is created, then there was a time when God could not, or did not speak, hence He was a dumb God. As soon as He spoke, He changed from one state to another—an intolerable violation of their doctrine of the immutability of God.

The same arguments hold for the Spirit of God. If He exists eternally with Allah, this is the unforgivable sin of *shirk*. If the Spirit is created, then there was a time in the past when God was dead—He had no Spirit. By most reckoning, it is the Muslims who are tortured with the charge of having three gods: Allah, The Word of God, and The Spirit of God existing as separate entities with no way to get them together in a unity.

When one looks at the Christian situation in contrast with all other possibilities, we are in a most felicitous condition. We know God as a loving Father, an understanding Son and fellow human, and as a life-giving Spirit, all held together in the happy unity of love. God is eternally alive in His Spirit, perfectly expressed in the Living Word, His Son, and our Father.

I believe that Islam, by presenting us with its untenable alternatives of either having three "gods," or of having a dumb and lifeless Allah at sometime in the past, has given us wonderful grounds for appreciating the intrinsic genius of the One Triune God: Father, Son [Word] and Holy Spirit.

> Oh, the depth of the riches of the wisdom and knowledge of God! How unsearchable his judgments, and his paths beyond tracing out! "Who has known the mind of the Lord? Or who has been his counselor?" "Who has ever given to God, that God should repay him?" For from him and through him and to him are all things. To him be the glory forever! Amen (Rom. 11:33-36).

CHAPTER 32

MUHAMMAD'S CLAIM TO PROPHETHOOD

I stood there, sweating, in the circle of a dozen police officers who were staring at me intently. I had just been asked the question: "Sir, you have been a missionary in our country for a long time. You know us and our religion. What do think of Muhammad?" This was in Pakistan, a land where it is now a capital offense to speak against Muhammad.

The Lord Jesus said not to worry about what to say in such situations because the Holy Spirit would tell us (Matt. 10:20). I prayed and trusted God for the answer: "Sirs, I have read the Quran and studied the life of Muhammad. I have studied the Bible and am thoroughly familiar with the life of Christ, and I am in love with Jesus Christ." Dead silence. I had not fallen into the trap of either badmouthing Muhammad or giving him praise in violation of my deep reservations about him, and I had borne witness to my faith in Christ, a boldness that Muslims respect.

But there comes a time, at least privately, when one has to form an opinion about Muhammad. By his daring claims, Muhammad and his followers force you to take a stand. In the following pages, we shall be taking up the claims he has made about himself in the Quran and the claims his followers have made for him. The purpose of undertaking such a study is to dispel the fuzzy thinking in Christian circles about Muhammad's status. Many good things could be said about Muhammad, and we have mentioned them earlier in the book. But here, we will address only those controversial issues that Muslims force upon us by their claims.

1. <u>Muhammad Puts Himself in the Class</u>
<u>of Biblical Prophets</u>

Following are selected verses of the Quran in which Muhammad makes claims for himself:

> Say: "O men! I am sent unto you all, as the Apostle of God, to Whom belongeth the dominion of the heavens and the earth: there is no god but He: it is He that giveth both life and death. So believe in God and His Apostle, the unlettered Prophet, who believeth in God and His Words: follow him that (so) ye may be guided" (Q. 7:158).

> The Apostle believeth in what hath been revealed to him from his Lord, as do the men of faith. Each one (of them) believeth in God, His angels, His books, and His apostles. "We make no distinction (they say) between one and another of His apostles" (Q. 2:285).

> We have sent thee inspiration, as We sent it to Noah and the Messengers after him: We sent inspiration to Abraham, Ismail, Isaac, Jacob and the Tribes, to Jesus ... O Mankind! the Apostle hath come to you in truth from God: believe in him: it is best for you (Q. 4:163, 170).

These quotations pose an enormous problem for Muslims. Let us just note the claims that Muhammad makes:

1. He claims to be an apostle of God.
2. He asks the world to follow him.
3. He professes faith in the "Books" and apostles before him.
4. He claims equality with biblical prophets.
5. He claims the same level of inspiration as Jesus.
6. He lists Ishmael as a prophet.

These are prodigious claims. Because over one billion Muslims take them seriously, we must examine them to see if they are true.

First, we need to look at the central theme and function of God's redemptive plan in the Bible from start to finish. As we do, we are impressed with the continuity of theme that prevails throughout. Starting with the fall of man in the Garden of Eden, we note that the Lord Himself was there and prophesied that the offspring of the woman would crush the head of the serpent (Satan) and the serpent would strike the heel of this person (Gen. 3:15). This offspring would take on and defeat our mortal enemy, Satan, who deceived Adam and Eve and caused mankind to stray from God.

Then we see how the Old Testament Prophets upheld the Mosaic Law with its sacrificial system, a system that foreshadowed the Lamb of God who would take away the sin of the world, setting us free from the power of sin and hence of Satan (John 8:36). In due time, the inspired writers of Scripture realized that this "seed of the woman" in Genesis 3:15 was ultimately Jesus the Messiah and that this was a prophecy about His death on the cross. And Jesus is clearly represented in Scripture as divine, as integral to the Godhead, along with the Father and the Spirit. It was through the crucifixion that He fulfilled the demands of the law on behalf of guilty sinners and simultaneously broke the power of Satan who worked through our sinfulness to hold us in his power (Col. 2:15). The apostle John wrote, "The reason the Son of God appeared was to destroy the devil's work" (1 John 3:8). The original apostles witnessed the crucifixion and resurrection of Christ. Later apostles bore witness to the central events of the crucifixion and resurrection in all their teaching. The last book of the Bible closes with the picture of God throwing the Devil into the lake of fire where he would burn forever and ever (Rev. 20:10).

So we see that the major theme of the Bible from Genesis to Revelation is God's great redemptive plan to save man from sin, Satan and death, and that the central figure in this plan is Jesus Christ. Even though there may have been long time gaps between various prophets, for example from Malachi to John the Baptist, they all fit in God's great redemptive scheme. There is not only a progression in the development of the theme, but an astonishing unity to the whole.

Second, we must define what a biblical prophet is. Muhammad considered a prophet to be anyone who was the vehicle for reciting God's revelation to a particular generation. Thus in the Quran Muhammad refers to such figures as Ishmael and the Tribes as prophets. Biblical prophets, however, are defined and identified by the various functions they performed in the Bible. These functions can be summarized as follows:

1. Out of their intimate relationship with God they speak on His behalf either to give us His Word, for example, the Law (Moses), or to call us back to the Word of the Lord.

2. They prophesy about, and point believers to, the Christ who was to come: the first time to die for the sins of the whole world, and the second and last time to bring full salvation to those who believe in Him and to judge the rest of mankind who rejected Him as their Savior and Lord, the Son of God.

3. They either provide guidance, warn of impending doom, or help prepare God's people for disasters about to happen.

4. From time to time, throughout the period of biblical revelation, signs and wonders or some manifestation of the miraculous have accompanied various prophets.

5. Since the birth of the church, we now find that the Spirit of God lives in the whole body of believers. In a sense, therefore, the church as a whole functions in a prophetic way as God's voice to the world, in addition to certain individuals who have and exercise the prophetic gift inside local congregations.

As we examine the claims of Muhammad, the following criteria will help us determine if he fits in the long and distinguished line of biblical prophets:

1. He should be in agreement with God's central plan for the salvation of man.

2. If there is any point where Muhammad's words differ from the ancient Scriptures, his words should evidence at least an equal, if not superior, morality or ethic over that which came before.

3. His prophecies about the future should expound upon biblical prophecies.

When we examine Muhammad's words in the Quran, we find that they do not meet any of the above criteria. Not only do they disagree with the Law of Moses in the Old Testament, but they attack the very core of the Gospel message in the New Testament. Muhammad maintained that God could neither become a man nor have a Son, consequently Jesus was not the Son of God; that Jesus was not crucified but was rescued by God and taken to heaven alive without going through death and resurrection; that no one could die for someone else; and that God could not possibly reveal Himself as one triune God—Father, Son and Spirit.

Any other points of agreement between the Quran and the Bible notwithstanding, these crucial attacks by Muhammad on the cardinal points of faith and revelation exclude him from the category of being a biblical Prophet or Apostle. It is not a question of Muhammad being inferior to true biblical prophets and apostles, it is that Muhammad was diametrically opposed to all that God has done through the previous prophets, and to the very heart and purpose of God in sending Christ as Savior and Lord of all mankind.

Even if we left aside these fatal differences and focused on the ethical and moral content of the Quran, we find that it falls far short of the ideals set forth and embodied by Jesus. Muhammad's teaching, for example, on marriage, divorce, forgiveness and peacemaking, to name a few, do not begin to measure up to what is taught in the Bible.

Furthermore, there is no supernatural attestation to this so-called "revelation" that God supposedly gave to Muhammad through the angel Gabriel. When we note that the lives of both Moses and Jesus, whom Muhammad claimed to supersede, were accompanied by great miracles, the lack of supernatural attestation to Muhammad's "revelation" is glaring.

We might add that Muhammad showed total ignorance of the Bible by listing Ishmael as a Prophet. Nowhere does the Bible do that. In fact, in Genesis 17:19, God explicitly says the missionary covenant will be with Isaac. Thus, Isaac will play the prophetic role to the world, to all peoples. And Ishmael and his descendants will be among those who are the object of this prophetic missionary activity.

Based on the above observations, we are forced to conclude that Muhammad's claims for his name to be included in the long line of biblical prophets will not pass the test of these simple criteria listed above. According to biblical criteria, he is neither a prophet nor an apostle. According to the apostle John, whoever denies the Son has also denied the Father and John calls that person an antichrist (1 John 2:18-23; 1 John 4:15). For my Muslim reader, please note that it is the inspired Scriptures which make these evaluations, not an individual believer. For a Muslim to contradict this Scripture is to take on the whole of Christian history for the last twenty centuries.

2. Muhammad's Claim That Jesus Prophesied His Coming

> And remember, Jesus, the son of Mary, said: "O Children of Israel! I am the Apostle of God (sent) to you, confirming the Law (which came) before me, and giving Glad Tidings of an Apostle to come after me, whose name shall be Ahmad" (Q. 61:6).

The prevalent understanding in the Middle East in Muhammad's day was that each prophet, before he died, prophesied who the next prophet would be (a widely known Zoroastrian idea). *Ahmad*, by the way, is considered by most Muslims as a variant form of *Muhammad*. Both words are from the same Arabic tri-literal root, "h-m-d," the root word for "praise." Even though the two words do not have the exact same meaning (*Ahmad* = "whose name is praised"; *Muhammad* = "the praised one"), most Muslims see them as equivalents.

It is interesting to note that Muslims have searched diligently in the Gospels for some passage that would support this idea that Jesus prophesied the coming of Muhammad. And in due time, they thought they found it. To follow their argument one needs to know Greek. In John 14:16, 17 we read: "And I will ask the Father, and he will give you another Counselor [*parakletos*] to be with you forever—the Spirit of truth." In classical Greek, there is a word that looks similar but uses different vowels: *periklutos*. This word can be translated "Praised One." The word "Muhammad" also means the "Praised One."

When Greek scholars have pointed out to Muslims that the two words are different, and that there is no textual history of the word *periklutos* ever being in the Bible, Muslims have countered by accusing Christians of tampering with the text and changing the vowels. All efforts to get Muslims to read the context and realize that Muhammad could not possibly fulfill all the roles assigned to the Holy Spirit in these passages (John 14:16, 17, 26; 15:26; 16:7-11, 13-15) are of no avail. As long as Muslims stay locked into their belief in the Quran, they will not be open to reason. If they ever do become open to reason, the untenability of such claims will rapidly become apparent in the light of Jesus' teaching in the Gospel.

It is only when a Muslim is willing to read and trust the Bible that he or she begins to realize there is something wrong with the Quran. It takes a great deal of patience to work through these problems with your Muslim friends. Just remember that you are demolishing their whole worldview, and that is a very terrifying thing for anyone. In the beginning of your relationship, they may not be able to see the truth of the Bible. This is where the strength of your friendship and intercessory prayer will have to carry them through this traumatic experience of abandoning their familiar Muslim worldview for a biblical one.

3. Muhammad's Claim to Be the Seal of the Prophets

It was a frightening scene. A handful of young men were running with cans of gasoline in their hands toward a small library building next to our property. They were shouting vigorously, "*Allahu Akbar*" (God is greater). Then they doused the building with gasoline and burned it down. It belonged to a heretical sect of Muslims called Ahmadi. Remember that this sect believes their founder, Mirza Ghulam Ahmad, had been raised up as a reforming prophet of God in the last century to lead a new "messianic" movement within Islam. The High Court of Pakistan had just declared that the Ahmadi Movement was non-Muslim (1974) and

Orthodox Muslims had taken to the streets everywhere and were burning down Ahmadi properties. The reasons were not hard to find.

The Ahmadis challenged the age-old Orthodox Islamic belief that Muhammad was the last and greatest of all the prophets, and after him there could be no other. This is based on a key passage in the Quran (33:40): "Muhammad is not the father of any of your men, but (he is) the Apostle of God, and the Seal of the Prophets: and God has full knowledge of all things." Yusuf Ali's comment on this verse is most interesting. He states: "The Holy Prophet Muhammad closed the long line of apostles ..." (1977:1119).

All of the above illustrate the Orthodox Muslim insistence that Muhammad, indeed, is "the Seal of the Prophets," and there can be none after him. But, is the claim valid? Is he really God's last "Word" to the human race?

The answer, of course, is no. Muhammad, having the qualifications of neither an Old Testament prophet nor a New Testament apostle, could not possibly be "the Seal of the Prophets." It was Jesus who said, "Salvation is from the Jews" (John 4:22). God chose to spell out His whole strategy of redemption through an obscure group of people called the Jews—and this included Jesus. The work was completed by Jesus. There would be no need for another "seal of the prophets" or another religion.

In addition, the New Testament indicates that the gift of prophecy is still in operation and will be so until the return of Christ. God continues to speak to His Church.

4. Muhammad's Insistence on Obedience to His Words

Instead of upholding the Mosaic Law that Christ came to fulfill, we find that Muhammad wanted to supplant it with a law of his own. Moreover, he wanted people to believe that their future state in eternity depended completely on what they did with his words; that is, *Muhammad's* words.

There is an absolutely dangerous aspect to many passages in the Quran in which Muhammad links his name to God's and then either offers the delight of a sensual paradise to those who obey him, or threatens those who will not listen to him with the torments of hell. Listed below are a few illustrations:

He who obeys the Apostle, obeys God (Q. 4:80).

Believe in God and His Apostle ... For, those of you who believe and spend (in charity),—for them is a great Reward ... "This day shall no ransom be accepted of you, nor of those who rejected God. Your abode is the Fire: that is the proper place to claim you: and an evil refuge it is!" (Q. 57:7, 15).

Obey God and His Apostle, if you do believe (Q. 8:1).

If any contend against God and his Apostle, God is strict in punishment (Q. 8:13).

Obey God and his Apostle, and turn not away from him when ye hear (him speak) (Q. 8:20).

And obey God and his Apostle ... (Q. 8:46).

Fight those who believe not in God nor the Last Day, Nor hold that forbidden which hath been forbidden by God and His Apostle, Nor acknowledge the Religion of Truth [Islam], (even if they are) of the People of the Book [Christians and Jews], until they pay the *Jizya* with willing submission, and feel themselves subdued (Q. 9:29).

This is truly a frightening teaching: If you obey the apostle Muhammad, you will receive great reward. And if you don't, you are to be subdued, caused to pay a punitive tax and ultimately abide in the fire of hell. Even more frightening, Muhammad is in essence making himself the voice of God.

However, the Bible is clear that nothing more needs to be written. The Scripture says of itself that it is enough for our salvation (John 20:30, 31). And the concluding book of the Bible (Revelation) gives a severe warning concerning anyone who would add or subtract from it (Rev. 22:18, 19). If this only refers to the Book of Revelation, then Muhammad is only guilty of ignorance and that would explain why he developed his own ideas of what end times would be like. If John was referring to all of Scripture, then Muhammad is in big trouble with God for seeking to add the whole of the Quran to God's revealed Scriptures.

The Dark Side of Muhammad's Personality

After Muhammad's early attempts to persuade the Jews and Christians that he was a true apostle of God had failed (the Jews mocked him and the Christians rejected him), he turned against them. He told his followers never to take a Christian as a friend (Q. 5:54). He banished two of the Jewish tribes of Medina, massacred all the men of another and sold their wives and children into slavery (Watt 1961:130, 150, 173). He signaled this turning away from the Jews and Christians when he changed the direction one was to face while praying from Jerusalem to Mecca (Q. 2:142).

On the question of the treatment of women, Muslims try to justify Muhammad's teaching by saying he improved their lot over what it was before. This may be true, but it fails to reach the Bible's standard that both male and female are made in God's image, and that Christ has removed any inequalities between them in terms of salvation. The Quran allows that some wives will go to paradise, but there is much more material in the *Hadith* which points the other way. Moreover, what Jesus taught about marital relations, Muhammad contradicted by both his teaching and his practice. Muhammad taught that a man may have four wives at one time, and that divorce could be initiated by a man but not by a woman.

It is on the subject of the sword that Muhammad stands forth in stark contrast to Jesus Christ. Both faced the prospect of assassination in the capital city of their respective people—Jesus in Jerusalem, Muhammad in Mecca. Jesus went up to Jerusalem to be crucified, to give His life as a ransom for many (Mark 10:45). He refused to take the sword (John 18:36), or to mobilize an army. He tasted death for every person (Heb. 2:9). Muhammad, when faced with the prospect of martyrdom in Mecca, chose to flee and to mobilize his followers in his newly adopted city of Yathrib. As Muhammad took up the prevalent Arab custom of raiding enemy caravans, he justified it by saying he was fighting against blasphemers in the cause of God. But what grew out of this was an untamable monstrosity.

To this day, "holy war" has been enshrined forever in the practices of Islam. Fazlur Rahman, one of the great modern-day authorities on Islam, wrote the following in his book, *Islam*:

> It is not merely the case that in the *Hadith* and in the orthodox teaching the doctrine of *jihad* lies permanently enshrined, but that the actual example of the Prophet and the early Community teaches a positive participation in the direct entry into and changing of the state of affairs (1979:211).

One of the hallmarks of Muhammad's teaching was his unrelenting emphasis on the oneness or unity of God. On the one hand, this led him to attack the Christian doctrine of the Trinity, however he understood it, and on the other to insist on tying every facet of life into this doctrine, including *jihad*. Bishop Kenneth Cragg, an expert on Islam, wrote that Muhammad's use of force grew out of this doctrine:

> If, as again seems likely, a confident combativeness on behalf of God emerges as the primary lesson of the Prophet's whole career, then it will be fair to ask at the end whether the divine imperative and the Muhammadan militancy are well conjoined. As founded by the Prophet and found in Islam, faith in the unity of God is historically united with the structure of religious community politically expressed and enforced (1984:14).

Monotheism, the belief in the one true God, lived on in the "descendants" of Ishmael. It is highly significant that the name of Muhammad's father was Abdullah, "Servant of God." Moreover, the Mecca of Muhammad's day held a group of monotheists called *Hanif*. Montgomery Watt states that in the Quran, this word is used to mean "a monotheist who is neither a Jew nor a Christian" and that the Muslims preferred to say they followed "the religion of Abraham, the *Hanif*, the Muslim" (1964:117).

Cragg feels that Muhammad's greatest contribution to our world was "to bring about a vast human practice, or ruling consciousness, of God's reality as Lord" (1984:148). It has been a tremendous accomplishment on the part of Islam. And even though we take issue with Muhammad's and the Muslim's perception of God, and this subject will be discussed later, we, nevertheless, are grateful for this emphasis on belief in the One and Only Creator God.

On the negative side, by choosing to identify with Abraham through Ishmael and emphasizing his racial link to him, Muhammad unwittingly took upon himself, and hence for all of Islam, the biblical prophecy concerning Ishmael which said that his hand would be against everyone and everyone's hand would be against him, and that he would live in hostility toward all his brothers (Gen. 16:12). This certainly is borne out in Muhammad's teaching on war.

> O Apostle! rouse the Believers to the fight. If there are twenty amongst you, patient and persevering, they will vanquish two hundred: if a hundred, they will vanquish a thousand of the Unbelievers: for these are a people without understanding (Q. 8:65).

> But when the forbidden months are past, then fight and slay the pagans wherever ye find them, and seize them, and beleaguer them, and lie in wait for them in every stratagem (of war); but if they repent, and establish regular prayers and practice regular charity, then open the way for them: for God is oft-forgiving, most merciful (Q. 9:5).

This kind of teaching was even encouraged in warring against the Jews and the Christians. For example:

> Fight those who believe not in God nor the Last Day, nor hold that forbidden which hath been forbidden by God and His Apostle, nor acknowledge the Religion of truth, (even if they are) of the People of the Book, until

they pay the *Jizya* with willing submission, and feel themselves subdued (Q. 9:29).

To this should be added complete intolerance against any Muslim who decides to change his religion, whether to become a Christian or anything else. "But if they turn renegades, seize them and slay them wherever you find them" (Q. 4:89). In Muhammad's own lifetime, this verse was applied only to those new Arab tribal converts to Islam who fled from the field of battle. Later, it developed into a general understanding against anyone who forsakes Islam. Abd Allah ibn Umar Baidiawi (d. 1291), a well-recognized commentator, says of this verse: "Whosoever turns back from his belief [Islam], openly or secretly, take him and kill him wheresoever ye find him, like any other infidel" (Zwemer 1924:33)! To this day, Orthodox Islam generally holds this harsh position, but does not usually act upon it; although stories abound of Muslims who became Christians and were put to death.

Naturally, the Christian who attempts to work in this environment will be beset with tremendous difficulties, especially if the Muslims tend to be strict observers of Islamic Law. Many of us have been asked hundreds of times by Muslims what we think of Muhammad. For Christians who love the Lord Jesus, Muhammad does not compare favorably. The problem is that Muslims will not tolerate unfavorable comments about their "Prophet." Therefore, it behooves the Christian to say what he or she can that is favorable about Muhammad or to say nothing at all. Montgomery Watt wrote of Muhammad:

> In his day and generation he was a social reformer, even a reformer in the sphere of morals. He created a new system of social security and a new family structure, both of which were a vast improvement on what went before (Watt 1961:234).

Naguib Mahfouz, the Egyptian Nobel Laureate for Literature was equally kind but injected a sly twist at the end of his assessment:

> He combined strength and gentleness, wisdom and simplicity, lordliness and humility, was an honest trustee

273

and was both feared and loved. Moreover he was witty, friendly and correct ... He was an affectionate companion, quite apart from having good taste and a love for songs and jokes ... the truth was that for every one time that they admired his character, they admired his virility and love of women many times. In our alley, the capacity to love women is a thing men boast of and it gives a man prestige as great as or greater than that of being a chief (Mahfouz 1981:286).

5. Muslims Claim Many Biblical Prophecies for Muhammad

Muhammad's followers, now that they have access to the Bible, have been very busy trying to ferret out prophecies from the Old Testament as well as the New, showing that Muhammad, rather than Jesus, is the fulfillment of those prophesies. We will not have space to take up all the attempts to capture these biblical prophecies for Muhammad. But we will take up the one that is the most commonly used. It is found in Deuteronomy 18:15, 19, and reads as follows:

> The Lord your God will raise up for you a prophet like me [Moses] from among your own brothers. You must listen to him ... "I [God] will put my words in his mouth, and he will tell them everything I command him. If anyone does not listen to my words that the prophet speaks in my name, I myself will call him to account."

This prophecy is applied exclusively to Jesus Christ in the New Testament (Acts 3:22; 7:37). In spite of this, Muslims press the claim that this Mosaic prophesy is about Muhammad. Their reasoning goes something like this:

- Moses and Muhammad were both married.
- Moses and Muhammad led armies to victory.
- Moses and Muhammad both gave a "Law" to the world.

- Muhammad was descended from Ishmael, a brother to Isaac; Jesus was not descended from among the brethren (meaning Ishmael).
- Moses and Muhammad both liberated their people from the yoke of oppression.

It is easy to show our Muslim friends how Jesus really is the fulfillment of that prophecy. In the prophecy quoted above, Moses was speaking to his fellow Israelites—the 12 tribes, his brothers. Jesus came from one of those tribes—the tribe of Judah. Moses and Jesus both gave us "covenants" sealed in blood. Jesus' Law was the fulfillment of the Mosaic Law. Both performed extraordinary miracles: Muhammad had none. Both Moses and Jesus were instrumental in providing bread in the wilderness. And both showed authority over the sea: one parted it, the other walked on it. Perhaps most important, Moses taught about the need for blood sacrifices as atonement for sins. Jesus fulfilled the intent of those sacrifices by the shedding of his own blood as atonement for our sins.

For the worker who would like to know more about these Muslim efforts to claim biblical prophecies for Muhammad, the following three books are widely circulated today among Muslims: *Muhammad in the Bible* by Jamal Badawi, *What the Bible Says About Muhammad* by Ahmad Deedat, and *Evidence of the Bible About Muhammad* by Abdul Hamid. Those workers who have to face these kinds of issues would do well to read these books and learn to refute such issues, for the sake of both Muslims who should not be allowed to go on in their deception as well as Christians who might be confused by such presentations.

6. Muslim Use of the Gospel of Barnabas to Support Muhammad

The *Gospel of Barnabas* was first brought to my attention when I was still working in Pakistan. My Muslim students put this book in my hands and showed me that in this "gospel" Jesus clearly foretold the coming of Muhammad. The book in its present form is 273 pages long and was printed at Fazleesons, Karachi, Pakistan, in 1973. It reinforces Muslim charges that Jesus is not the Son of God, that He did not die on the cross, and as we mentioned above, that Jesus prophesied the coming of Muhammad.

From the vantage point of literary criticism, it can be demonstrated that this so-called "gospel" was written sometime after 1300 (McDowell and Gilchrist 1983:99). It is filled with anachronisms. The author made serious mistakes in the geography of Palestine, showing that he had never been there. Some quotations in the work are taken from the poetry of the Italian writer Dante (1245-1321). The author denies that Jesus was the Messiah and assigns that title to Muhammad. Thus this forgery agrees with neither the Bible nor the Quran! An analysis of the literary style shows that whoever wrote this forgery was fluent in Italian (it was first written in Italian), but probably lived in Spain. Josh McDowell's and John Gilchrist's conclusion is that it was "an attempt to mold the life of Jesus into the Quranic and Islamic tradition" (1983:103).

I am indebted to Dr. Youssef Kamell of Colorado College for the following assessments of the *Gospel of Barnabas* from his unpublished paper on the subject, in which he quotes two eminent Egyptian Muslim scholars: "A false gospel, composed by a European person in the fifteenth century containing gross mistakes and descriptions of the political and religious situation in Jerusalem [during the era of Jesus Christ]" (Professor Muhammad Shafik Ghorbal of Cairo), and "This gospel is full of mistakes and would not be acceptable by any Muslim if he could understand how it contradicts the Quran" (Abbas Mahmood al-Accad). Again, as tedious as it may be for the Christian worker, it is necessary to do one's homework in refuting such unworthy efforts to bolster Muhammad's claim that Jesus foretold his coming. Again, we refer to the apostle Paul's counsel on such matters: "And the Lord's servant must not quarrel; instead, he must be kind to everyone, able to teach, not resentful. Those who oppose him he must gently instruct, in the hope that God will grant them repentance ... " (2 Tim. 2:24, 25).

A word of caution: Muslims are incredibly sensitive to what you say about Muhammad. Whether due to their tremendous sense of insecurity or to the demonic empowerment of the cultic aspect of Muhammad's followers, the reason is not important. Generally speaking, Muslims have not reached that level of tolerance and objectivity in scholarship where they will allow an open examination of Muhammad's life and the legends surrounding him. Therefore, in spite of the conclusions reached when comparing Muhammad's life with that of Christ and testing his teaching by biblical criteria, you had best keep your opinions to yourself when working with your Muslim friends.

Perhaps a day will come in their lives when they realize Christ is greater than Muhammad, even in the Quran, and are willing to reach such conclusions on their own. The best that we can do, in light of our love for Muslims, is gently encourage them to undertake such studies for themselves. Meanwhile, go on praying and asking God to remove the veil from their minds that they might see the glory of God in the face of Jesus Christ. Do your best to focus them on Christ.

For the Christian reader who has read the Quran and the *Hadith* and is conversant with the life of Christ in the Gospels, the contrast between Muhammad and Christ is startling. On many issues they are diametrically opposed. Living in the light of the Bible, the Christian finds it difficult, if not impossible, to admit that Muhammad measures up to a biblical definition of a prophet. When one goes on to compare the life of Muhammad with that of Christ, the list of ways in which Christ excels is long indeed. Following is a comparative chart of the two men.

Muhammad	**Christ**
Reflected the qualities of a seventh century Arab man	Reflected the Image of God
Instituted holy war in God's name	Taught disciples not to fight
Institutionalized looting of war victims	Warned against covetousness
Taught vengeance	Taught forgiveness
Legalized polygamy and concubinage	Upheld ideal of monogamy
Demeaned the role of women	Honored women
Made divorce easy for men, but not for women	Spoke against divorce

Muhammad	Christ
Taught sensuous view of paradise	Indicated an afterlife on a higher plane in presence of the Father
Institutionalized Arabic Middle Eastern rituals of religious duties	Taught that true worship was in spirit and truth
Advocated once-in-a lifetime pilgrimage to Mecca	Taught that we are life-long pilgrims in this world
Substituted his law for Mosaic Law	Fulfilled Mosaic Law in love
Ignored the need for blood sacrifice for sins	Came to give his life, shed his blood for the sins of others
Maintained atonement sins was not possible	Came to make atonement for for our sins
Denied the crucifixion	His life culminated in crucifixion and resurrection and ascension
Had no power over Satan or demons	Broke Satan's power in life and at the cross
Had no power to give his disciples	Gave his disciples power and authority over demons
Assumed Islam was the expression of the kingdom of God	Introduced the kingdom of God and Himself as King
Reduced Jesus to being a prophet for his age only	Jesus was the culmination of offices of Prophet, Priest and King for all time

Muhammad	Christ
He cursed those who thought Jesus was the Son of God	Jesus said he who honors the Son honors the Father
No concept of God as our Father	Came to bring us back to our Heavenly Father
Confessed he could do no miracles	Attested the presence of the kingdom with his miracles
Died	Died and then rose from the dead

For the open-minded Muslim who may be reading this material, may I suggest a more detailed comparative study of the life of Christ and the life of Muhammad. The issues for comparison should include such topics as: sinlessness, holiness, purity, forgiveness, marital relations, healing, reconciliation, peace, love, and suffering. This list is not exhaustive, but it offers suggestions by which one can make a comparative evaluation.

Just a final word of caution to the Christian reader. As tempting as it is to speak against Muhammad and his teaching because of the untold suffering he has caused Christians down through history, Muslims have made it a capital offense, in those countries where *Shariah* Law has been imposed, to speak against Muhammad. We could well take the apostle Paul's resolution as our own. He instructed us to "slander no one, to be peaceable and considerate, and to show true humility toward all men" (Titus 3:2). And his words to the believers in Corinth were:

> For I resolved to know nothing while I was with you except Jesus Christ and him crucified. I came to you in weakness and fear, and with much trembling. My message and my preaching were not with wise and persuasive words, but with a demonstration of the Spirit's power, so that your faith might not rest on men's wisdom, but on God's power (1 Cor. 2:2-4).

The father of Abdiyah Akbar Abdul-Haqq, the late Pastor Abdul-Haqq, a brilliant Muslim who converted to Christianity as a young man and went on to become the foremost living debater against Muslims in the Indian subcontinent, said to me when he was in his seventies, "If I had my life to live over again, I never would have entered into debates with Muslim scholars over all those issues [including the prophethood of Muhammad]; I would simply preach Jesus Christ as the crucified, risen and living Lord."

CHAPTER 33

MUHAMMAD'S CLAIMS FOR THE QURAN

Verily this is no less than a Message to (all) the worlds:
(with profit) to whoever among you wills to go straight
(Q. 81:27, 28).

What Muhammad claims for the Quran in the Quran itself is not a challenge that can be taken lightly. For the more than one billion souls in the Muslim world, this is the book that points the way either to heaven or hell. In the quote at the head of the chapter, we see that Muhammad intended it for the whole world. And his qualifying statement in the text is that it is a message for you if you are one of those people who want "to go straight." I am sure most people want to go straight. Therefore, let's examine his claims to see if the guidance in this book will lead us on the straight path.

1. The Quran Confirms All Previous Scripture

For those of us who are Christians, the supreme question is, "Is the teaching of the Quran in accord with that of the Bible?" Repeatedly, Muhammad claims this is the case. For example, note the following quotes: "To thee We sent the Scripture in truth, confirming the scripture that came before it, and guarding it in safety ... " (Q. 5:51), and "This Quran is not such as can be produced by other than God (Q. 10:37); "And before this, was the Book of Moses as a guide and a mercy: and this Book [The Quran] confirms (it) in the Arabic tongue; to admonish the unjust, and as Glad Tidings to those who do right" (Q. 46:12).

A summary of these claims, then, would contain the following points:

- The Quran confirms all the revelations that came before it.
- The Quran guards all revelations that came before it.

- The Quran is from God—the Lord of the Worlds.
- The Quran is a fuller explanation of what went before.
- The Quran is a warning to the unjust.
- The Quran is good news to those who do right.

When we look at the Quran to see if it fulfills its claims, that is not what we find. First of all, there is a great lack of material concerning all of the Old and New Testaments. And when we do examine the subject matter common to both, we find discrepancies, for example, in the life of Abraham, Joseph, the family of Jesus, the circumstances attending Jesus' birth, Zechariah's dumbness, and most of all, the denial of Jesus' Sonship, crucifixion, atoning death, resurrection and deity. Instead of getting a fuller explanation of the true Scriptures, we actually get less detailed accounts, and they are erroneous, they even contradict the Scriptures.

This author's conclusion is that Muhammad never saw the real Bible. Based on the literary criticism technique of analyzing the Quran, I find that it reflects Muhammad's dependence on hearsay material available to him from the Jews and Christians among his acquaintances, none of whom had the canonical Scriptures available to them in Arabic.

Therefore, we cannot accept the claims that Muhammad and his followers make for the Quran. If they are going to insist on these claims, the burden is on them to show how the Quran confirms, guards and more fully explains biblical material. They will have to produce evidence for this to be believable.

2. The Quran is Equal to All Previous Scripture

In the following quote, Muhammad claims that there is "no difference between one and another of them," meaning the revelations given to biblical characters starting with Abraham and ending with Jesus. Let us look at the verse in full:

> We believe in God, and the revelation given to us, and to Abraham, Ismail, Isaac, Jacob, and the Tribes, and that given to Moses and Jesus, and that given to (all) Prophets from their Lord: We make no difference between one and another of them: and we bow to God (in Islam) (Q. 2:136).

Again, we find much that is troubling in this claim. If we take Muhammad's expression "the revelation given to" the various biblical and even non-biblical prophets listed in the Quran, and apply it in the same way we understand Muhammad to have received revelation, then we find Muhammad is in a difficult position. For example, there is no evidence in the Bible that either God or the angel Gabriel ever spoke directly to Ishmael. Nor can we find any material to indicate that God gave "revelations" to the "tribes," presumably, the immediate descendants of Jacob's twelve sons.

Muhammad is in further trouble when he includes in the Quran, for example, Adam and Lot among the biblical prophets. Nowhere in Scripture are they ever referred to as prophets, nor are they ever seen performing a prophetic function. All in all, we find, then, a notable lack of understanding on Muhammad's part as to what was biblical revelation. For these reasons and others in the area of ethical content, which we will not go into here, we find that the Quran is not of the same quality as true biblical revelation. In fact, we find it in opposition to true biblical revelation. Again, the burden is on the Muslim to examine biblical material and compare it with Quranic material to see if Muhammad's claim is truly valid.

3. The Quran Supersedes All Previous Scripture

Inherent in Muhammad's claim that he is "the Seal of the Prophets," is the related idea that the Quran is, by virtue of being the last revelation, the most important one. It is hard to find Quranic verses that say this in just so many words. But the one listed below could be indicative of this assumption on the part of Muslims concerning the preeminence of the Quran over previous Scriptures:

> O People of the Book [Jews and Christians]! There hath come to you our Apostle, revealing to you much that ye used to hide in the Book, and passing over much (that is now unnecessary): There hath come to you from God a (new) light and a perspicuous Book,—wherewith God guideth all who seek His good pleasure to ways of peace and safety, and leadeth them out of darkness, by His Will, unto the light,—guideth them to a path that is straight (Q. 5:16-18).

The following points are extremely interesting in this passage. First, Muhammad charges the Jews and Christians with hiding things that were in their Holy Books, presumably material he thought would support his position. Second, Muhammad asserts that he is now passing over material from their Holy Books that is no longer necessary. This might be a possible reference to the Christian abandonment of the Mosaic ceremonial law, including the sacrifices and all that vanished along with the destruction of the temple. Third, Muhammad claims that with his teaching comes new light in the form of a "perspicuous" book. Yusuf Ali has a long footnote on the meaning of "perspicuous" (1977:246, footnote 716). The gist of his explanation is that this word means something like a "shining light" which makes things clear and helps us distinguish truth from the fiction. Fourth, God, through the Quran, supposedly guides "The People of the Book" out of darkness into light. The clear implication is that Christians and Jews needed more light or "new light" which was only provided in the Quran. And last, the Quran will guide "The People of the Book" to "a path that is straight." Again, the implication is that they were on a crooked path.

It could be argued that Muhammad was speaking to the heretical excesses that he saw among both the Jews and the Christians. Unfortunately, Muhammad considered the very heart of the Gospel heretical. The fruit of this kind of teaching is that Muslims today are made to think that they do not really need to know the Bible, that Muhammad has summarized it correctly for them, and even served as a corrective to those parts of it not handled properly by Jews and Christians. For these reasons, then, we understand why Muslims think that the Quran has superseded the Bible.

The burden on the Christian worker is to find ways to make the full teaching of the Bible known, to defend the authenticity of the Scriptures, and to show their inherent beauty and adequacy for serving every need of a true seeker after God. Again, this calls for much patience, a thorough knowledge of the Scriptures, and an ability to teach it to one's Muslim friends.

4. Muhammad Claims the Words of the Quran Are God's, Not His

One of the constant roadblocks for the Christian who wants to communicate the Gospel to a Muslim is the idea that the Quran is actually the Word of God, possibly even eternal, brought down to earth by an angel (possibly Gabriel) and given to Muhammad as he needed it in discharging his apostleship. There are several Quranic passages that promulgate this idea. The one cited below is typical:

> This Quran is not such as can be produced by other than God; on the contrary it is a confirmation of (revelations) that went before it, and a fuller explanation of the Book—wherein there is no doubt—from the Lord of the Worlds (Q. 10:37).

The true Muslim is convinced that the Quran is actually the Word of God. By holding to this presupposition, when faced with the material of the Bible which does not agree with the Quran, Muslims take one of two positions. Either they conclude the Quran is sufficient for all matters and there is no need to read the Bible, or that Christians must have altered the Bible. They have no other explanation for why the Quran doesn't agree with the Bible.

In this situation, the Christian worker is faced with a double-edged problem. First is to show that the Bible, as we have it, is authentic, genuine, reliable, adequate and a true guide to man's salvation. Concerning the authenticity of the Bible, the reader can refer back to the material at the beginning of chapter 31. There you will find the evidences to show that the Bible has not been tampered with and is essentially the same today as it was in the original.

The second task is not so pleasant. It involves demonstrating the human and possibly alien spiritual sources from which Muhammad got his ideas. John Blair's book, mentioned before, is the best single volume identifying Muhammad's sources in Jewish Talmudic and Mishnaic material, spurious non-canonical gospels in Arabia in his day, the teachings of Zoroastrianism from nearby Persia, and other bits and pieces of ideas from pre-Islamic Bedouin culture, as well as ideas from as far away as Egypt, Ethiopia and India. Again, the student will be well rewarded for such research. It removes the mystery as to where Muhammad got his ideas. Virtually everything in the Quran can be traced to sources in Muhammad's environment.

What is unique about the Quran can be explained as follows. Muhammad was extremely gifted with words. He often challenged others to try to imitate him. His ability to synthesize all of his source material into semi-poetic, ecstatic religious utterances that mesmerized his hearers was astonishing. And he did show a unique ability to adapt his material to the exigencies of each situation as it developed in his life.

Again, a word of warning to the Christian worker. These are explosive issues. It is true that we have been commissioned to "demolish arguments and every pretension that sets itself up against the knowledge of God …" (2 Cor. 10:5). But the corollary to this is that we also have been commissioned to try to win as many as possible. We have to trust the Holy Spirit to fill us with love and wisdom as we handle these sensitive issues while we attempt to bring Muslims back to their heavenly Father through the Good News of Jesus Christ.

PART SEVEN

CONCERNS IN DISCIPLING (BRINGING MUSLIMS INTO ABRAHAM'S FAMILY)

I say to you that many will come from the east and the west and will take their places at the feast with Abraham, Isaac and Jacob in the kingdom of heaven (Matt. 8:11).

Before this faith came, we were held prisoners by the law, locked up until faith should be revealed. So the law was put in charge to lead us to Christ that we might be justified by faith. Now that faith has come, we are no longer under the supervision of the law. You are all sons of God through faith in Christ Jesus, for all of you who were baptized into Christ have clothed yourselves with Christ. There is neither Jew nor Greek, slave nor free, male nor female, for you are all one in Christ Jesus. If you belong to Christ, then you are Abraham's seed, and heirs according to the promise (Gal. 3:23-29).

INTRODUCTION

As we come to the concluding section of this book, let us look again at our starting point. God called Abraham to be the human agency of blessing to all the rest of ruined mankind. "All peoples on earth will be blessed through you" (Gen. 12:3). But, there was a domestic tragedy in Abraham's family right at the beginning of the missionary venture. Instead of waiting for God's miraculous provision of a son (Isaac), Abraham and Sarah took matters into their own hands and consented to have a child through a surrogate mother, Sarah's Egyptian slave girl, Hagar. This ultimately led to a spirit of rivalry between Hagar and Sarah, and at least two ruptures in the family. The first was when Hagar ran away; the second, when she was expelled. But God took an active interest in the problem of Hagar and Ishmael. Hagar, too, was to become a mother, through Ishmael, of many nations, with descendants too numerous to count. These descendants, along with the other races of humankind, were to be the objects of God's great redemptive love.

We traced the tenuous link from Hagar and Ishmael, through Nebaioth and Kedar, Ishmael's sons, to the seventh century "prophet," Muhammad. We learned how he founded a new religion, Islam, and wove into it the ancient story of Hagar and Ishmael, even having pilgrims reenact their search for water by transplanting the biblical account from Beersheba to the vicinity of Mecca.

Next, we described the religion that Muhammad established and the various kinds of Muslims on a theological spectrum, suggesting possible approaches to each type. The underlying assumption is that there will be a rich harvest of Muslims coming to Christ, from every language group, ethnic background and theological persuasion. We also know that there will be violent opposition, inevitable martyrdoms, and heartbreaking setbacks.

In this final section, we will consider several important issues involved in bringing about reconciliation in Abraham's broken family. This kind of endeavor is costly to everyone involved. After all, it cost Jesus His painful death on the cross. We, too, will have prices to pay in bringing Muslims to Christ. And the Muslims themselves, who forsake their allegiance to Muhammad and give it to Christ, will have prices to pay. We will start with the factors that contribute to the trauma of conversion, and suggest how to prepare the Christian worker to play a sympathetic and supportive role for those who dare to leave Islam. Then we will discuss how costly it may be to the Christian worker who wants to do the discipling of their young converts. We will present ideas about having clear goals in discipling, and we will mention possible models of how to incorporate those who come out of Islam into the Body of Christ. In the last chapter we will look at the model of our Savior as He labored in Galilee during the days of His earthly ministry. From His example we will draw applications for the yet unfinished task of evangelism throughout the Muslim World.

CHAPTER 34

THE TRAUMA OF CONVERSION

Do not suppose that I have come to bring peace to the earth. I did not come to bring peace, but a sword. For I have come to turn 'a man against his father, a daughter against her mother, a daughter-in-law against her mother-in-law. A man's enemies will be the members of his own household.' Anyone who loves his father or mother more than me is not worthy of me; anyone who loves his son or daughter more than me is not worthy of me; and anyone who does not take his cross and follow me is not worthy of me. Whoever finds his life will lose it, and whoever loses his life for my sake will find it (Matt. 10:34-39).

True conversion, under most circumstances, is traumatic. There is the trauma of being "born again" (John 3:3), of leaving one spiritual state and entering another, of leaving one master and embracing another. Jesus, in an excruciating way, through unbelievable pain and ultimately through death itself, transited from one state (His pre-resurrection state) to another (His post-resurrection state). In speaking of His own impending death and resurrection, Jesus said: "The Son of Man must suffer many things and be rejected by the elders, chief priests and teachers of the law, and he must be killed and on the third day be raised to life" (Luke 9:22). In a very real way, He modeled being born again. In describing the perils of following Him, He said to His disciples: "If anyone would come after me, he must deny himself and take up his cross daily and follow me. For whoever wants to save his life will lose it, but whoever loses his life for me will save it" (Luke 9:23, 24).

Here in the West, where we have a great deal of freedom and tolerance, those words don't seem so ominous. But in many parts of the Muslim world they are terrifying. Even though there are exceptions, such as in some parts of Indonesia, where the people tend to be tolerant and gentle and where several million "Folk Muslims" have become Christians, in other parts of the Muslim world the spirit of Islam has taken a decidedly more unfriendly turn. There, to declare oneself a Christian normally results in persecution and, depending on which country you are in, could cost your life.

In Pakistan, for example, during the period of 1989 and 1990, the leading Afghan Christian convert was tortured to death at the order of a leader of one of the guerrilla groups. The same group is reported to have abducted and tortured to death a key worker of a Western relief agency. His only "sin" was helping Afghan widows and orphans and making Bibles available to them. In Sind Province, the son of a leading ex-Muslim pastor was first warned and then gunned down in a drive-by shooting in the streets of Hyderabad.

In Malaysia, a recent convert from Islam was jailed along with those who led him to the Lord. He was later released because existing laws could not be used to support his arrest. Since then, the government has changed the law in order to make such arrests "legal."

In Egypt, three converts were jailed in 1990. Another convert died under torture the previous year. The three who had been severely beaten in jail were released only after they once again professed Islam under torture. Thank God for the others, who, for whatever reason, have not been jailed; probably because the authorities do not know about them. When it is known to the authorities that a Christian worker is effective in leading Muslims to Christ, that person is usually jailed or, if a foreigner, told to leave the country.

Where does all this hatred and intolerance come from? It finds its source in the Quran and in the *Hadith*. For a full treatment of this subject, one should read Samuel Zwemer's, *The Law of Apostasy in Islam* (1924). Let's look again at those passages in the Quran which are used as the basis for the imprisonment, torturing, and even murdering of Christians who come out of Islam.

Why should ye be divided into two parties about the Hypocrites? God hath upset them for their (evil) deeds. Would ye guide those whom God hath thrown out of the Way? For those whom God hath thrown out of the Way, never shalt thou find the Way. They but wish that ye would reject Faith, as they do, and thus be on the same footing (as they): but take not friends from their ranks until they flee in the way of God (from what is forbidden). But if they turn renegades, seize them and slay them wherever ye find them; and (in any case) take no friends or helpers from their ranks (Q. 4:88, 89).

O ye who believe! If any from among you turn back from his faith, soon will God produce a people whom He will love as they will love Him,—lowly with the Believers, mighty against the Rejecters, fighting in the Way of God, and never afraid of the reproaches of such as find fault. That is the Grace of God, which He will bestow on whom He pleaseth. And God encompasses all, and He knoweth all things (Q. 5:57).

Any one who, after accepting faith in God, utters Unbelief,—except under compulsion, his heart remaining firm in Faith—but such as open their breast to Unbelief,—on them is Wrath from God, and theirs will be a dreadful Penalty (Q. 16:106).

During the period of Muhammad's rule (A.D. 622-632) in Medina, these verses were used to threaten people who either wanted to turn back to their old ways of idol worship, or who wanted to desert Muhammad's army in the days of fighting, or both. They were not used, apparently, against Muslims who became Christians (Woodberry 1992:28-31). But later, following the death of Muhammad, these above verses were applied to Muslims who became Christians. Major Muslim commentators almost universally interpret these verses to mean any Muslim who leaves Islam (becomes a Christian) should be put to death. Zwemer quotes al-Baydawi (died 1291), considered the soundest and most authoritative of all Muslim commentators, who wrote in his *The Lights of Revelation and the Secrets of Interpretation:*

> Whosoever turns back from his belief, openly or secretly, take him and kill him wheresoever ye find him, like any other infidel. Separate yourself from him altogether. Do not accept intercession in his regard (Zwemer 1924:33, 34).

Two of the original *Hadith* chroniclers, Bukhari (died 870) and Muslim (died 875), reported that the Prophet said, "Kill those who change their religion" (English translation by James Robson, 1975:752). To the reader unacquainted with Islam and the place of *Hadith* in it, please note that along with the Quran, the *Hadith* has been of extreme importance in molding the attitude of Muslims. Generally, the more fundamentalist the Muslims are, the more apt they are to enforce this, and the more syncretistic they are, the more tolerant they are apt to be. Because of the widespread acceptance of this "Law of Apostasy" by Muslims, there is a dreadful fear that attends the whole decision-making process when a Muslim becomes a Christian. In most cases, this fear is fully justified, and is probably the greatest single reason why more Muslims do not become Christians.

Even though there is a verse in the Quran that says, "Let there be no compulsion in religion ..." (Q. 2:256), it does not contravene the above mentioned authorities who advocate killing a Muslim who becomes a Christian. It should be noted that when Orthodox Muslims discuss the idea of "religious freedom," they mean that all others are free to become Muslims, but Muslims are not free to change their religion.

As we return to the discussion of conversion, we should remember that for the inquiring Muslim, right from the beginning, it is a question of life or death. Thank God that earlier in this century millions of Indonesian Muslims became Christians without losing their lives. Recent riots between Christians and Muslims in Indonesia indicate that the mood of tolerance may be giving way to communal fighting. Nevertheless, the threat is ever present, and often hangs like a pall over the Muslim groping toward faith in Christ. It is not uncommon when Muslims come to Christ, if their lives are not actually in danger, for them to be disowned by their families, fired from their jobs and thrown out of their universities. If they are married, many have their spouses and children taken away from them; if they are single, many are denied the privilege of marrying among their own people. Many are denied the possibility of future employment and excluded from the mosque and all religious festivities. In general, they are cut off from all normal family and societal relationships. In other words, they become outcasts. Let us just stop and think about the levels of trauma a person may have to go through to leave Islam.

The Trauma of Change of Allegiance

When Paul was commissioned to work among the non-Jews, the Lord said to him:

> I am sending you to them to open their eyes and turn them from darkness to light, and from the power of Satan to God, so that they may receive forgiveness of sins and a place among those who are sanctified by faith in me (Acts 26:17, 18).

For a Muslim, the first shock is "seeing" Islam with open eyes. In the light of Jesus Christ, its basic anti-Christian spirit becomes clear. The function of the Christian worker, using the Word of God and relying on the Spirit of God, is to enable the Muslim to "see" the truth of Jesus Christ as well as the contrasting untruth of the tenets of Islam. The trauma, then, is in tearing oneself away from one power (Satan) and entering the embrace of another (Christ). During this process, Satan, or his underlings, usually stir up people to threaten the new believer with physical harm. Shock is inevitable as the new believer realizes that what he or she considered an acceptable religion before was actually bondage to the very enemy of God.

The Trauma of Broken Pride

Islam, as a system, subtly appeals to human pride. If you do all of the required duties of Islam you will supposedly achieve, by your own effort, admission to paradise. Muslims believe people are born weak but not sinful.

When Muslims come to Christ, however, it is often with the realization that they really are sinful and need a Savior. The late Dr. Muhammad Kamil Hussein, a well-known surgeon and writer in Cairo, is perhaps the first Muslim of distinction to comment on what the crucifixion (or the attempted crucifixion, from the Muslim point of view) of Jesus by the religious Jews has to say about unjustified human religious pride and its failure to defend a just man. In his *City of Wrong: A Friday in Jerusalem*, he writes:

> From the purely human point of view, however, there is no doubt that what they did was wrong. They left the right in all its unmistakability to suffer outrage. They exposed their religion to extinction, their prophet [Jesus] to foul wrong and themselves to destruction ... without doubt the line of action their reason had approved and the guidance deriving from their reflection and their intuitions were alike invalid (Husain 1959:120).

The knowledge that they were partners in the wrong and that their action followed a line of communal consent did not save the disciples from self-reproach because they saw themselves as individually responsible (Husain 1959:123).

To a sensitive person like Hussein, the conclusion was inescapable. Religious men and women, at their best, failed, thus leaving no grounds for human pride. Conversion, then, for a Muslim involves breaking religious pride. Unfortunately, most Muslims have taken the position that people can be saved by their own good deeds. These Muslims believe that Jesus was not crucified for man's sins; rather, that God rescued Jesus and took Him alive to heaven before He could die.

The Trauma of Death to Self

"If anyone would come after me, he must deny himself and take up his cross daily and follow me" (Luke 9:23).

How many times in all of these years of working with Muslims have I heard the words, "Sir, the teaching of Christianity is impractical, even impossible. It is not 'natural' to have a pure mind. People cannot help having sexual thoughts all the time. It is impossible to love your enemy. You are supposed to hate him and to seek revenge. Come to Islam. It is the religion of the natural man. It was designed for human beings the way we are." The idea of "new birth" is utterly foreign to Islam. "Come as you are. Simply confess that 'there is no God but God and Muhammad is the Messenger of God,' and you are okay." Becoming a Muslim is so easy, so effortless; getting out is another matter, as we have pointed out earlier.

"New birth" implies leaving one world to enter another; leaving the kingdom of darkness to enter the kingdom of God's dear Son. It implies failing to justify oneself in God's eyes. It admits the failure of family, community, and nation to provide a "right" way of living. The need to be re-made, re-created in the image of God, is a traumatic and crushing blow to those who had formerly sought to justify themselves by their "good" deeds.

The Trauma of Placing God Above Family

For the average Muslim, at least in the Middle East, family is everything. The idea of hyper-individualism, as we know it in the West, is utterly foreign to Islam. Families make decisions. Marriages are arranged. Next to the extended family, the wider community is considered the focus of loyalty. In Islam, it is almost unheard of for a Muslim to contemplate leaving his or her family and community. A Muslim may ask, "Where else is there to go? What other basis of security is there? To whom do I belong? From where do I derive my significance? What is my identity?" Humanly speaking, the Muslim finds his ultimate significance in belonging to the household of Islam (*Dar al-Islam*). One of the common questions that goes through a Muslim's mind as he or she contemplates conversion is: "Who will be my new community, my new family, my new social context?" Yes, the trauma of leaving father, mother, wife, children or lands is, indeed, very great for the average Muslim. "Would ye guide those whom God hath thrown out of the Way?" These words from Quran 4:88, quoted earlier, forbid members of the Muslim community from helping their family members or former friends after they have become Christians.

Three cases of Saudi young men who became Christians could be used to illustrate this. All three converted while living abroad. In each case, they had the good sense to phone home and tell their fathers what had happened. These are the three responses from their respective fathers:

1. "Don't ever come home again. We will have to kill you if you do."

2. "Come home, clear up all your personal affairs, and get out of this country. There is no place here for you."

3. "You may come home and retain your faith privately if you promise not to share this with anyone."

If one survives inside the country, the sense of alienation is almost overwhelming. Very few in Saudi Arabia, until recently, had the courage or the stamina to maintain their faith under such rejection. The third father's response quoted above raises the whole question of "secret believers." Is a person who keeps silent really a believer? I personally do not wish to judge such a situation. But I do know that Jesus was uncompromising in requiring public witness to Himself:

> If anyone would come after me, he must deny himself and take up his cross and follow me. For whoever wants to save his life will lose it, but whoever loses his life for me and for the gospel will save it. What good is it for a man to gain the whole world, yet forfeit his soul? Or what can a man give in exchange for his soul? If anyone is ashamed of me and my words in this adulterous and sinful generation, the Son of Man will be ashamed of him when he comes in his Father's glory with the holy angels (Mark 8:34-38).

The Trauma of Losing a Spouse, and/or Children

The *Hadith* clearly states that in the case of apostasy of a married man, the wife is to be taken from him, as well as the children. In the case of a woman who becomes a Christian, the Muslim husband may do with her as he wishes, either keep her or divorce her (Zwemer 1924:34). In the case of the single person, there is virtually no prospect of finding a spouse. The consequences of coming to Christ are so starkly cruel. The new believer is left in the most unnatural state of facing life without a wife or husband and with no prospect of building a family.

Ministering to the Traumatized

In no way is a member of the Muslim community to help or intercede for a Muslim who apostatizes (Q.4:88). He or she is considered a traitor to the community and a renegade from the faith. No mercy is to be extended. In the case of educational institutions, he or she is to be denied admission. In no way is this person to be allowed to advance his or her career. Even more ominous is the growth of fundamentalism in the Arab world today. In Egypt, spokesmen for Muslim fundamentalists have openly declared that they are going to drive the Christians out of their country. Qaddafi of Libya has said there should be no such thing as an Arab Christian. His formula for peace in Lebanon, you'll recall, is to kill converts or drive all Arab Christians out of Lebanon. All of the above constitute a worst case scenario. In the Arab heartland, if Islamic fundamentalists gain control, this is the way it will be. But the amazing thing is that even under these most adverse circumstances, Muslims are coming to Jesus, even in Saudi Arabia. The Christian worker must be aware of the tremendous risk the Muslim is taking to come to Christ and must, if at all possible, do everything to minister to these victims from one of the world's worst totalitarian systems. "However, if you suffer as a Christian, do not be ashamed, but praise God that you bear that name" (1 Peter 4:16).

CHAPTER 35

THE COST OF DISCIPLING

> We were gentle among you, like a mother caring for her little children. We loved you so much that we were delighted to share with you not only the gospel of God but our lives as well, because you had become so dear to us (1 Thess. 2:7, 8).

For the Christian discipler living in a wonderfully free Western society, discipling is costly, as illustrated by the verses above. It involves commitment of significant time and energy, but it fits into the normal rhythm of one's daily life. No police, no unusual crises, possibly no financial burden is incurred; probably there is no stigma, no shame, and certainly, no danger. In a closed totalitarian society, security can change suddenly and dramatically. Relatives of your disciple inform the police of suspicious activity. The police visit your disciple. There is an interrogation. Your name may come up. Employers are informed. Your disciple is fired. His or her in-laws attempt to take the children away, and in the case of a married male convert, to take his wife from him. Your disciple enters a period of deep depression. And your career as a missionary or tentmaker may be in jeopardy. The above scenario has endless variations.

What will your role be? How can you be supportive? Suppose you live in the same country, even the same city? Will your disciple want to see you? Are you an embarrassment to him or her? How can you stay in touch? Suppose you live outside the country? You are a non-residential discipler. What are you going to do? Or suppose you are a national brother or sister living nearby. Further activity on your part may involve you with the police, too. Will you risk it in order to be supportive? These are the questions the worker may have to live with in a closed totalitarian Muslim country. The following are cases in point.

In Malaysia, Chinese Christians who were instrumental in leading Muslims to Jesus were jailed, along with the new converts. Those who escaped the police dragnet emigrated. In Morocco, expatriate workers are periodically thrown out of the country (God sends new ones in later). In Turkey, titanic legal battles involving Muslims who have come to Jesus rage in a few major cities. Foreign workers are always under investigation. In Nigeria, scores of churches have been burned to the ground and pastors have been killed in the northern Muslim areas of the country. In Saudi Arabia, the religious police confiscate Bibles, shut down prayer meetings and forbid church services for expatriate Christians. Tension is rising in poverty-stricken Egypt. Thousands of nominal Coptic orthodox "Christians" have caved in to cruel Muslim economic pressure and such threats as having their irrigation water shut off to their farms. They are becoming Muslims. A recent convert from Islam died under torture in that country. And expatriate workers wonder when one of their disciples will talk under interrogation and tell the police who it was who helped him or her to become a Christian.

As incredible as it may seem, in spite of the examples listed above, discipling is going on, not only in the countries listed above, but in virtually every Muslim country of the world and even among Muslim minorities in non-Muslim countries. It is a mark of the universal love of God for these lost peoples that He arranges for His workers to find ways to evangelize and disciple in the face of such opposition.

What can be done under such adverse circumstances? Following are ideas and suggestions that may be helpful. Some of these are universal concerns and should be emphasized under any circumstances, whether we are living under restriction or in relative freedom. Others will not be necessary in societies that exhibit more freedom and tolerance.

The Indispensability of Intercessory Prayer in the Life of the Discipler

Even before discussing what to do in live person-to-person discipling, one other concern may be the most important thing you do: practicing intercessory prayer.

One of the most fascinating stories coming out of the lives of missionaries working in the Overseas Missionary Fellowship, formerly called the China Inland Mission, is of the missionary who had a vast territory to cover in difficult mountainous terrain. God graciously gave him a fruitful ministry in various villages and towns of his far-flung ministry. Because of the difficulty of travel and time, he found that he could not visit his disciples as often as he wished. He decided to spend extra time in prayer for those disciples whom he could not find time to visit very often. After some months, it became apparent that the disciples for whom he spent more time in prayer did better than those that he was able to visit more frequently. To be sure, the conclusions one could draw from this are subjective. Nevertheless, I am inclined to believe that their improved growth was directly linked to that earnest intercessory prayer time that was invested in their lives. It is God who is ultimately responsible for the growth of a believer. Prayer, on our part, releases God to do what He longs to do for His own. Let us look at one of the examples of Jesus Himself.

Jesus, knowing full well what His men were made of, and foreseeing the worst in the case of Simon Peter, prayed for him. Do you remember the story? Simon Peter, the "Rock," faltered at the time of Jesus' arrest. And after having boasted that even if all the other disciples forsook Jesus, he would not! Simon Peter denied Jesus three times! But all was not lost. It was Simon Peter who delivered that mighty sermon on the day of Pentecost when three thousand came to the Lord. What was it that made this remarkable transformation possible? Jesus had prayed for him, even before his denial happened: "Simon, Simon, Satan has asked to sift you as wheat. But I have prayed for you, Simon, that your faith may not fail. And when you have turned back, strengthen your brothers" (Luke 22:31, 32). Simon Peter's faith faltered briefly, but overall, it prevailed. Simon Peter was not lost because Jesus foresaw his fall. He expected it. He prayed for him, went back to him, questioned him publicly in front of all the Apostles and elicited from him a three-fold reaffirmation of faith. This was accompanied each time by a re-commissioning: "Feed my lambs... Take care of my sheep ... Feed my sheep" (John 21:15-17). Jesus understood. He recovered Peter. But even before that restoration, there was that prayer. The Scriptures do not tell us much about the contents of Jesus' prayers. That is why the recording of this particular prayer is so significant.

In Muslim work, where persecution is so fierce, shouldn't praying that the faith of our disciples not fail, but prevail be one of our basic activities? In the life of Paul, several passages reveal his heart and the importance of intercessory prayer for his disciples. Note the following:

> How constantly I remember you in my prayers at all times ... (Rom. 1:9, 10).

> I have not stopped giving thanks for you, remembering you in my prayers. I keep asking that the God of our Lord Jesus Christ, the glorious Father, may give you the Spirit of wisdom and revelation, so that you may know him better. I pray also that the eyes of your heart may be enlightened in order that you may know the hope to which he has called you, the riches of his glorious inheritance in the saints, and his incomparably great power for us who believe (Eph. 1:16-19).

> I pray that out of his glorious riches he may strengthen you with power through his Spirit in your inner being, so that Christ may dwell in your hearts through faith. And I pray that you, being rooted and established in love, may have power, together with all the saints, to grasp how wide and long and high and deep is the love of Christ, and to know this love that surpasses knowledge—that you may be filled to the measure of all the fullness of God (Eph. 3:16-19).

> I thank my God every time I remember you. In all my prayers for all of you, I always pray with joy because of your partnership in the gospel from the first day until now, being confident of this, that he who began a good work in you will carry it on to completion until the day of Christ Jesus. It is right for me to feel this way about all of you, since I have you in my heart ... how I long for all of you with the affection of Christ Jesus (Phil. 1:3-8).

What a heart for his disciples! He thanked God always for them. His ultimate goal was to see them filled with all the fullness of God. He wanted them to be filled with hope, understand God's love, and operate in the power of God. He wanted them to know God better. He wanted Christ to dwell in their hearts by faith. He spent time praying these qualities into the lives of his disciples. And he felt confident that God would answer his prayers because he held his disciples "in his heart."

The Need to Demonstrate Affection

In addition to his habit of intercessory prayer, Paul demonstrated a personal concern and affection for his disciples. The devil knows how to prey on suffering people by creating a sense of loneliness, alienation and rejection. "No one cares. Turn back, you will be accepted. This suffering will all be over, if you just come back to Islam." In the absence of affection and a caring discipler or fellowship group, misunderstanding or bitterness or even anger may take root in the heart of the young believer, opening the door for the Devil.

As incredible as it may seem to us, God has apparently given to us the privilege and responsibility of caring for these young believers. And what we do matters. Perhaps this could be illustrated from the rearing of newborn babies. Where there is love and caring, touch and affection, babies thrive. Where they are left to themselves without personal touch and affection, they tend to become sickly and even die. Is it possible that people react spiritually in a similar fashion? I think so. Unfortunately, I know of no documented studies to prove this, just personal observations over a long period of time. People need love, affirmation, affection, touch, a sense of significance and of being cared for, and the assurance that someone is concerned for what happens to them. Perhaps for those coming out of hostile Islam, this is an even more critical concern.

It is true that Jesus Himself has promised never to leave us or forsake us (Matt. 28:20; Heb. 13:5). Some new believers have this sense of the Lord's presence right from the beginning and never seem to lose it. Others have to grow into it, usually by learning it from an older, more mature Christian. In the life of our Lord, we see that He invited His disciples to be with Him. They could sense His caring and His love at all times. He continued teaching, training, and sharing His power, wisdom, and vision with them. He washed their feet. In the end, He died for them.

In case we think that Jesus is an exception and His model is unattainable, God chose an ordinary man, Rabbi Saul of Tarsus, even a killer of Christians, a man cut from the same piece of cloth as we are, to model for us this same kind of loving concern. At the beginning of this chapter, we quoted from Paul's letter to the Thessalonians. In it, we learned that Paul was as gentle as a mother among her children, caring for them, loving them even to the point of giving his life for them. He said, "I long for all of you with the affection of Christ Jesus" (Phil. 1:8). "The affection of Christ Jesus." Jesus gave Himself for us all. His Spirit lived on in Paul, just as He does in us today. Look at how that love moved Paul to follow up with his disciples: "Some time later Paul said to Barnabas, 'Let us go back and visit the brothers in all the towns where we preached the word of the Lord and see how they are doing'" (Acts 15:36). When Paul could not visit people personally, he either sent someone to represent him, or he wrote letters, or both. Notice the following references to his sending of others in his place.

To the Disciples in Ephesus
Tychicus, the dear brother and faithful servant in the Lord, will tell you everything, so that you also may know how I am and what I am doing. I am sending him to you for this very purpose, that you may know how we are, and that he may encourage you (Eph. 6:21, 22).

To the Disciples in Colosse
Tychicus will tell you all the news about me. He is a dear brother, a faithful minister and fellow servant in the Lord. I am sending him to you for the express purpose that you may know about our circumstances and that he may encourage your hearts (Col. 4:7, 8).

To the Disciples in Philippi
I hope in the Lord Jesus to send Timothy to you soon, that I also may be cheered when I receive news about you ... I hope therefore, to send him as soon as I see how things go with me (Phil. 2:19, 23).

In addition to sending personal emissaries both to comfort and encourage, Paul took time to write letters to individuals (Timothy, Titus, Philemon), to churches that he had helped to plant (Galatians, Ephesians, Philippians, Thessalonians), and to groups of believers in places he had not visited (Colosse and Rome). Those letters took time to write. Even though they are only letters, they turned out to be treasure houses of practical pastoral advice, theological treatises of the first order, and lessons in mission philosophy and strategy. Paul also used these letters to exchange greetings with all kinds of people and even conveyed other people's greetings to his readership, thus giving the sense of unity and mutual concern for one another in the growing body of Christ. This latter function can have a very steadying effect on isolated new believers who may wonder about the significance of what they have joined. All of the above activity takes an enormous commitment of time and energy. In fact, it becomes a fulltime occupation. There is risk of every kind involved in the cause of winning and discipling new believers. Study intently this list of hardships that Paul cites as the "cost of discipling":

> I have ... been in prison ... been flogged ... been exposed to death again and again. Five times I received ... the forty lashes minus one. Three times I was beaten with rods, once I was stoned, three times I was shipwrecked, I spent a night and a day in the open sea, I have been constantly on the move. I have been in danger ... from false brothers. I have labored and toiled and have often gone without sleep; I have known hunger and thirst and have often gone without food; I have been cold and naked. Besides everything else, I face daily the pressure of my concern for all the churches (2 Cor. 11:23-28).

The above point out the nature and extent of commitment involved in giving yourself to the discipling of young believers. To say it is costly is too trite; it may cost your life. The result of your love and commitment to your disciple is that a bridge of trust is established and the disciple will respond to your leadership and teaching. Without this bond of trust, especially when the environment is so hostile, discipling may not take place.

Carrying out this type of ministry in certain "restricted access" Muslim countries may be difficult, but not impossible. With Muslim governments controlling visas, with their ubiquitous secret police, and with "good" Muslim neighbors and relatives acting as informants for the police, it can be very tough. Yet surprisingly, discipling goes on. The inventiveness of God's servants is incredible. Disciplers, both male and female, can go as tourists, business people, or people with professional skills, or as students or teachers. The discipler can also work through trained nationals who are willing to go in and out of these "closed" countries. Also there is a great benefit to the use of radio programs, mail, audio-cassettes, videotapes and hand-carried material. The most important thing in the life of the discipler is to have the heart to do it. Where there is such a heart, there will be a way. You will find a way.

Perhaps at this point we should remember that God Himself takes an active role in this discipling. Paul wrote in 1 Corinthians 3:6, "I planted the seed, Apollos watered it, but God made it grow." And God has His own way of enabling disciples to grow: dreams, visions, the promptings of the Holy Spirit, bringing to attention passages from the Word of God, and simply manifesting His wonderful presence. I am sure that these phenomena are a result of our prayers for the young believers. But, insofar as possible, we are expected to do our part. Discipling, even under ideal circumstances in a free society, is costly. It involves investing your life in another. In closing this chapter on the cost of discipling, we could use no better words than those Jesus spoke to explain the purpose of His life: "For even the Son of Man did not come to be served, but to serve, and to give his life as a ransom for many" (Mark 10:45).

CHAPTER 36

CLEAR OBJECTIVES IN DISCIPLING

My dear children, for whom I am again in the pains of childbirth until Christ is formed in you (Gal. 4:19).

What a wonderful way for the apostle Paul to state his concern for the disciples in Galatia, "until Christ is formed in you." What does it really mean? What is it all about? How does it work? It is very different from Islam. Muslims are very concerned with what to do. "How do I 'do' this religion?" "What is the correct posture for prayer?" "How do I ritually cleanse myself?" "What are the exact good deeds I should do to earn my way to paradise?" Behind it all is the deeper question: "How would Muhammad do this?" Unconsciously, the Muslim takes into himself or herself something of the character of Muhammad and the spirit that inspired him. Discipling Muslims who are becoming Christians then has to do with weaning the disciple away from the teaching and spirit of Muhammad, and enabling Christ to be formed in the new believer.

To understand this we must go back to the first chapter of the Bible. There we read: "So God created man in his own image, in the image of God he created him; male and female he created them" (Gen. 1:27). Once, when speaking to a gathering in a restricted country, I noticed there was a young Malay man in the audience among the Chinese and Indian believers. Afterwards, I asked him to tell me how he became a Christian. With a twinkle in his eye he said, "By reading chapter 1 of Genesis." He explained that there is no teaching in all of Islam about man being made in the image of God. Islam teaches us that God is high, transcendent, unknowable. In Islam no one knows what God is really like. So these words "man in the image of God" fascinated him. With a Christian friend and a Bible, he studied this theme. He discovered that Jesus is "the radiance of God's glory and the exact representation of his being …" (Heb. 1:3).

Jesus himself said, "Anyone who has seen me has seen the Father" (John 14:9).

God can be seen, understood and known in the life of Jesus the Messiah. Jesus was called both "The Son of God" and "The Son of Man." Jesus was a living model of the "Image of God" in human form. The man realized that Jesus was the example of what he was supposed to be.

The young Malaysian also discovered Paul's words that we all need to "reach unity in the faith and in the knowledge of the Son of God and become mature, attaining to the whole measure of the fullness of Christ" (Eph. 4:13). And "for in Christ all the fullness of the Deity lives in bodily form, and you have been given fullness in Christ ..." (Col. 2:9, 10).

He also read the same idea in 2 Corinthians 3:18: "And we, who with unveiled faces all reflect the Lord's glory, are being transformed into his likeness with ever-increasing glory, which comes from the Lord, who is the Spirit."

From other passages, the Malaysian learned that Christ said He wanted to abide in him (John 15:5), that his body was the temple of the Holy Spirit (1 Cor. 3:16), and that the Holy Spirit is referred to as "the Spirit of God," and "the Spirit of Christ" (Rom. 8:9).

It all became an overwhelming, breathtaking revelation. God originally made man in His image. All of that was spoiled by man's rebellion. Christ came to restore in us God's image. God Himself wanted to live in us. It all came together. Suddenly, the young man knew who he was and what he was supposed to be. He recognized God's provision for making it all happen by His Spirit, the Spirit of Christ, indwelling him. He saw the absolute centrality of Christ Jesus as the key to becoming what God wanted him to be and to his very understanding of God. The man realized that God wants the image of His Son to be formed in him. And he realized that Christ is the one who opens the door to fellowship with God.

This young believer, not knowing where else to begin, read Genesis and discovered in the first chapter who he was. This led him to further research what it meant to be made or remade in God's image and he discovered the necessity, the centrality of Jesus in God's plan for man. He also saw the interchangeable roles of God the Father, of Jesus and of the Holy Spirit in this redemptive process, because various passages used one or the other role to describe God's indwelling presence. This helped the man understand the unity of God, a problem for people of Muslim background.

In discipling, we know the ultimate goal is God Himself, being recreated in His image, yes, being indwelt by Him. The goal of discipling, then, is helping the young believer develop this relationship, this walk with God as intimate as having Christ abide in us and we in Him (John 15:5). All other aspects of discipling revolve around this central goal of Christ living in us. This is what we want to communicate, to teach, and to build into the lives of young disciples. They must see the radiancy of the indwelling Christ in us. We, by the power of the Spirit, engender this in our disciples.

The Role of the Holy Spirit

The initial concern, then, is to teach the new believer the need to be filled with the Holy Spirit. Paul wrote to the believers in Corinth, "Do you not know that your body is a temple of the Holy Spirit, who is in you, whom you have received from God?" (1 Cor. 6:19). At Pentecost, Peter explained it so clearly, "Repent and be baptized, every one of you, in the name of Jesus Christ for the forgiveness of your sins. And you will receive the gift of the Holy Spirit" (Acts 2:38). Jesus instructed His first band of disciples to tarry in Jerusalem until they were "clothed with power from on high" (Luke 24:49). On another occasion He said, "But you will receive power when the Holy Spirit comes on you; and you will be my witnesses … to the ends of the earth" (Acts 1:8). The concern here is not with doctrine or how to do this or that. The concern is with God's presence and power. Jesus said, "Apart from me you can do nothing" (John 15:5).

There are only two powers in this world and we are under the influence of either one or the other. The apostle John wrote, "We know that … the whole world is under the control [power] of the evil one" (1 John 5:19). The issue, then, is the question, "Under which power will we live?" Since the whole world is under the power of the evil one, it is imperative that we teach new believers how to be indwelt by Christ, to be filled with the presence and power of God's Spirit.

You, the discipler, must teach the new believer about his or her tremendous resource in the Holy Spirit. Peter taught that when a person repents and is baptized in the name of Jesus Christ for the forgiveness of sins, he or she receives the gift of the Holy Spirit (Acts 2:38). Paul, in arguing for the unity of the body, points out that "we were all baptized by one Spirit into one body... (1 Cor. 12:13). To the Church in Ephesus, Paul wrote, "Be filled with the Spirit..."(Eph. 5:18). It is imperative that the new believer understand and appropriate by faith this tremendous resource of God's Spirit. In other words, the believer needs to consciously walk in the Spirit at all times. Otherwise, he or she may lapse back into trying to do everything in his or her own strength.

The following functions of the Holy Spirit should be taught to the new believer and he or she should be taught to appropriate by faith what God wants to give.

1. Jesus comes to live in us by His Spirit (John 14:17, 18).

2. The Holy Spirit teaches us all things and reminds us of everything Jesus has said (John 14:26).

3. The Holy Spirit is the one who bears witness of the reality of Jesus to others (John 15:26).

4. It is the Holy Spirit who convicts the world of sin, righteousness and judgment (John 16:8-11).

5. The Holy Spirit will guide us into all truth; He will tell us of things to come and will make Christ's things known to believers (John 16:13).

6. It is the Holy Spirit who bears in us the "fruit of the Spirit," the manifestation of the image of Christ (Gal. 5:22, 23).

7. It is the Holy Spirit who appoints people to the various ministries in the church (Eph. 4:11).

8. It is the Holy Spirit who gives spiritual gifts (1 Cor. 12:28-30).

9. It is the Holy Spirit who anoints us with power to witness (Acts 1:8; 4:31; 5:32).

10. It is the Holy Spirit who gives the visions and dreams out of which advances in the work of the kingdom of God are achieved (Joel 2:28).

It is interesting to note the role of the Holy Spirit in Jesus' life and teaching. He obviously understood the very nature of how everything works in God's kingdom. God Himself, God the Spirit, works through filled believers. Note Jesus' baptism. Heaven opened and the Spirit of God descended upon Him. In fact, in John's gospel, it says, "For the one whom God has sent speaks the words of God, for God gives the Spirit without limit" (John 3:34). Zechariah prophesied hundreds of years before Jesus came: "This is the word of the Lord ... 'Not by might, nor by power, but by my Spirit' says the Lord Almighty" (Zech. 4:6).

Spiritual Warfare
Closely following this teaching about the Holy Spirit should come teaching on the reality of spiritual warfare. No greater disservice could a discipler render to a young believer than to keep him or her in the dark about the spiritual battles that have raged and will rage over his or her soul and over his or her tribe, clan, people and nation, yes, over the whole world. At this point you may want to review the material in chapter 21 on the use of spiritual power. That material was initially for you, the Christian worker. Now you must teach what you yourself believe and practice in this war. Even though this may be review for you, the following should be fundamental in your discipling.

The Devil was here on earth when Adam and Eve were created and was instrumental in their downfall by deceiving them and getting them to doubt the goodness and wisdom of God and to disregard His Word (Genesis 3:1-5). God pronounced eternal enmity between Satan and mankind, hinting at the war that was about to begin. In this war, Satan would fatally wound Jesus, but God also prophesied the crushing of Satan under Jesus' feet, the latter to be done in two stages. Stage one occurred when Christ died on the cross for the sins of the whole world thus robbing

Satan of his power to accuse and condemn believers (Col. 2:14, 15). Stage two will occur at the final return of the Lord Jesus Christ when He will carry out the ultimate and irrevocable sentence of judgment against Satan (2 Thess. 2:8).

By virtue of our Lord Jesus' great victory over Satan at the cross, and His indwelling presence in us by His Spirit, we have a certain degree of authority and power over the forces of darkness now. We have power to drive out demons and heal (Matt. 10:1), power to resist the devil and see him flee from us (James 4:7), divine power to demolish strongholds and every argument and pretension that sets itself up against the knowledge of God (2 Cor. 10:4, 5), and power to ultimately crush Satan under our feet (Rom. 16:20). But we do not yet see him crushed under our feet. The war rages on, "for our struggle is not against flesh and blood ..." (Eph. 6:12). "The weapons we fight with are not the weapons of this world ... they have divine power to demolish strongholds" (2 Cor. 10:4). We have been taught that "he who is in us is greater than he who is in the world" (1 John 4:4). We are taught to actively resist Satan (James 4:7). We are warned that the devil walks about as a roaring lion seeking people to devour (1 Peter 5:8). Teach your disciples, by all means, the nature of spiritual warfare, the reality of the spiritual enemy of all mankind, and how to exercise authority and power over him in Jesus' name.

The Indispensable Role of the Word of God

When we examine the account of the temptation of Jesus, we are amazed that instead of using His own name and authority, He, as a human, modeled for us the use of Scriptures. To each of Satan's temptations, He answered by saying, "It is written." Then, He quoted the appropriate responses from God's Word (Matt. 4:1-11). It was in the Garden of Eden that Adam and Eve failed on this very point ("Did God really say?" [Gen. 3:1]). In Jesus' test, it was not in a garden, but in a barren wilderness (perhaps made that way as a consequence of sin—and certainly symbolic of where man is today since the Fall) that Jesus met and successfully resisted Satan by quoting God's Word.

Taking just one of Jesus' responses as an example, we read, "Man does not live on bread alone, but on every word that comes from the mouth of God" (Matt. 4:4, a quote from Deut. 8:3).

Around 1400 B.C., God spoke to Joshua (the Hebrew version of the name Jesus) in the following words: "Do not let this Book of the Law depart from your mouth; meditate on it day and night, so that you may be careful to do everything written in it. Then you will be prosperous and successful" (Josh. 1:8). Four hundred years later (around 1,000 B.C.), King David, the man who gave us the Psalms, reiterated this profound teaching in writing of how the righteous should behave: "But his delight is in the law of the Lord, and on his law he meditates day and night. He is like a tree planted by streams of water, which yields its fruit in season and whose leaf does not wither. Whatever he does prospers" (Ps. 1:2, 3). Approximately three hundred years after David, around 700 B.C., the prophet Isaiah wrote: "This is the one I esteem: he who is humble and contrite in spirit, and trembles at my word" (Isa. 66:2).

Jesus, in teaching His immediate disciples, and hence, all of us, said: "If you remain in me and my words remain in you, ask whatever you wish, and it will be given you" (John 15:7). Paul, perhaps thirty years after Jesus ascended to heaven, wrote to the Colossians (3:16) "Let the word of Christ dwell in you richly as you teach and admonish one another with all wisdom, and as you sing psalms, hymns and spiritual songs with gratitude in your hearts to God." To the above sampling of quotes could be added scores of others about the indispensability of the Word of God in the life of the believer.

The practical side concerns how to make the Word of God available to your disciples and how to get them to ingest the Word of God to the point where they can meditate on it day and night and have it remain as the living word in the core of their being. Let us divide the challenge into two parts. First of all, there are many ways to make the Word of God available: through translation, publication and distribution of the printed Word, the use of audio cassettes, the chanting of the Word of God over radio, and person-to-person memorization sessions. Each situation calls for its own solution about how to make the Word of God available. The second aspect of using the Word of God in discipling depends a lot on personal style and training. The point is to work through a program that will meet the young believers' needs. At the same time, try to build into their lives habits that will become, if possible, permanent. Teach them to meditate on God's Word day and night to the end that its truths may be applied to their lives in a practical way.

In large parts of the Muslim world, due to illiteracy and even methods of teaching, people have phenomenal memories. We advocate not only the memorization of selected verses, but also the memorization of whole passages so that the believer will be able to draw on them, even if his or her Bible is confiscated or he or she faces imprisonment and solitary confinement. The purpose of the meditation, of course, is to lead the believer to apply the teaching of that Word to his or her life. If you are at a loss as to where to begin, I would suggest Leroy Eims' book, *The Lost Art of Disciple-Making* (1978). He has developed a list of 30 qualities or emphases he would like to see in the life of his disciple and has suggested study approaches and relevant Scriptural passages for each topic.

In situations where there is more leisure to meet regularly with your disciple, you may want to go systematically through certain books of the Bible, but always in such a way as to apply the truths to the disciple's life. You may want to take time to explain the structure of the whole Bible to your disciples and assign selected readings to cover what you consider the important parts. My own preference, for what it is worth, is to start with one of the Gospels, and after the Gospels, I would suggest a study of the book of Acts of the Apostles, followed by selected Epistles that may relate to the situation in the life of the believers. Later, I would lead them to gain familiarity with the books of Genesis, Exodus and Deuteronomy. Simultaneously, I would want to introduce the believers to the books of Psalms and Proverbs and map out a way of going through them once a month. After that, it is up to you to develop in them a familiarity with the rest of the Bible.

While you are teaching your disciples the Word of God, always keep in mind your overall goal to see Christ formed in them. Because you know this happens only by the power of the Holy Spirit, teach and practice life in the Spirit. Be careful how you teach the Word of God. It is not to impart a new legalism; it is to see that Christ is formed in your disciples, and then for the application of the Word of God to all of life's relationships and responsibilities. Always keep the whole process bathed in intercessory prayer.

The Art and Practice of Prayer

Not only should prayer be a big part of your life as a discipler, but you have the privilege of teaching your disciples how to pray. Remember, you are not in the business of transferring a lot of knowledge from your brain to that of your disciples. You are there to see that Christ is formed in their lives. Prayer is an integral part of this process. Notice just a few references on prayer throughout the Scriptures:

"Call to me and I will answer you and tell you great and unsearchable things you do not know" (Jer. 33:3). "Then Jesus told his disciples a parable to show them that they should always pray and not give up" (Luke 18:1). "Until now you have not asked for anything in my name. Ask and you will receive, and your joy will be complete" (John 16:24). "Do not be anxious about anything, but in everything, by prayer and petition, with thanksgiving, present your requests to God. And the peace of God, which transcends all understanding, will guard your hearts and your minds in Christ Jesus" (Phil. 4:6, 7). "And pray in the Spirit on all occasions with all kinds of prayers and requests. With this in mind, be alert and always keep on praying for all the saints" (Eph. 6:18). "Be joyful always; pray continually; give thanks in all circumstances, for this is God's will for you in Christ Jesus" (1 Thess. 5:16-18).

God invites us to "call on Him," to pray to Him. Jesus taught us to keep on praying and not give up. He suggested that we learn to pray in His name. We are to make all our requests known to God with thanksgiving. We are to pray in the energy and power of the Holy Spirit. And we are to rejoice in God's presence as we continue in prayer. The results of our prayers are that God answers with "great and unsearchable things." He gives us a peace that passes understanding. Our hearts and minds are kept by Christ Jesus. And we can have the assurance, as we rejoice in the Lord and pray constantly, that we are in the center of God's will. And, of course, God will answer our prayers according to His will.

Your disciples must see this in your life. They will learn by praying with you. You will encourage them by praying with them and coaching them as they grow in their capacity to pray. If you can't do this in person, you will have to leave tapes or written-out suggestions so that they can learn the habit of prayer. In due time, they will discover the great prayers of the Bible and take them for models. Assuming you have been able to influence them to meditate on the Word of God day and night, they will have ample biblical material to draw on for both content and inspiration as they grow in prayer.

The Place and Music of Worship

Theoretically, music and worship might better belong in the next chapter on incorporating new believers into the body of Christ. But individuals can learn singing and worship from you on a one-to-one basis. You may have to be very innovative here in translating new material into their language as you teach them to sing and worship the Lord. Remember, discipling is more than discipline. It is teaching a young believer to walk in the presence of the Lord, thanking, praising, adoring, rejoicing in Him as he or she prays and is nourished by the Word of God. If as the ancients used to say, "The chief end of man is to glorify God and enjoy Him forever," then surely worship, including singing, is an essential part of this. Because of the oppressive nature of many Muslim regimes, the new believer may be unable to meet with other believers for worship and singing. This is why I advocate the teaching of singing "psalms, hymns and spiritual songs" as part of the discipling process.

The Need for Fellowship

In a previous chapter, we saw that Paul thought follow-up was so very important. He knew that young believers needed encouragement. They needed to know that someone cared and was staying in touch with them. It is equally important that the new believer be taught the need, on his or her part, to seek fellowship. And that is what the next chapter is about: possible models of being incorporated into the fellowship of the body of Christ.

CHAPTER 37

MODELS OF COMMUNITY FORMATION

Consequently, you are no longer foreigners and aliens, but fellow citizens with God's people and members of God's household, built on the foundation of the apostles and prophets, with Christ Jesus himself as the chief cornerstone. In him the whole building is joined together and rises to become a holy temple in the Lord. And in him you too are being built together to become a dwelling in which God lives by his Spirit (Eph. 2:19-22).

In this inspired text, we have a great revelation of the very heart of God for His people. The consummation of God's plan is for Him to live in the midst of His people. God has been working toward this for millennia. Foundations were laid starting with Abraham. Moses, the Lawgiver, played a key role. David was the kingdom-establisher. Prophets, such as Isaiah, Jeremiah and Daniel, gave intimations of the coming kingdom. Jesus became the keystone in the foundation, along with the apostles. Century by century, following Christ's ascension to Heaven and the outpouring of the Holy Spirit, the world has witnessed the building up of God's great masterpiece, a living, multi-ethnic body of many generations, a temple of redeemed children among whom He chooses to live by His Spirit for all eternity.

In His church, the visible expression of His kingdom, we see the reconciliation of all things through the shed blood of Christ. God is calling out for Himself a new humankind from every tongue, tribe, people and nation to be part of His everlasting fellowship. Sons of Ishmael, the Muslims, are part of this great redemption. Through Jesus, healing has come to the broken family of Abraham. By His great sacrifice on the cross, Jesus has reconciled all things to God. The old stone temple is gone. The new living temple of human believers has come. Pilgrimage is no longer to a place, it is to God Himself. Worship is no longer an empty word used by the inventors of religions, it is now something done in Spirit and in Truth. This new living body is united as one, even though believers speak many languages and come from many tribes. Reconciliation has been achieved between God and humankind, and between all human beings, including former Muslims from every tongue, tribe, people and nation. The division between the descendants of Isaac and Ishmael is being healed by the great redemptive work of Jesus.

Not only should this be your vision, but you must impart this to your young disciples. They need to see the greatness of God's plan of which they are an integral part. It is important that the new believer sees beyond the local church to the worldwide, transgenerational church comprising peoples from every age. In the light of this vision, this reality, believers understand who they are and the significance they have in God's kingdom.

What Abraham began as a man of faith, has come to fruition among the people of faith. And through Jesus, his promised seed, the race of believers has been unified. Healing has come to the broken family of Abraham. Ishmael's children have been and are being won to the Lord. Muslims, especially Arab Muslims, who have always seen themselves as proud and distinct, destined to rule, are now won over to a Godly humility. They, too, have been broken at the cross, at least the ones who believe, and are now being integrated into the body of Christ.

In the preceding chapter, we wrote of Christ being formed in the life of each disciple. In this chapter, our theme is to show the disciples their significance in the worldwide Body of Christ. Remember, the new believers may be totally cut off from their families. They may be under persecution. They will certainly have moments of wondering who they are, what their significance is, and to what or whom they belong. This is why it is so important to teach them how they should perceive themselves from the perspective of God's Word. For it is here, in the worldwide Church, a manifestation of God's kingdom, that the healing of Abraham's broken family first occurs. The stigma of Ishmael's alienation is overcome, the family re-united. Forgiveness, reconciliation and peace are the fruit of God's great redemptive work through Christ on the cross.

Before developing this theme, it would be good to review Islamic teaching on related subjects and show how the Christian reality corrects and transcends it. For all of its purported claims to be the religion that supplants all of its predecessors, we find that Islam does not measure up. The new believer, having come freshly out of Islam, needs to know this. Otherwise, failing to comprehend this reality, the new disciple may under stress fall back into the old and familiar Islamic way of thinking.

For example, Muhammad used to pray in the direction of Jerusalem. When the Jews rejected him as a prophet, he turned to the pagan shrine center of his hometown, Mecca. That ancient idol center, the *Kaaba*, was renamed by the voice that spoke to Muhammad as "My House." Today, Muslims call it the "House of God" (Q. 2:125). Muhammad's idea was to designate an Arab place as the center of the earth and the place of pilgrimage. He completely missed the point. The old temple in Jerusalem was only a temporary object lesson, pointing to something in the future far more beautiful and glorious, namely a living temple made up of believers from all ages and races. God wants to dwell in the midst of His people. This idea never entered Muhammad's mind, nor is it found anywhere in the teaching of Islam. And failing to understand God's plan, he degenerated into the role of a rival, trying to provide an alternative to Jerusalem, not knowing that the physical Jerusalem was only the hint of the heavenly one to come (Gal. 4:26).

Muhammad also missed God's plan in another way. He failed to understand the scope of God's great redemptive plan, encompassing as it does believers of all ages and from every ethnolinguistic background who are being built into a glorious living temple for God Himself. Muhammad perceived Islam in purely racial terms: an Arab prophet, an Arabic Quran, the *Kaaba* as the center of the earth, and the relocation of the scene of Hagar and Ishmael's brush with death from the desert of Beersheba to the environs of Mecca. In the place of this living temple, what we get is a picture of Arab pride and the desire to establish Mecca as the center of the world.

In discipling, you must help the new believer to be filled with the hope and the glory that attends this beautiful biblical vision. Needless to say, you need to be filled with this vision too. Otherwise, you will find yourself teaching that the local church is all there is. Before the new believer is introduced to a local church, he or she needs to know that this is only a manifestation of the larger universal Church. In place of the *Ummah* of Islam, there is now this wonderful worldwide fellowship of believers with God Himself living in its midst. Understanding this reality will help the new believer tolerate the ups and downs that go with a struggling local church.

Moving from the concept of the universal Church, we need to take up the question of what constitutes a local church. Perhaps the briefest definition of a church is two or more believers meeting together to worship and serve the Lord in the power of the Spirit and under the headship of Jesus Christ. This allows a lot of latitude in style and composition of members. True as this may be, it doesn't say enough for most situations. Each mission and church, no doubt, has developed its own idea of what constitutes a local church. Arab World Ministries has developed a suggested set of criteria for what constitutes a local "church." They are:

1. About ten baptized believers (flexible).
2. The desirability of starting with families rather than singles.
3. Scripturally qualified, recognized local leaders.
4. Meeting places of their own (not in a missionary house).
5. The local group accepts the responsibility for its own finances and for propagating the Gospel (Schlorff 1981:11).

To this I would add the ideas of worship, study of the Word of God, the practice of baptism, celebration of the Lord's Supper and the exercise of discipline (when needed). At the other extreme, this could mean becoming part of an ancient church with inbred traditions into which a new believer is absorbed. In between are hundreds of variations in size, style, traditions (or lack of them), and patterns of self-organization. These churches can be of one ethnic background or multi-ethnic. Throughout the world, they will function in hundreds of languages with many different preferences in musical instruments and concepts of music or in some rare cases, even the absence of music. There will be endless variations in the choice of meeting places, dress codes, and differing concepts on the role of women in the church.

Before discussing patterns of ways to gather into churches, certain basic truths need to characterize the group you form or to which you introduce the new believer. First and foremost is the question of who the head of this church is. All too often, human organizations are substituted for what God intended to be a living temple with Himself as the head. The apostle Paul's words to the Colossians were so clear: "And he [Jesus] is the head of the body, the church; he is the beginning and the firstborn from among the dead, so that in everything he might have the supremacy" (Col. 1:18). Jesus exercises His rule by His Spirit. Our worship is to be in Spirit and in Truth (John 4:24). Without the Spirit, without this focus on Jesus as the Head, our worship either becomes dead (the absence of the Spirit) or compromised (untruthful). We must remember that the local church is a living body of believers with Jesus as the Head, ruling through His Spirit. Local elders and pastors are not the head of the local church, but stewards and servants to the rest of the body.

In spite of the great varieties of churches in the world, they are characterized by a marvelous unity. To the Ephesians, Paul wrote: "There is one body and one Spirit—just as you were called to one hope when you were called—one Lord, one faith, one baptism, one God and Father of all, who is over all and through all and in all" (Eph. 4:4-6). Unless you teach this to your disciples, they will not be able to integrate the confusing picture of varieties of local churches and denominations. It is best if you explain to your new believers why there are so many varieties of churches. They need to know the historical reasons, the role of traditions or the absence of them, the ethnic reasons, the linguistic reasons, the cultural reasons, and the role that human failure plays in developing local bodies of believers. One way to help them understand is to point out to them the reasons for the tremendous numbers of sects among Muslims.

Many new believers will want to know why the Word of God is not more explicit in teaching a uniform way of worship and organizing the church. You will have to explain why you think the Scriptures are silent on these questions. My opinion, for what it is worth, is that God did not want to impose a uniform way of doing everything because He wanted people to be free to respond to the Gospel in their own cultural context. He wanted them to be free to choose styles of music, architectural designs and patterns of worship that were appropriate for them. Up to the time of the Reformation, Christians in the West had no choices. The Roman Catholic Church forced its ideas on all. Luther and his followers evaluated many practices in the church in the light of Scripture. If Scripture did not forbid it and it aided in worship, they kept it. On the other hand, the Anabaptists said that if the Bible does not tell you explicitly to do something a certain way, you should *not* do it. Apparently, God remained silent on this great issue because He did not want to impose a culturally absolutistic way of doing things on believers of every age and place. He must have enjoyed the luxuriant diversity of cultures, and thought that local churches should reflect it, possibly out of concern for the maximum expansion of the Church among all tongues, tribes, peoples and nations.

By way of precaution, remember that God did tell us enough in Scripture to keep us from falling into fatal compromise with godless elements from the religious and cultural background from which new believers would come. This is why it is so important to know Islam well. Otherwise, we might use elements that would compromise the Gospel.

Having cleared the ground with the above kind of teaching, it is now time to take up the issue of gathering believers together into fellowship groups, either into existing churches or by forming new ones. I would like to discuss this from the pragmatic side rather than the idea of imposing a theoretical model on new believers. There are five patterns of incorporating believers into churches that I think will cover most of the examples in the world.

<u>Model One: Total Integration</u>

By far, the most common way of bringing new believers into the church is the pattern that we shall call total integration into an existing body. No matter what the ethnic or linguistic background of the former Muslims may be, they are taken into the existing local church. The new believers have to make all the adjustments. They may have to learn a new language, strange music, new customs, new styles of dress, and a host of other practices if they want to be truly accepted. In essence, the new believers have to undergo two conversions: the spiritual one to Christ and the conversion to the culture of the local host church. If the converts are from a different cultural background from that of the local church, then we describe this as "extracting" the former Muslims from their cultural context and integrating them into that of the local church.

Model Two: Mother-Daughter Churches
of Differing Cultures

A second model is what may be called a mother-daughter church pattern where the mother church is of one ethnic background and the daughter church is of another. In this situation, those in the mother church realize it is not right to force a linguistic cultural conversion upon new believers. And so, the people of the mother church deliberately set out to create another church different from itself, and yet with the approval and blessing of the mother church. In this model, those in the mother church may impose their own organizational and worship pattern on the daughter church, only allowing people to use a different language, or it may give permission for the new converts to develop patterns more congenial to the culture from which they have come. Not only will the language, the music and the dress code be different, but the patterns of organizing themselves and styles of worship will likely be different, too.

Model Three: Dual Membership Pattern

A third pattern I have observed is what I call dual membership. For whatever reason, the new believers feel that they should belong to an established church, even though they may not fully understand the language of worship or be attracted by the style. So they attend the regular services of that body. But in addition to that, they have another fellowship meeting with their own kind of people in their own language and in a manner more culturally comfortable for them. These friends feel they must belong to what is already there, and yet simultaneously, they hold their own meetings in a style congenial to their own culture.

Model Four: The Contextualized Church

The fourth model is the one most controversial for believers from a non-Muslim background as it offers a great deal of freedom to the new believers, former Muslims, to develop a pattern of their own choosing, independent of all others. The reasons for this could be many. There may be no church near them to join. Or the existing church or churches of a different ethnolinguistic background may not want these former Muslims worshiping with them. Or the existing church may be so corrupt that no one would want to associate with them, much less imitate them.

For those who choose this model, certain fundamental assumptions underlie this approach. One is that "extractionism" is wrong, that is, the new believers should not be totally drawn out of their cultural context and forced into another. This approach attempts to resist the potential cultural imperialism of the existing church. The second assumption, in this model, is that God has given all peoples freedom to respond to Him in worship styles congenial to their cultures. It implies that although God is interested in spiritual unity among all believers, He does not insist on total uniformity in style and structure.

Generally speaking, the way this model develops is that the believers sit down with an open Bible in their own cultural context. They then try to decide what would be compatible with God's Word. In working with this approach, I have found it helpful to divide the religious elements of the existing Muslim culture into three categories: those which are compatible with Scriptural teaching, those which are totally unacceptable, and those which are apparently neutral; that is, they have no bearing on the issues. Great care has to be taken with this method since the old Islamic forms, if used, may carry with them unacceptable Islamic meanings. Appropriating and or adapting Islamic forms is only valid if the meaning of the old form dies and is filled with new Christian meaning.

Denis Green has done us all a great service in showing that the Book of Hebrews in the New Testament was written to converted Jews who retained too much of their old religious forms. They were in grave danger of falling into a fatal syncretism, by holding onto the old Judaistic patterns. In the new Messianic Jewish community the danger was of the old Judaistic meanings overwhelming the intended new Christian meaning (Green 1989:233-250).

Phil Parshall, on the other hand, one of the primary advocates of the contextualized approach in Muslim work, has written the first modern book on the subject, *New Paths in Muslim Evangelism* (1980). The Lombaro Case Study mentioned in this book was worked out much the way we suggested above; that is, sitting down with an open Bible and deciding what could be appropriated, what had to be rejected and what was, relatively speaking, neutral. Nine years later, Parshall wrote an article titled, "Lessons Learned in Contextualization" (Parshall 1989:251-265). Although there are many useful comments and insights in his article, the following paragraph seems to capture the gist of his thought. He wrote:

As yet, it is impossible to give a thorough evaluation of the effort. But it is fair to say that initial reports have been favorable. Converts are appreciative of the opportunity to worship with others from an Islamic background. Biblical forms of prostration, chanting God's Word, fasting, and use of familiar words have all contributed to believers making a smooth transition to the new community. And most importantly... converts have remained as salt and light among their Muslim relatives and friends. They have not become the typical extracted, persecuted ones and twos that make exciting biography, but are dead-ends as far as church growth potential is concerned (Parshall 1989:254).

I would like to make the following comments based on my own understanding of the Scriptures and my observations of this work in Bangladesh. First of all, as Parshall has stated that it is too early to make a proper evaluation of whether or not the "contextualized" church mentioned in the case study will survive the current persecution. Even if it does, it is too early to tell whether it will come through as a syncretistic church, retaining too much of the old Islamic meaning.

One of the great controversial steps these ex-Muslim Christians in Bangladesh have taken is to say, "We are not Christians; we are Muslims who follow the way of *Isa*." Those who know the Arabic Quran, will recognize that *Isa* is the Quranic corruption of the name Jesus (*Yeshua* in the Hebrew). There is no doubt that the Quranic *Isa* is a distortion of the Christ as He is set forth in the Scriptures. (Refer back to chapter 28 for the Quranic treatment of Jesus and the Scriptural rebuttals.) I question the wisdom (or lack of it) for choosing a Quranic name for Jesus. The biblical word *Jesus* (or *Yeshua*) has in its root meaning the idea of "savior" and "deliverer." The Quranic word *Isa*, in reality, stands for nothing more than a prophet superseded by Muhammad. Naguib Mahfouz, the Nobel Prize Winner for Literature in 1988, goes so far as to reduce Jesus to a snake-charming exorcist in his parody in *The Children of Gebelaawi* (1981:137-198). Sooner or later, an ex-Muslim disciple is going to have to come face to face with biblical meaning and nomenclature. Why not from the beginning? We would not dare corrupt the spelling or the pronunciation of the name "Muhammad." Why should we treat Jesus with less respect than Muhammad?

The second concern is the thought that, perhaps, contextualization is a way to avoid persecution. It is interesting to note that in Bangladesh, even though the leaders of the new movement said they were not Christians but followers of *Isa*, the Muslim Chairman of the Union Council there took the New Testament, kicked it into the lake and said, "As long as you are reading this book, you are in fact Christians" (A missionary newsletter, July 16, 1990). Should we not face the prospect of persecution head on? Should we not rather take our cues from God's "Casebook," the Bible, and teach the inevitability of persecution? Let's look at Luke's early description of how the first apostles perceived persecution:

> The apostles left the Sanhedrin, rejoicing because they had been counted worthy of suffering disgrace for the Name. Day after day, in the temple courts and from house to house, they never stopped teaching and proclaiming the good news that Jesus is the Christ (Acts 5:41, 42).

Later on, Peter wrote on the same subject: "However, if you suffer as a Christian, do not be ashamed, but praise God that you bear that name" (1 Peter 4:16).

The third area of concern is that we do not yet know if the new believers cited in Parshall's quote have actually discarded the Islamic meanings and truly filled their old forms with Christian content.

Parshall himself, in another book, *Beyond the Mosque*, hints that whatever new thing emerges when thousands of Muslims come to Christ, such as in Bangladesh, it will not be housed in the old mosques, it will be something new, something "beyond the mosque" (1985:184). The implication from this is that the mosque should be abandoned and new structures be created for new believers.

My final concern with this model has to do with the great danger of the new group becoming schismatic, that is, not wanting to identify with other parts of the Body of Christ. For example, in Bangladesh, by refusing to say they were "Christian," the new believers, all former Muslims, were saying, "We do not want to be identified with the existing Christians because they are all from a Hindu Untouchable background, and tainted by contact with Westerners." This violates the spirit of Jesus' great priestly prayer in John 17:20, 21:

> My prayer is not for them alone [His present disciples].
> I pray also for those who will believe in me through their
> message, that all of them may be one, Father, just as you
> are in me and I am in you. May they also be in us so that
> the world may believe that you have sent me.

If no effort is made to maintain the unity of Christ's body in the bond of peace, the message of the oneness of Christ and the Father, the oneness of the body, and the fellowship between God and the church may be violated. Great care must be taken not to divide the body or communicate a wrong message to the non-Christian world.

Model Five: Staying Inside Islam

Recently, there have been experiments (where the experimenters prefer to remain anonymous) in which the new believers are urged to remain within Islam. In this model, the believer still claims to be a Muslim and shuns the title of "Christian." In this approach, the person may retain almost all Islamic forms and customs. It appears that two camps are emerging in this group. One group is willing to retain the idea of Muhammad as a prophet of God without actually meaning what the Bible means by that term. The other group is not willing to concede that Muhammad is a prophet of God. When reciting the creed, this latter group substitutes "Jesus" for "Muhammad." And again, there are further variations. The two versions go something like this:

1. "There is no God but God and *Isa* is the Word of God." *Isa* is a Quranic name for Jesus and this keeps the door open to perceive Jesus as divine, at least in the mind of this "believer."

2. "There is no God but God and Jesus is the apostle of God." This particular affirmation has a certain ambiguity to it in that

329

the Muslim already believes Jesus is an apostle, but no more than an apostle. Whereas, the Christian may believe that Jesus, although an apostle, is much more than an apostle, without having to say so.

I find two reasons why I cannot agree with model five. First, by retaining everything Islamic, the danger of old forms containing old Islamic meanings is so great that syncretism is inevitable. Second, there is too much room for deception in this model. The unconverted Muslims can perceive these new "believers" as Muslims, while the new "believers" perceive themselves as Christians without the label. As we have noted in our comments in model four, Scripture seems to indicate that persecution is one of the marks of being a true Christian. Bearing shame for the name of Christ and the name "Christian" is a privilege. Therefore, designing an approach merely to escape persecution is not a valid motive. Moreover, this model allows for no real breaking out of the old mold of Islam. The whole witness to the truth of the Gospel is blunted by this total submersion within the forms of Islam.

CHAPTER 38

COMPLETING THE TASK

The Lord had said to Abram, "Leave your country, your people and your father's household and go to the land I will show you. I will make you into a great nation and I will bless you; I will make your name great, and you will be a blessing. I will bless those who bless you, and whoever curses you I will curse; and all peoples on earth will be blessed through you" (Gen. 12:1-3).

And they sang a new song: "You are worthy to take the scroll and to open its seals, because you were slain, and with your blood you purchased men for God from every tribe and language and people and nation. You have made them to be a kingdom and priests to serve our God, and they will reign on the earth" (Rev. 5:9, 10).

In the first passage quoted above, God's Word commissions Abraham to bring blessing to all the peoples of the earth. In the second passage, the song of exultation at the end of human history celebrates Christ's (Abraham's promised "seed") accomplishment of the mission. The harvest is made up of men, women and children from every tongue, tribe, people and nation. Among them, of course, will be the descendants of Ishmael. This would include Muslims of every kind.

In another passage, called by biblical scholars "an endtimes passage," Jesus spoke of the completion of the missionary task as the one great contingency upon which His final return depended. Here are His words: "And this gospel of the kingdom will be preached in the whole world as a testimony to all nations [Greek, *ta ethne*], and then the end will come" (Matt. 24:14). There is justification for translating *ta ethne* as ethnic groups of people, rather than "nations." And again we point out, this would include

Muslims of every ethnic variety. If this is true, and this author certainly thinks it is, then there is a sense in which we could say that our reluctance to disciple all ethnic varieties of Muslim peoples is one of the big impediments to the return of Christ. (When we have won believers to Christ from every tongue, tribe, people and nation, Muslim and non-Muslim, the stage is set for Jesus' return.)

The Place of Intercessory Prayer

The following passage on intercessory prayer seems to indicate that this activity is related to God's desire to see all people saved:

> I urge, then, first of all, that requests, prayers, intercession and thanksgiving be made for everyone—for kings and all those in authority, that we may live peaceful and quiet lives in all godliness and holiness. This is good, and pleases God our Savior, who wants all men to be saved and to come to a knowledge of the truth. For there is one God and one mediator between God and men, the man Christ Jesus, who gave himself as a ransom for all men—the testimony given in its proper time (1 Tim. 2:1-6).

Paul wrote those words when the worldly powers of Rome and the Jews were arrayed against him. Yet he understood the innate connection between intercessory prayer (with thanksgiving) for rulers and God's desire to see all people saved. The lesson for us is to follow this pattern. As awkward as it may seem, for example, to pray for Muslim rulers because of all the destruction they have caused, there is some connection between our prayers obediently prayed, and the salvation of the people in Iraq and Libya. And the same would apply to the other 47 countries of the Muslim world.

The Need to Enter the Harvest Fields

But we have to do more than pray. Again, I would like to refer back to the example of our Lord Jesus Christ in the days of His earthly ministry. The passage we will look at is Matthew 9:35-38:

Jesus went through all the towns and villages, teaching in their synagogues, preaching the good news of the kingdom and healing every disease and sickness. When he saw the crowds, he had compassion on them, because they were harassed and helpless, like sheep without a shepherd. Then he said to his disciples, "The harvest is plentiful but the workers are few. Ask the Lord of the harvest, therefore, to send out workers into his harvest field."

The Need for a Comprehensive Strategy

I would like to draw attention to the following lessons from this wonderful glimpse into the ministry of our Lord. First of all, notice the comprehensiveness of Jesus' Galilean ministry. He "went through all the towns and villages." Scholars tell us that this amounts to more than two hundred and fifty towns and villages. Jesus went through all of them. What a model of thoroughness. For us, the lesson is that we should be working with the same thoroughness with Muslims everywhere. We should start with the thousands of Muslim students God has brought into our midst in America. We should also work among the millions of immigrants who have come here from distant lands. And we should be going to Muslims of every tongue, tribe, people and nation. Our work is not finished until we do. And I might repeat that Jesus will not return until we do (Matt. 24:14).

Teaching in Synagogues and Mosques

The next lesson that catches our eye is that Jesus taught in their synagogues. "Synagogue" is a Greek word that simply means "gathering place." In the Arabic language, *jamia masjid* means the gathering place of those who bow down before God. *Jamia masjid* is better known to us as "mosque." What would it mean if Jesus were here today? I think He would go to mosques (if they would let Him in), the places where Muslims gather to say their prayers and listen to the sermons preached from the Quran. Once inside, He would teach the Good News of the kingdom of God.

Before proceeding any further, it is necessary to comment on the Arabic word for "good news." In the Quran, it is a curious thing to read the word *injil* for "Good News." This obviously is an Arabic corruption of the Greek word, *euangelion*, for "Good News." Neither Muhammad, nor Muslims ever since, have any idea what "Good News" means in the New Testament sense. Similarly, the expression "kingdom of God" is mentioned several times in the Quran, but with no indication that Muhammad understood the relationship of the kingdom of God to the advent and ministry of Jesus Christ the King.

But this is where you and I, Christian reader, come in. We do know what the kingdom of God is. In fact, we possess the "keys of the kingdom." We have been given the power of the kingdom. We have the authority and the privilege of using the name of the King. We know the nature of the kingdom, the principles upon which it stands. We know that the kingdom is now present in the hearts of believers in Jesus Christ, and that the kingdom will be fully consummated at the final return of the King. We know that we are to communicate the Good News of the kingdom to the whole human race: men, women and children of every tongue, tribe, people and nation. We know that Jesus the King is yearning to return and will do so when we have completed the task He has given us to do. So, we have no choice but to go to all the peoples of the world and teach and preach the Good News of Jesus Christ's kingdom.

By way of review, lest we use the term "kingdom of God" too glibly, we need to remind ourselves that the heart of that Good News is that God sent His only Son as the Lamb of God to take away the sins of the world by sacrificing Himself on the cross. For Muslims, as for the rest of humankind, the Good News is that Jesus died for their sins, tasted death for every one of them and then rose victorious over death to share with all who will believe the fruits of that glorious victory—the right to everlasting life in the presence of God.

It is our privilege to preach and teach this, whether in a mosque or marketplace, over the radio or on cassettes, in person or by printed page. This Gospel must be made known to all Muslims.

The Power and Authority to Heal

But there is more. As we read on, we discover that wherever Jesus went, He healed every disease and sickness. By these mighty miracles, Jesus demonstrated both the love and the power of God, the presence of the kingdom in the person of Himself. What is even more astounding is that He has given us His authority and power today to bring healing and, where needed, deliverance from demonic possession. These "signs and wonders" are not given simply to prove the Gospel is true: they are manifestations of the love and power of God wedded together to minister the presence of the King, and the reality of His kingdom in the midst of all the other kingdoms of the world. This is the ultimate fulfillment of that prophecy of long ago that Abraham and his "seed" would bring blessing to all the peoples of the earth. Jesus, in the days of His Galilean ministry, was a marvelous model for how we should do this throughout the Muslim world today.

Compassion on the Harassed and Helpless

But there are still more lessons in this passage. How did Jesus look at the crowds of humanity He encountered from place to place? How do you look at crowds of Iraqis, for example, screaming in the streets of Baghdad? Or Iranians in the streets of Tehran? Or the shuffling multitudes of the poor in Bangladesh? When Jesus moved through the crowds during the days of His earthly ministry, He was not overcome with despair. He saw their true condition. He saw through the foolish slogans and misplaced loyalties. In fact, He saw them as harassed and helpless, like sheep without a shepherd. Being the Good Shepherd, He discerned the true condition of these lost sheep. He was moved with compassion by what He saw. Do we have eyes to see as Jesus saw? We must see beyond the madness of shouting multitudes to the masses who are poor, harassed and helpless, dying without a Savior. Jesus would have us go out among them. He died for them as He did for us all. And, He expects us to follow His example— to go and make disciples among each of these crowds of ethnolinguistic groups of Muslim peoples (Matt. 28:18-20).

Harvest Eyes

We also note that Jesus had the faith to believe that multitudes would come to Him. He said: "The harvest is plentiful, but the workers are few" (Matt. 9:37). Thank God for Jesus' irrepressible love, hope and faith, all blended together in His assessment of the people's receptivity. Jesus had what we call a harvest mentality. He believed God for it. He could see men, women and children from every tongue, tribe, people and nation gathered into His eternal and blessed kingdom.

Praying for Workers

But Jesus also noticed that the workers were few. The implication is that the harvest would go unharvested without adequate workers. Jesus and His early band of disciples could have tried to prolong their lives in order to harvest as much as they could in their own lifetimes. But Jesus went beyond this kind of shortsightedness. He envisioned a vast harvest down through the centuries from every corner of the globe. He simply said: "Ask the Lord of the harvest, therefore, to send out workers into his harvest field" (Matt. 9:38).

It was my privilege a few years ago to be in the country of Guinea when it was a "closed" country. At that time, a corrupt dictator by the name of Seko Toure ruled the country. As we walked through the city of Conakry, we passed the city jail where we heard the screams of the political prisoners being tortured. It so happened that during the very days we were there, President Toure staged a national day of celebrating his own coming to power. As we sat in the stadium watching this exercise in self-praise, the screams of those being tortured still echoed in our ears. The Spirit of God moved the three of us to leave the stands and find a quiet place to pray. This is what we prayed: "O God, if this man has the capacity to repent, then we ask you to soften his heart, stop his cruelty, and cause him to open up this country to the Gospel. But, if he is a 'Pharaoh' who will not repent, then please remove him and bring another, kinder ruler to power who will open this country to the Gospel." Within a year he died of natural causes and was replaced by a man who opened up Guinea to missionaries.

On the same trip, we also went inland to the Telakoro Bible Institute where we met with a small group of pastors. During our time together, maps of the country were put up on the chapel wall and various ethnolinguistic groups of people were delineated on the map. Then we prayed to the Lord of the harvest to send workers into each one of these groups. Today, either national or expatriate workers are laboring in every one of those harvest fields. If God could order the affairs of one country,

Guinea, in such a way, couldn't He do the same for every Muslim country? Of course He could.

Since this book is about working with Muslims, and Muslims claim identity with Abraham, let us work toward healing Abraham's broken family until the full number of Muslims who can be saved are saved. Through the Gospel of Jesus Christ, we shall see healing in Abraham's broken family.

APPENDIX A

THE DEMOGRAPHICS OF THE MUSLIM WORLD

A number of sources have been used to determine the population of the Muslim World. The primary source has been the 1998 World Population Data Sheet. *The 1988 Demography of Islamic Nations*, by John Weeks has been a great help, as well as Richard Weekes' two-volume work, *Muslim Peoples* (1983), and Patrick Johnstone's *Operation World* (1993). For Spain, I have relied on the research of Project Maghreb.

In general, I have rounded numbers to the nearest 1,000 and have not listed any country with less than 10,000 Muslims. When reviewing these figures, one must remember that they are approximations. In many countries, no census has been taken for years. In others, the figures are distorted for political purposes. Following are the Muslim population figures by the major regions of the world. The total population for the Muslim world is 1,244,652,000 or 21.0% of the world's population (mid-1998).

ASIA

Country	Percent Muslim	Muslim Population
Indonesia	82.9%	171,935,000
India	14.0%	138,418,000
Pakistan	96.7%	137,217,000
Bangladesh	87.0%	107,358,000
China	2.4%	29,820,000
Afghanistan	99.0%	24,552,000
Uzbekistan	68.2%	16,436,000
Russia	8.7%	12,780,000
Malaysia	55.0%	12,210,000
Kazakstan	40.0%	6,240,000
Azerbaijan	80.0%	6,160,000
Philippines	8.0%	6,024,000
Tajikistan	82.3%	5,020,000
Turkmenistan	76.0%	3,572,000
Kyrgyzstan	60.0%	2,820,000
Thailand	4.0%	2,444,000
Myanmar (Burma)	3.8%	1,790,000
Sri Lanka	7.8%	1,474,000
Georgia	21.3%	1,150,000
Nepal	3.5%	830,000
Singapore	15.4%	601,000
Cambodia	2.9%	313,000
Maldives	99.4%	298,000
Japan	0.2%	253,000
Brunei	71.0%	213,000
Vietnam	0.2%	157,000
Armenia	3.3%	125,000
Taiwan	0.5%	109,000
Mongolia	4.0%	96,000
China, Hong Kong	1.0%	67,000
Laos	1.0%	53,000
Bhutan	5.0%	40,000
South Korea	0.06%	28,000

Total   **690,603,000**

OCEANIA

Country	Percent Muslim	Muslim Population
Australia	1.5%	281,000
Fiji	7.5%	60,000
Total		**341,000**

THE MIDDLE EAST

THE ARAB MIDDLE EAST WITHOUT NORTH AFRICA

Country	Percent Muslim	Muslim Population
Iraq	95.4%	20,797,000
Saudi Arabia	93.4%	18,867,000
Yemen	99.9%	15,784,000
Syria	90.5%	14,118,000
Jordan	94.0%	4,324,000
Oman	95.5%	2,388,000
United Arab Emirates	84.6%	2,284,000
Lebanon	53.0%	2,173,000
Kuwait	89.9%	1,708,000
West Bank	82.1%	1,478,000
Gaza	98.0%	1,078,000
Israel	14.5%	870,000
Bahrain	85.0%	510,000
Qatar	91.4%	457,000
Total		**86,836,000**

NORTH AFRICA

Country	Percent Muslim	Muslim Population
Egypt	85.4%	55,937,000
Algeria	99.4%	30,019,000
Morocco	99.8%	27,645,000
Sudan	70.0%	19,950,000
Tunisia	99.5%	9,453,000
Libya	96.0%	5,472,000
Total		**148,476,000**
Total Arab World (Middle East and North Africa)		**235,312,000**

NON-ARAB MIDDLE EASTERN COUNTRIES

Country	Percent Muslim	Muslim Population
Turkey	99.8%	64,670,000
Iran	99.0%	63,459,000
Cyprus	22.0%	154,000
Total		**128,283,000**
Total for All Middle East and North Africa		**363,595,000**

SUB-SAHARAN AFRICA

Country	Percent Muslim	Muslim Population
Nigeria	40.0%	48,720,000
Ethiopia	35.0%	20,440,000
Tanzania	35.0%	10,710,000
Somalia	99.96%	10,696,000
Niger	90.5%	9,141,000
Mali	86.3%	8,716,000
Senegal	90.8%	8,172,000
Guinea	83.1%	6,233,000
Côte d'Ivoire (Ivory Coast)	38.7%	6,037,000
Burkina Faso	48.0%	5,424,000
Cameroon	24.0%	3,432,000
Chad	45.5%	3,367,000
Ghana	16.0%	3,024,000
Mauritania	99.7%	2,493,000
Mozambique	13.0%	2,418,000
Sierra Leone	43.1%	1,983,000
Eritrea	51.0%	1,938,000
Kenya	6.0%	1,698,000
Uganda	8.0%	1,680,000
Malawi	14.5%	1,421,000
Gambia	95.4%	1,145,000
Togo	21.0%	1,029,000
Benin	17.0%	1,020,000
Rwanda	10.0%	800,000
Dem. Rep. of Congo (Zaire)	1.4%	686,000
Djibouti	94.6%	662,000
Comoros	98.0%	490,000
South Africa	1.25%	486,000
Guinea-Bissau	44.0%	484,000
Liberia	13.3%	372,000
Madagascar	2.2%	308,000
Zimbabwe	1.6%	176,000
Mauritius	12.5%	150,000
Central African Republic	3.3%	112,000
Zambia	1.0%	95,000
Burundi	1.0%	55,000
Gabon	4.2%	50,000
Congo	1.3%	35,000
Reunion	4.2%	29,000

Total   **165,927,000**

Total North Africa   **148,476,000**

Total for All of Africa   **314,403,000**

EUROPE
EASTERN AND SOUTHERN EUROPE

Country	Percent Muslim	Muslim Population
Yugoslavia	17.0%	1,802,000
Bosnia-Herzegovina	40.0%	1,600,000
Albania	40.0%	1,320,000
Bulgaria	13.9%	1,154,000
Italy	1.9%	1,096,000
Macedonia	25.0%	500,000
Spain	0.77%	303,000
Ukraine	0.47%	236,000
Romania	1.0%	225,000
Croatia	5.0%	210,000
Greece	1.5%	158,000
Belarus	0.2%	20,000
Estonia	1.0%	14,000
Hungary	0.1%	10,000
Latvia	0.4%	10,000
Total		**8,658,000**

WESTERN EUROPE

Country	Percent Muslim	Muslim Population
France	7.7%	4,528,000
Germany	2.5%	2,058,000
United Kingdom	2.5%	1,478,000
Netherlands	2.7%	424,000
Belgium	3.1%	316,000
Austria	1.4%	113,000
Switzerland	1.0%	71,000
Sweden	0.8%	71,000
Denmark	1.0%	53,000
Norway	0.5%	22,000
Portugal	0.2%	20,000
Total		**9,154,000**
Total for All of Europe		**17,812,000**

NORTH AMERICA

Country	Percent Muslim	Muslim Population
United States	1.8%	4,864,000
Canada	0.8%	245,000
Total		**5,109,000**

LATIN AMERICA

Country	Percent Muslim	Muslim Population
Argentina	1.5%	542,000
Brazil	0.1%	162,000
Panama	4.5%	126,000
Suriname	24.0%	96,000
Venezuela	0.4%	93,000
Trinidad-Tobago	5.9%	77,000
Colombia	0.2%	77,000
Guyana	9.0%	63,000
Mexico	0.03%	29,000
Total		**1,265,000**
Total for Western Hemisphere		**6,374,000**
World Total	21.0%	**1,244,652,000**

APPENDIX B

THE MUSLIM COUNTRIES OF THE WORLD

Listed below are the forty-nine countries of the world that have at least fifty percent Muslim population or a Muslim plurality. The total population of these countries is 963,278,000 or 77% of all the Muslims of the world. The countries are listed according to the actual size of their Muslim populations, not their total population.

Country	Percent Muslim	Muslim Population
Indonesia	82.9%	171,935,000
Pakistan	96.7%	137,217,000
Bangladesh	87.0%	107,358,000
Turkey	99.8%	64,670,000
Iran	99.0%	63,459,000
Egypt	85.4%	55,937,000
Nigeria*	40.0%	48,720,000
Algeria	99.4%	30,019,000
Morocco	99.8%	27,645,000
Afghanistan	99.0%	24,552,000
Iraq	95.4%	20,797,000
Sudan	70.0%	19,950,000
Saudi Arabia	93.4%	18,867,000
Uzbekistan	68.2%	16,436,000
Yemen	99.9%	15,784,000
Syria	90.5%	14,118,000
Malaysia	55.0%	12,210,000
Somalia	99.96%	10,696,000
Tunisia	99.5%	9,453,000

Niger	90.5%	9,141,000
Mali	86.3%	8,716,000
Senegal	90.8%	8,172,000
Kazakstan*	40.0%	6,240,000
Guinea	83.1%	6,233,000
Azerbaijan	80.0%	6,160,000
Libya	96.0%	5,472,000
Tajikistan	82.3%	5,020,000
Jordan	94.0%	4,324,000
Turkmenistan	76.0%	3,572,000
Chad*	45.5%	3,367,000
Kyrgyzstan	60.0%	2,820,000
Mauritania	99.7%	2,493,000
Oman	95.5%	2,388,000
United Arab Emirates	84.6%	2,284,000
Lebanon	53.0%	2,173,000
Sierra Leone*	43.1%	1,983,000
Eritrea	51.0%	1,938,000
Kuwait	89.9%	1,708,000
Bosnia-Herzegovina*	40.0%	1,600,000
West Bank	82.1%	1,478,000
Albania*	40.0%	1,320,000
Gambia	95.4%	1,145,000
Gaza	98.0%	1,078,000
Djibouti	94.6%	662,000
Bahrain	85.0%	510,000
Comoros	98.0%	490,000
Qatar	91.4%	457,000
Maldives	99.4%	298,000
Brunei	71.0%	213,000
Total	77% (of Muslim World)	**963,278,000**

* Countries that have either a Muslim plurality or control of the government.

APPENDIX C

DATES OF LIBERATION OF OCCUPIED MUSLIM LANDS

This chart is confined to those countries with a majority of Muslims. No effort was made to mention those countries with Muslim minorities who suffered under colonial occupation. For this reason, you will neither find the Muslims of Russia, China or India mentioned; nor will you find America listed as a colonial power, although she did occupy the Philippines with its Muslim minority from 1898 until 1946, excluding the Japanese occupation during World War II.

	Name of Country	Occupied by	Year Liberated
1.	Gaza	Israel	Still Occupied
2.	Mayotte	France	Still Occupied
3	West. Sahara	Morocco	Still Occupied
4.	Azerbaijan	Russia	1991
5.	Bosnia-Herzegovina	Yugoslavia	1991
6.	Kazakstan*	Russia	1991
7.	Kyrgyzstan	Russia	1991
8.	Tajikistan	Russia	1991
9.	Turkmenistan	Russia	1991
10.	Uzbekistan	Russia	1991
11.	Afghanistan	Soviet Union	1989
12.	Brunei	Britain	1984
13.	West. Sahara	Spain	1984
14	Djibouti	France	1977
15.	Comoros	France	1975
16.	Maldives	Britain	1975
17.	Qatar	Britain	1974
18.	Bahrain	Britain	1971
19.	United Arab Emirates	Britain	1971
20.	Oman	Britain	1970
21.	Yemen	Britain	1967

22.	Gambia	Britain	1965
23.	Malaysia	Britain	1963
24.	Algeria	France	1962
25.	Kuwait	Britain	1961
26.	Sierra Leone*	Britain	1961
27.	Chad*	France	1960
28.	Mali	France	1960
29.	Mauritania	France	1960
30.	Niger	France	1960
31.	Nigeria*	Britain	1960
32.	Senegal	France	1960
33.	Somalia	Britain/Italy	1960
34.	Guinea	France	1958
35.	Egypt	Britain	1956
36.	Morocco	France	1956
37.	Sudan	Britain/Egypt	1956
38.	Tunisia	France	1956
39.	Libya	Britain/Italy	1951
40.	Indonesia	Netherlands	1949
41.	Bangladesh	Britain	1947
42.	Pakistan	Britain	1947
43.	Jordan	Britain	1946
44.	Albania*	Italy	1945
45.	Lebanon	France	1943
46.	Syria	France	1943
47.	Tunisia	Britain/Greece	1922
48.	Iran	Britain	1921
49.	Iraq	Britain	1921
50.	Turkey	Russia/Italy/France	1921
51.	Saudi Arabia	Turkey/Britain	1918

* Countries with a Muslim plurality, but with less than a 50% Muslim population.

Note: Technically, no Muslim should live under non-Muslim rule. It is possible that we will see many other Muslim enclaves around the world attempt to declare themselves independent.

APPENDIX D

THE MUSLIM LUNAR YEAR AND MAJOR FESTIVALS

The lunar year is used for religious observances and the feasts are celebrated universally by most Muslims. The Shias have additional special days of celebration. And in various countries, under the umbrella of Folk Islam, there are usually additional seasonal holidays related to the Solar Calendar and special holidays connected with the birth or death dates of various saints. The lunar year is only 354 days long, approximately 11 days shorter than the solar year. So the lunar years advance through our calendar by eleven days every year. Therefore, approximately every 33 years the lunar years lap or gain a year on the solar calendar. Since the Muslim calendar starts with the Christian year of A.D. 622, one would expect A.D. 1990 to be A.H. 1369; but instead it is the year A.H. 1410, which is 1369 plus 41 additional years of the lunar calendar.

The letters "A.H." before the Muslim lunar year stand for the words *anno Hegirae*, the year of Muhammad's flight from Mecca to Medina. This occurred in A.D. 622.

Months of the Muslim Lunar Year
1. Muharram
2. Safar
3. Rabi-al-Awwal
4. Rabi-ath-Thani
5. Jumada-l-Ula
6. Jumada-th-Thaniyyah
7. Rajab
8. Shaban
9. Ramadan
10. Shawwal
11. Dhu-l-Qadah
12. Dhu'l-Hijjah

351

THE MAJOR FESTIVALS OF THE MUSLIM YEAR

First of Muhharam = New Year's Day

Tenth of Muharram = Ashura, coincides with
Jewish Day of Atonement

Twelfth of Rabi al-Awwal = Mawlid an-Nabi,
Muhammad's Birthday

Twenty-seventh of Rajab = Laylat al-Miraj,
The Night Journey

Fifteenth of Shaban = Laylat al-Baraah,
The Night of Destinies

Ramadan = The Month of Fasting

Twenty-seventh of Ramadan = Laylat al-Qadr,
The Night of Descent

First of Shawwal = Id al-Fitr,
The Feast of Breaking the Fast
(3 days)

Eight, Ninth, Tenth of Dhu-l-Hijjah = Id al-Adha,
The Feast of Abraham's
Sacrifice

APPENDIX E

MUSLIM COUNTRIES' STANDARD OF LIVING

Oil-Rich Muslim Countries:

Country	Standard of Living as Percentage of U.S. Economy
United Arab Emirates	87.0%
Kuwait	73.0%
Brunei	67.0%
Bahrain	49.0%
Qatar	47.0%
Saudi Arabia	28.0%
Libya	26.0%
Oman	24.0%
Algeria	10.0%
Malaysia	10.0%
Iran	8.5%

Non-Oil-Rich Muslim Countries:

Country	Percentage of U.S. Economy
Kyrgyzstan	11.0%
Tajikistan	8.0%
Jordan	6.2%
Turkey	6.2%
Tunisia	6.1%
Syria	4.8%
Morocco	4.1%
Lebanon	4.0%
Senegal	3.3%

Non-Oil-Rich Muslim Countries (Continued):

Turkmenistan	3.3%
Yemen	3.0%
Egypt	2.9%
Djibouti	2.3%
Indonesia	2.3%
Mauritania	2.2%
Comoros	2.0%
Maldives	2.0%
Sudan	2.0%
Pakistan	1.7%
Mali	1.5%
Niger	1.5%
Nigeria	1.5%
Guinea	1.4%
Albania	1.2%
Afghanistan	1.1%
Gambia	1.1%
Sierra Leone	1.0%
Chad	0.9%
Bangladesh	0.85%
Iraq	*

* Since the war with Iran, and more recently (1991) the war with Kuwait, there has been a serious economic setback to the economy of Iraq, and no statistics are available.

Note: Statistics are not available for the following countries: Azerbaijan, Bosnia-Herzegovina, Eritrea, Gaza, Kazakhstan, Mayotte, Somalia, Uzbekistan and West Bank.

GLOSSARY

FOREIGN WORDS AND NAMES

Abdullah A word meaning "servant of God."

ahl-i-Kitab A Quranic expression for the People of the Book, the Jews and Christians who had their holy books before Muhammad. This phrase can also include Zoroastrians.

Ahmad Meaning "the one who is praised," this word is used in the Quran to refer to Jesus' prophecy of the one who would follow Him.

Ahmadi The name of a follower of Ghulam Ahmad Mirza.

Ahmadiyya The name of the sect of Muslims who are called Ahmadis.

Allah The Arabic word for God.

Allahu Akbar A common Muslim expression meaning, "God is greater."

Al-Manar The name of an Arabic periodical, which means "The Lighthouse."

Amal Literally meaning "hope," the name of a Shia sect.

Arafat The name of a plain several miles from Mecca.

asr The name for afternoon prayers.

Ashura The name of the Jewish Day of Atonement; this day coincides with the tenth of Muharram, the day Shias celebrate the death of Husayn.

ayatollah The name of the highest type of religious rank in Shia Islam, literally meaning "sign of God."

Bairam An alternate name for the Great Feast in Islam, *Id al-Kabir*, or *Id al-Adha*, or *Id al-Qurban*.

baraka A blessing, often thought to pass from one person or thing to another.

caliph (khalifa) A ruler of Muslims, the successor to Muhammad.

Dajjal A Muslim word for the Antichrist.

Dar al-Harb A term meaning "the House of Resistors": those upon whom holy war is to be waged until they submit or are killed.

Dar al-Islam A term meaning "the House of Islam": those who have submitted to Muhammad's teaching.

dhimmi	A word for "clients," Jews and Christians who submit to Muslim rule and who pay special taxes.
din	The duties of religion, which are a response to Muhammad's law.
Druze	A sect of Shia Islam located in Lebanon.
dua	A word for extemporaneous prayer in Islam.
euangelion	The Greek word for "good news."
Hadith	The written traditions of Islam, based on *Sunnah*.
hajj	The annual pilgrimage to Mecca.
Hanif	A Meccan monotheist in Muhammed's day who was neither a Jew nor a Christian but claimed to follow the religion of Abraham, the Hanif, the Muslim.
hijra	A term meaning "emigration"; Muhammad's flight from Mecca to Medina.
Hizbollah	A Shia sect in Lebanon meaning, "party of God."
Id al-Adha	The "Feast of Sacrifice" commemorating Abraham's attempted sacrifice of his son.
Id al-Fitra	The Feast of Fast-Breaking, which occurs at the end of Ramadan.
Id al-Kabir	The Great Feast, the Feast of Sacrifice.
ihram	The word for the ritual state of purity when on pilgrimage.
ilm	A term meaning "intellectual knowledge."
imam	The leader of prayers in Sunni Islam; a much more important title of religious functionary in Shia Islam.
Imami	A branch of Shia Islam that follows the disappeared and occulted twelfth imam.
iman	A term for "faith," the six key articles of the Muslim creed.
Injil	Muhammad's name for the Gospel or "book" he thought God gave to Jesus.
Islam	A word meaning "submission"; specifically, submission to Muhammad's teaching.
Ismaili	A branch of Shia Islam which follows the disappeared seventh imam.
isnad	The chain of reference for the Written Traditions.
jihad	"To exert" (on behalf of God), meaning any means to further Islam, including holy war.
jinn	An order of spiritual beings, not angels, supposedly created out of fire and usually considered to be evil in nature.

Jizya	A special poll tax levied on Jews and Christians.
Kaaba	The cubical building inside the mosque in Mecca which is thought to be the House of God.
kenosis	A Greek word meaning "emptying."
Khadijah	Muhammad's first wife.
Kharijites	A fanatical sect of Muslims whose members feel they must revolt against rulers who have sinned.
khutbah	The sermon preached at mosques on Friday afternoon.
Mahdi	A term meaning "the rightly guided one," the one who will come back at the end of the age to purify Islam.
marifah	A term for mystical knowledge of God.
Marwa	One of the two hills between which pilgrims run as they reenact Hagar's search for water.
masa	The name for the sunset and evening prayers.
masjid	The word for a mosque, "the place of bowing down."
matn	The text of a written tradition.
Maulvi	The title of a religious scholar.
Mecca	The city of Muhammad's birth; the center of pilgrimage.
Medina	The city from which Muhammad ruled A.D. 622-632.
Mina	The site where Muslims claim Abraham sacrificed an animal God provided in place of his son.
Mirzai	A follower of Ghulam Ahmad Mirza.
Mizan-ul-Haqq	*The Balance of Truth*, a book of Dr. Karl Pfander's apologetic answers to Muslim questioning of Christian doctrine.
mosque	The accepted English version of the French word for a Muslim place of worship: a *masjid*.
mufti	A Muslim jurisprudent, a high court judge.
mujahidin	A Muslim holy warrior who fights in a *jihad*.
mullah	A narrowly-educated Muslim teacher.
Muslim	One who has submitted to Muhammad and his teaching.
pir	A non-Arabic word for a holy man in the Indian subcontinent.
qadi	A religious judge in Islam.
Qadiani	A follower of Ghulam Ahmad Mirza whose home town was Qadian in India.
Quran	The name of the collected recitations of Muhammad, the Muslim holy book.
razzia	The practice of raiding an enemy's caravan.

sadaqat	Meaning "righteousness," this term means gifts for the poor.
Safa	One of the two hills between which pilgrims run as they reenact Hagar's search for water.
salat	The word for ritual prayers in Islam.
sawm	The word for the Muslim fast.
shahadah	The word for the Muslim confession of faith.
Shariah	"The pathway to water," the word for Islamic Law.
shaykh	A variant of Sheikh, a religious leader or holy man.
Shia	The sect of Islam that follows Ali as their leader.
Shirk	The unforgivable sin in Islam of associating anyone else with God (God has no partners).
sijda	The act of bowing down or prostrating oneself in prayer.
subh	Meaning "morning," the time for the first prayer of the day.
suf	The Arabic word for wool.
Sufi	A Muslim mystic who originally wore robes of wool or "suf," hence the nickname, "Sufi."
Sufism	The name of the Muslim religious practice of mysticism.
sultan	The title of a Muslim ruler and leader, distinguished from a caliph.
Sunnah	"The trodden path," the living tradition concerning what Muhammad did and said.
Sunni	One who follows the model behavior and teaching of Muhammad.
surah	The word used for a chapter in the Quran.
ta ethne	The Greek expression for "the nations," better translated, "the ethno-linguistic groups of peoples."
Taurat	The book God gave to Moses (The Mosaic Law).
tawaf	Circumambulating around the Kaaba, the huge cubical building inside the great mosque of Mecca.
ulama	The word for religious scholars; the plural of *alam*.
Ummah	A term meaning "the Community of the Faithful," used to refer to Muslims.
Yathrib	The original name of the city of Medina.
zakat	The obligatory alms, about 2.5 % of one's income.
zilli	The word used for a reforming prophet, as distinguished from an inspired prophet; this word is applied to Ghulam Ahmad Mirza.

BIBLICAL REFERENCES

QURANIC REFERENCES

REFERENCES CITED

Abdul-Haqq, A. Akbar
    1980   *Sharing Your Faith with a Muslim.* Minneapolis: Bethany Fellowship, Inc.

Ajayi, J.F.A., and Crowder, Michael
    1985   *Historical Atlas of Africa.* New York: Cambridge University Press.

Ali, Maulana Muhammad
    1973   *The Holy Qur'an.* Lahore: Ahmadiyyah Anjuman Isha'at Islam.

Ali, A. Yusuf
    1977   *The Glorious Qur'an.* 2nd Edition. Bloomington: The American Trust Publications.

Andrae, Tor
    1955   *Les Origines de l'Islam et le Christianisme.* Paris: Librairie d'Americaque et d'Orient: Adrien-Maisonneuve.

    1960   *Mohammed: The Man and His Faith.* New York: Harper and Row.

Arberry, Arthur J.
    1980   *The Koran Interpreted.* London: George Allen & Unwin Publishers. (First One Volume Edition.)

Badawi, Jamal
    1982   *Muhammad in the Bible.* Halifax (Canada): Islamic Information Foundation.

Barton, James L.
    1918   *The Christian Approach to Islam.* Boston: Pilgrim Press.

Battle, V. DuWayne
    1988   "The Influence of Al-Islam in America on the Black Community." *The Black Scholar* 19:33-44.

Bell, Richard
    1958   *Introduction to the Qur'an.* Edinburgh: The University of
                 Edinburgh Press.

Bentley, David
    1992   *Rights of Muslims.* Pasadena: Zwemer Institute of Muslim
                 Studies.

Berger, Morroe
    1964   "The Black Muslim." *Horizon* 6:49-64.

Blair, John C.
    1925   *The Sources of Islam.* Madras: The Christian Literature Society
                 for India.

Burton, John
    1977   *The Collection of the Quran.* Cambridge: The Cambridge
                 University Press.

Calverley, E. E.
    1958   *Islam: An Introduction.* Cairo: The American University at
                 Cairo.

Chapman, Colin
    1989   "Second Thoughts about the Ishmael Theme." *Seedbed* 4:50-
                 57.

Cole, R. I. and Keddie, Nikki R.
    1986   *Shi'ism and Social Protest.* New Haven: Yale University Press.

Cragg, Kenneth A.
    1956   *The Call of the Minaret.* New York: Oxford University Press.

Cragg, Kenneth A.
    1965   *Islamic Surveys.* Edinburgh: Edinburgh University Press.

Cragg, Kenneth A.
    1969   *The House of Islam.* Belmont (California): Dickenson
                 Publishing Company, Inc.

Cragg, Kenneth A. and Speight, R. Marston
1980   *Islam from within: Anthology of a Religion.* Belmont: Wadsworth Publishing Company.

Cragg, Kenneth A.
1984   *Muhammad and the Christian: A Question of Response.* London: Darton, Longman and Todd.

Cragg, Kenneth A.
1985   *The Pen and the Faith.* London: George Allen & Unwin Publishers, Ltd.

Cragg, Kenneth A.
1988   *Readings in the Quran.* London: Collins.

Da Costa, Isaac
1972   "Hagar." *In de Slag Bij Nieupoort.* Buitnedijk: Thieme, Zutphen (Translated into English by Marten Vogelaar, 1990.)

Dawood, N. J.
1956   *The Koran.* Baltimore: Penguin Books, Ltd.

Deedat, Ahmad
1976   *What the Bible Says about Muhammad.* Durban (South Africa): Islamic Propogation Centre.

Eims, Leroy
1978   *The Lost Art of Disciple Making.* Grand Rapids: Zondervan Publishing House.

Esposito, John L.
1983   *Voices of Resurgent Islam.* New York: Oxford University Press.

Esposito, John L.
1984   *Islam and Politics.* Syracuse: Syracuse University Press

Esposito, John L.
1991   *Islam: The Staight Path.* New York: Oxford University Press.

Farah, Ceasar E.
1968   *Islam.* Woodbury (New York): Barron's Educational Series, Inc.

Gaudefroy-Demombynes, Maurice
1968   *Muslim Institutions.* London: George Allen & Unwin, Ltd.

Geertz, Clifford
1968   *Islam Observed.* Chicago: The University of Chicago Press.

Gibb, Hamilton A. R.
1949   *Islam: A Historical Survey.* (Formerly entitled *Mohammedanism.*) Oxford: Oxford University Press.

1962   "Pre-Islamic Monotheism in Arabia." In *The Harvard Theological Review*, Vol. LV, No. 4.

Gibb, Hamilton A. R. and Kramers, J. H. et al
1974   *Shorter Encyclopedia of Islam.* Leiden: E. J. Brill.

Glasse, Cyril
1989   *The Concise Encyclopedia of Islam.* San Fransisco: Harper & Row.

Goitein, S. D.
1968   *Studies in Islamic History and Institutions.* Leiden: E. J. Brill.

Green, Denis
1989   "Guidelines from Hebrews for Contextualization." In *Muslims and Christians on the Emmaus Road.* J. Dudley Woodberry, ed., pp. 233-250. Monrovia (California): MARC Publications.

Green, Michael
1981   *I Believe In Satan's Downfall.* Grand Rapids: Wm. B. Eerdmans Publishing Company.

Guillaume, Alfred
1954   *Islam.* Baltimore: Penguin Books, Inc.

Haley, Alex
    1976   *Roots.* Garden City: Doubleday.

Hamada, Louis Bahjat
    1990   *Understanding the Arab World.* Nashville: Thomas Nelson Publishers.

Hamid, Abdul
    1973   *Evidence of the Bible about Muhammed.* Karachi: Published by the author.

Hardy, P.
    1972   *The Muslims of British India.* Cambridge: At the University Press.

Haykal, Muhammad H.
    1976   *The Life of Muhammad.* Bloomington: The North American Trust Publications.

Henninger, Joseph
    1981   "Pre-Islamic Bedouin Religion" in *Studies in Islam,* ed. M. Swartz

Hiebert, Paul
    1989   "Power Encounter and Folk Islam." *Muslims and Christians on the Emmaus Road.* J. Dudley Woodberry, ed., pp. 45-61. Monrovia (California): MARC Publications.

Hitti, Philip K.
    1970   *Islam: A Way of Life.* Chicago: Henry Regnery Company.

Hunter, Edward
    1953   *Brainwashing in Red China.* New York: Vanguard Press.

Husain, Muhammad Kamil

    1959   *City of Wrong: A Friday in Jerusalem.* London: Geoffrey Bless Publishers.

Iranian Christian
    1986   In a public lecture at "Impetus '86," Columbo, Sri Lanka (name withheld).

Jeffrey, Arthur
    1938   *The Foreign Vocabulary of the Qur'an.* Baroda: Oriental Institute.

    1958   *Islam: Muhammad and His Religion.* New York: The Liberal Arts Press.

Johnstone, Patrick
    1993   *Operation World.* Grand Rapids: Zondervan Publishing House.

Kamell, Yousef
    1980   An Unpublished Paper on "Apologetic Approach to Muslims."

Karandikar, M. A.
    1968   *Islam in India's Transition to Modernity.* Delhi: Eastern Publishers.

Keil, C. F. and Delitzsch, F.
    1954   *Biblical Commentary on the Old Testament.* (Translated by James Martin) Grand Rapids: Wm. B. Eerdmans.

Kelso, James L.
    1968   *Archeology and the Ancient Testament.* Grand Rapids: Zondervan Publishing House.

Kraft, Charles H.
    1979   *Christianity in Culture.* Maryknoll: Orbis Books.

    1989   *Christianity with Power.* Ann Arbor: Servant Publications.

Lewis, Bernard
    1971   *Race and Color in Islam.* New York: Harper and Row (Torchbook edition).

Lewis, C. S.
1943   *Mere Christianity.* New York: Macmillan Publishing Company.

Lincoln, C. Eric
1973   *The Black Muslims in America* (Revised Edition). Boston: Beacon Press.

Mahfouz, Naguib
1981   *The Children of Gebelaawi.* (Translated by Philip Stewart) London.

1985   "Majib Mahfuz of Cairo." In *The Pen and the Faith.* London: George Allen & Unwin, Ltd

Margoliouth, D. S.
1928   *Mohammedanism.* London: Thornton Butterworth, Ltd., (Fourth Impression).

Massih, Bashir Abdol
1979   "The Incarnational Witness to the Muslim Heart." In *The Gospel and Islam: A 1978 Compendium.* Don McCurry, ed., pp. 85-96. Monrovia (California): MARC: World Vision International.

Maududi, Abul Ala
1973   *Towards Understanding Islam.* Indianapolis: American Trust Publications.

McDowell, Josh and Gilchrist, John
1983   *The Islam Debate.* San Bernardino: Here's Life Publishers, Inc.

McGavran, Donald A.
1979   *Ethnic Realities.* Pasadena: William Carey Library.

Mujeeb, M.
1967   *The Indian Muslims.* London: George Allen & Unwin, Ltd.

Musk, Bill
1989   *The Unseen Face of Islam.* Eastbourne (U. K.): MARC, Europe.

Nazir-Ali, Michael
  1983   *Islam: A Christian Perspective.* Exeter: The Paternoster Press.

  1987   *Frontiers in Muslim-Christian Encounter.* Oxford: Regnum Books.

Nicholls, Bruce J.
  1979   "New Theological Approaches in Muslim Evangelism." In *The Gospel and Islam: A 1978 Compendium.* Don McCurry, ed., pp.155-162. Monrovia: MARC: World Vision International.

Nicholson, R. A.
  1907   *Studies in Islamic Mysticism.* Cambridge: At the Univerity Press.

O'Shaugnessy, Thomas
  1948   *The Koranic Concept of the Word of God.* Rome. Pontificio Instituto Biblico.

  1953   *The Development of the Meaning of Spirit in the Koran.* Rome: Pontificio Institutum Orientalium Studiorum.

Parrinder, Geoffrey
  1977   *Jesus in the Quran.* New York: Oxford University Press.

Parshall, Phil
  1980   *New Paths in Muslim Evangelism.* Grand Rapids: Baker Book House.

  1983   *Bridges to Islam.* Grand Rapids: Baker Book House.

  1985   *Beyond the Mosque.* Grand Rapids: Baker Book House.

  1989   "Lessons Learned in Contextualization." In *Muslims and Christians on the Emmaus Road.* J. Dudley Woodberry, ed., Monrovia: MARC: World Vision International.

Pfander, Carl G.
  1910   *The Mizan-ul-Haqq.* London: The Religious Tract Society.

Pipes, Daniel
    1983   *In the Path of God: Islam and Political Power.* New York: Basic Books, Inc. Publishers.

Pryce-Jones, David
    1989   *The Closed Circle: An Interpretation of the Arabs.* New York: Harper & Row Publishers.

Qaddafi, Muammer
    1989   Quoted in *News Network International.* December 13, p.18.

Rahbar, M. Daud
    1979   *The God of Justice.* Leiden: Brill Publishers.

Rahim, M. A.
    1973   *The Gospel of Barnabas.* Karachi: Fazleesons.

Rahman, Fazlur
    1979   *Islam.* 2nd Edition. Chicago: The University of Chicago Press.

Reyburn, William D.
    1979   "The Current Status of Bible Translations in Muslim Languages." *The Gospel and Islam: A 1978 Compendium.* Don M. McCurry, ed., Monrovia: MARC: World Vision International.

Roberts, D. S.
    1981   *Islam: A Concise Introduction.* San Francisco: Harper & Row, Publishers.

Roberts, Robert
    1925   *The Social Law of the Quran.* London: Williams and Northgate, Ltd.

Robson, James
    1975   *Mishkat Al-Masabih.* Lahore: Sh. Muhammad Ashraf, A 1981 Reprint. 2 Volumes.

Rodinson, Maxime
    1971   *Mohammed.* Bungay (Suffolk): The Chaucer Press.

Rushdie, Salman
    1989   *The Satanic Verses.* New York: Viking Penguin, Inc.

    1989   Quoted in *The Los Angeles Times.* February 14, and June 23, 1989.

    1990   Quoted in *Newsweek.* February 12, 1990.

Sale, George
    1850   *The Koran.* London: Frederick Warne and Company, Ltd. (Originally published in 1734.)

Sayres, Dorothy
    1964   *The Mind of the Maker.* New York: The World Publishing Company (1st ed. Harcourt, Brace & World, Inc. 1941.)

Schlorff, S. P.
    1981   *Discipleship in Islamic Society.* Marseille: North Africa Mission.

Shah, Idries
    1971   *The Sufis.* New York: Doubleday & Company (Anchor Books Edition).

Smith, Margaret
    1995   *Studies in Early Mysticism in the Near and Middle East.* Oxford: Oneworld Publications.

Stacey, Vivienne
    1986   *Christ Supreme over Satan: Spiritual Warfare, Folk Religion (Islamic), and the Occult.* Lahore: Masihi Isha'at Khana.

Subhan, John A.
    1938   *Sufism: Its Saints and Shrines.* Lucknow (India): Lucknow Publishing House.

Swartz, Merlin L.
1981   *Studies on Islam*. New York: Oxford University Press.

Tisdall, Wm. St. Clair
1910   *The Sources of the Quran*. London: The Society for the Promotion of Christian Knowledge.

Torrey, Charles C.
1933   *The Jewish Foundation of Islam*. New York: The Jewish Institute of Religion Press.

Trimingham, J. Spencer
1979   *Christianity among the Arabs in Pre-Islamic Times*. London: Longman Group Limited.

Tuchman, Barbara W.
1956   *Bible and Sword*. New York: Funk & Wagnalls.

Vander Werff, Lyle
1977   *Christian Mission to Muslims*. Pasadena: William Carey Library.

Vollmer, Philip
1912   *The Modern Student's Life of Christ*. New York: Fleming H. Revell Company.

Watt W. Montgomery
1974   *Muhammad: Prophet and Statesman*. Oxford: Oxford University Press. (Paperback: Galaxy Book Reprint.)

Weekes, Richard V.
1984   *Muslim Peoples: A World Ethnographic Survey*. Westport (Connecticut): Greenwood Press. 2 Volumes.

Weeks, John R.
1988   *The Demography of Islamic Nations*. Washington, D.C. A Publication of the Population Reference Bureau, Inc.

Whitehouse, Aubrey
   1981   *Topical Concordance to the Quran.* Lilydale (Victoria, Australia):
               Bible College of Victoria Press.

Williams, Don
   1989   *Signs, Wonders and the Kingdom of God.* Ann Arbor: Vine
               Books, Published by Servant Books.

Wilson, Marvin R.
   1989   *Our Father Abraham.* Grand Rapids: William B. Eerdmans
               Publishing Company.

Wimber, John and Springer, Kevin
   1987   *Power Healing.* San Fransisco: Harper & Row Publishers.

Woodberry, J. Dudley
   1989   *Muslims and Christians on the Emmaus Road.* Monrovia:
               MARC: World Vision International.

World Population Data Sheet
   1998   Washington, D.C.: Population Reference Bureau, Inc.

Wright, Robin
   1989   *In The Name of God: The Khomeini Decade.* New York: Simon
               & Shuster.

Yaghnazar, Samuel
   1991   Information from a private conversation.

Zeegers, Rolf
   1990   *The Soviet Union Republic Profiles.* Ermelo: Open Doors
               Research Department.

Zwemer, Samuel M.
   1924   *The Law of Apostasy in Islam.* London: Marshall Brothers,
               Ltd.

INDEX